The *Pirates' House*

COOK BOOK

SAVANNAH, GEORGIA

compiled and tested by
SARAH GAEDE

Copies of THE PIRATES' HOUSE COOKBOOK may be obtained from The Pirates' House, 20 East Broad St., Savannah, Ga. 31401

 Denotes recipes from The Pirates' House

 Denotes Hints

International Standard Book Number 0-939-11461-5
Printed in the United States of America
Wimmer Brothers Books
Memphis, Tennessee 38118
"Cookbooks of Distinction"™

"WHAT FOODS THESE MORSELS BE!"

So states the slogan we've been using for years to describe the delicious masterpieces created by our large staff of wonderful cooks. If you are among the thousands who have dined at The Pirates' House, we hope you agree with this slogan. On the other hand, if you have never crossed our threshold, then we hope you will agree after you have sampled some of the mouth-watering dishes that can be concocted so easily from the recipes in this fascinating cookbook.

From its modest beginning in February, 1950, when Frances McGrath first opened a petite but wonderful tea room here, to today's meandering maze of 23 unique dining rooms in nine connected old buildings, The Pirates' House has always boasted of superb food served in the original romantic setting of yesteryear. Frances's culinary talents were many and helped form the firm foundation upon which we have continued to build and grow into one of the nation's most unusual restaurants. New items have, of course, been added to our menu from time to time and this edition of The Pirates' House Cookbook contains practically all of them . . . plus many delicious surprises in the form of numerous never-before-published recipes contributed by family and friends.

We sincerely hope that you will enjoy reading and using this book . . . and as you do, be as thankful as we are that there was a Frances McGrath to kindle the flame here a long time ago! Be thankful, too, for the author of this 1982 edition, Sarah Gaede, a talented and knowledgeable food expert herself, who spent two years and endless hours assembling and testing every single recipe with the result that they are, as Sarah says, practically foolproof!

To those of you who do not live in Savannah we extend a warm invitation to visit us whenever you are in our beautiful, historic city. Natives, of course, can drop in ANY time! We'll be delighted to meet you in person, to show you our restaurant from Galley to Gift Shop and to answer any questions you may have concerning the preparation and serving of our specialties.

Bon appetit . . . and good luck!

Herb Traub

Herb Traub

ACKNOWLEDGEMENTS

Compiling, testing and editing the recipes for THE PIRATES' HOUSE COOKBOOK was an enormous undertaking, and I couldn't have done it without a lot of help. I'd like to thank Mr. Traub for deciding that it was time for a new cookbook. Kit Traub was my guiding light, mentor, proofreader and guinea pig. Thanks to Sheron George, Brenda Lain and Martha Summerour, who taught me so much about Southern cooking. Special thanks to my wonderful husband, Henry, who married me in the midst of this project and has the pounds to prove it (as does everyone within feeding distance of my kitchen.) He helped with proofreading and maintaining my sanity, and washed *lots* of dishes. My undying gratitude goes to the lovely ladies in the Pirates' House kitchen, who were so patient under the onslaught of all my questions (and without whom I absolutely could not have learned to cook Red Rice)—especially Queenie Mae Boyd, Gussie Stoney, Erma Grant, Eloise Kelly, Beverly Johnson, Rosa Lee Early and Edna Bryant.

Sarah Gaede

P.S. I mustn't forget Nathalie Dupree of Rich's Cooking School in Atlanta, who taught me to ask why and how.

TABLE OF CONTENTS

6

APPETIZERS

AFRICAN PICKLES

1 (46 oz.) jar whole Kosher dill pickles, or whole Kosher baby dills
1 teaspoon crushed red pepper flakes
3 cloves garlic, slivered
½ pound (1 cup firmly packed) light brown sugar

Drain pickles; reserve juice. Cut pickles in quarters lengthwise, then in half through middle, to get 8 pieces from each pickle. Put pickles back into jar, layering with red pepper and garlic. Dissolve brown sugar in pickle juice, holding back ½ cup juice which will be displaced by sugar. Pour over pickles in jar. Let sit at room temperature 24 hours, then refrigerate before serving.

NOTE: A great, inexpensive hors d'oeuvre.

Stephen Traub

AVOCADO MOUSSE

2 ripe avocados
¼ cup mayonnaise
1½ teaspoons unflavored gelatin, softened in:
1½ teaspoons fresh lemon juice
2 teaspoons grated onion
½ teaspoon Worcestershire sauce
½ teaspoon salt
¼ teaspoon freshly ground pepper
4 drops Tabasco
¼ cup sour cream
Cucumber slices for garnish, optional

Peel and pit avocados. Purée in food processor or blender. Add remaining ingredients except sour cream and cucumbers. Mix well. Turn into serving bowl. Whip sour cream lightly with fork and spread over mousse to prevent discoloration. Refrigerate until set. Serve cold, garnished with cucumber slices.

NOTE: This is similar to guacamole, and is good on corn chips.

BACON CRISPS

Waverly wafers   **½ strip bacon per cracker**

Wrap bacon around width of cracker—ends should hang out.
Place on rack in baking pan. Bake at 375° until bacon is brown,
about 15 to 20 minutes. Serve hot.
NOTE: Easy and delicious!

BACON-WRAPPED OYSTERS

1 pint select oysters,   **½ slice bacon per oyster**
  drained (or as many as
  you want)

Wrap bacon around oysters and secure with round toothpicks.
Place on rack in baking pan. Bake at 375° until bacon is crisp,
about 15 to 20 minutes. Serve hot.
NOTE: Chicken livers may be substituted for oysters. Try soaking them in soy sauce for 15 minutes before wrapping with
bacon.

BACON-WRAPPED WATERMELON RIND

Watermelon rind preserves   **½ strip bacon per**
                                watermelon rind chunk

Drain watermelon rind preserves. Wrap bacon around chunks
and secure with round toothpicks. Place on rack in baking pan.
Bake at 375° until bacon is crisp, about 15 to 20 minutes. Serve
hot.
NOTE: One of the most popular Pirates' House hors d'oeuvres.

HOT APPETIZER PIE

1 (2½ oz.) jar dried beef, finely chopped
1 (8 oz.) package cream cheese, softened
2 tablespoons milk
½ cup sour cream
2 tablespoons finely chopped green pepper
2 tablespoons finely chopped green onion
½ teaspoon black pepper
¼ cup chopped pecans or walnuts

Preheat oven to 350°. Blend cream cheese with milk. Beat in all other ingredients, except nuts, and blend until smooth, or just toss everything in the food processor. Spread in Pyrex pie plate and sprinkle nuts on top. May be mixed ahead and refrigerated until time to bake. Bake for 15 minutes. Serve on crackers or sturdy potato chips.

Ginny Barnett

HOT OLIVE CHEESE PUFFS

1 cup (4 oz.) grated extra sharp Cheddar cheese
3 tablespoons butter, softened
½ cup all-purpose flour
¼ teaspoon salt
½ teaspoon paprika
48 medium stuffed green olives, drained (approximately)

Blend cheese with butter, stir in flour, salt, and paprika and mix well. This can be done easily in a food processor. Pinch off a small amount of dough, flatten, wrap around olive and roll between palms to smooth out. Place on ungreased cookie sheet; bake in a preheated 400° oven for 10 to 15 minutes, or until browned on the bottom. Serve hot.
NOTE: To freeze: Freeze on baking sheet, transfer to Zip-loc bag when frozen. No need to thaw before baking. Recipe doubles easily.

BROCCOLI-FLOWER BOUQUET

1 head cauliflower
1 bunch broccoli
2 cloves garlic, peeled
1 lemon

3 tablespoons salt
1 bay leaf
1 pint cherry tomatoes,
　stemmed and washed

Cut the stems from cauliflower and broccoli and break the tops into similar-sized flowerets. Cut the rind from the lemon with a vegetable peeler—try not to get any white on the peel. Add lemon peel, garlic, salt, and bay leaf to a large pot of boiling water. Boil 5 minutes to flavor the water. Add the vegetable flowerets. Return to a boil and cook for 3 to 4 minutes, until broccoli is bright green and vegetables are crisp-tender. Do not overcook! Drain immediately in a colander and rinse with cold water. Shake dry. Discard seasonings. May be done in advance to this point; refrigerate vegetables in plastic bags. On a round tray or platter, arrange the broccoli in a ring around the outside, then a ring of cauliflower. Mound cherry tomatoes in the center. Serve with your favorite vegetable dip, or home-made mayonnaise flavored with lemon.
NOTE: Wonderful on a Christmas buffet.

"PLAINS SPECIAL" CHEESE RING

1 pound extra-sharp
　Cheddar cheese, grated
1 cup chopped pecans
1 small onion, grated
1 cup good quality
　mayonnaise

Black pepper to taste
Cayenne pepper to taste
Strawberry preserves

Mix everything but preserves together with hands and mold into a ring on serving platter. Chill. When ready to serve, fill center with strawberry preserves. Serve with crackers.

GINGER CREAM CHEESE

3 (8 oz.) packages cream cheese, softened
1 (16 oz.) jar Dundee's Ginger Preserve
1 cup blanched almonds (whole, sliced or slivered)

Sliced blanched almonds, toasted or not, optional
Fresh fruit for garnish

Throw everything in a food processor and let it rip until well-combined, scraping down sides occasionally. Pack in a well-oiled melon mold or pudding bowl. Refrigerate overnight. Run a knife around edge of mold and unmold onto serving platter. Cover with toasted or untoasted almonds, if desired, or smooth with knife. Garnish with fresh fruit—grapes or strawberries are nice.

NOTE: Especially good with Carr's Wheatmeal Biscuits, but Ritz crackers are okay too.

POTTED CHEESE

1 cup grated Cheddar cheese
¾ cup crumbled bleu cheese
¾ cup unsalted butter

1 teaspoon Dijon mustard
⅛ teaspoon freshly ground nutmeg
3 tablespoons brandy

Allow cheeses and butter to stand at room temperature until softened. Blend in remaining ingredients until smooth. Pack into a 2½ cup crock; cover and refrigerate overnight before using. Serve with crisp crackers, toast or celery.

NOTE: Instead of using brandy, flavor the cheese with port, sherry, or bourbon. For extra spiciness, add Worcestershire and Tabasco. Or substitute cream cheese for all or part of the butter and add chopped walnuts for texture. For a totally different taste, use a mild cheese such as Fontina instead of bleu cheese, and add a tablespoon or two of caraway seeds.

STUFFED BRIE WITH GRAPES AND NUTS

1 (1 kilogram) brie
½ cup unsalted butter,
  softened
Grapes—best are
  Thompson Seedless or
  Ribier

Chopped pecans or
  walnuts

Place brie in freezer for 1 hour; it will be much easier to cut. Prepare the board or platter on which you will serve the brie. Once it has been split and stuffed, it is very difficult to move. Unwrap brie. Get down to eye level with side of brie and mark a line all around the circumference with the point of a knife, dividing it in half horizontally. With your longest, thinnest knife, cut brie in half, moving around the circumference as you do. Peel off top half and place cut-side up on board or platter. Don't worry if there is more cheese on one half than the other. Just shave the excess off the high spot on one side and transfer it to the low spot on the other. Divide butter in half and spread evenly over both cut sides, using your fingers. Sprinkle nuts evenly over the half lying on the board. Cut grapes in half, remove seeds if necessary, and place over nuts, covering entire side 1 layer deep. Carefully place other half of brie cut-side down on top of stuffed half. Decorate top with grape and nut halves if desired. Serve at room temperature with Bremner wafers or Carr's Table Water crackers.

NOTE: If you are having a very large party, order a 2-kilogram brie from your cheese shop, and use 2 sticks of butter, one on each half. You may need someone to help you handle it.

 Taste, taste, taste! From beginning to end, at every stage of a recipe. It takes a lot of nerve to put an untasted dish in front of guests, or even family.

STUFFED BRIE IN BRIOCHE

Brioche Dough

1 package yeast
¼ cup warm milk (110°-115°)
1 tablespoon sugar
1 teaspoon salt
½ cup *frozen* butter, cut in 8 pieces

2 eggs, lightly beaten
1 egg, well beaten, for glaze
1 Stuffed Brie, see below

Proof yeast in warm milk with sugar. With metal blade in place in food processor, add flour, salt and butter to bowl. Process until butter is cut into flour mixture, about 20 seconds. Add yeast mixture and process until combined, about 5 seconds. Add 2 eggs and process until ball of dough forms on blade. (Add a little more flour if dough is sticky.) Turn dough out onto lightly floured counter and knead until smooth, 1 to 2 minutes, adding more flour if necessary. Place in an oiled bowl, turning to coat both sides. Cover with plastic wrap and let rise in a warm place until doubled. Punch down, knead several times and divide in half. Cover one half. Roll out other half in a circle about 4 inches wider than brie. Lay dough on baking sheet, slide stuffed brie from box lid onto dough, and trim dough to extend 1 inch around brie. Brush edge of dough with glaze. Roll out remaining dough, lay over brie, press down to cover brie tightly, and trim edge even with bottom circle. Roll edges towards brie and press all around with a fork to seal tightly. Brush all over with glaze. If desired, cut vines, leaves, or whatever you like from leftover dough to decorate top of brie. Brush with glaze. Let rise 30 minutes; no more. Bake at 375° for 30 minutes, or until dough is puffed and golden brown. Cool. Serve at room temperature. May be made the day before serving, refrigerated, and brought to room temperature before serving. Cut in wedges to serve.

Stuffed Brie for Brioche

1 (1 kilogram) brie   Walnuts, chopped
Dried apricots, snipped

To stuff brie: Stuff brie after dough has risen. See instructions for splitting brie under Stuffed Brie with Grapes and Nuts. Lay one half cut-side up on top of brie box. Cover with chopped walnuts and snipped apricots. No cheese should show through, but you don't want too thick a layer of stuffing. Lay top of brie cut-side down on stuffed half.

THAT WONDERFUL CRABMEAT-CAVIAR THING

1 envelope unflavored   1 pound fresh crabmeat
  gelatin   Red lumpfish caviar, as
Juice of 1 lemon   much as you can afford,
1 (8 oz.) package cream   but at least 2 (3½ oz.)
  cheese, softened   jars
1 (8 oz.) carton sour cream
1 medium onion, finely
  chopped

Soften gelatin in lemon juice. Beat cream cheese and sour cream until smooth and stir in onion. Or chop onion in food processor, throw in cream cheese and sour cream and process until smooth. Melt gelatin and lemon juice over low heat. Stir into cream cheese mixture. Spread a layer of cream cheese mixture on the bottom of a glass bowl, preferably a straight-sided soufflé dish. Top with a layer of crabmeat. Spread another layer of cream cheese, then a layer of caviar. Repeat layers, ending with a solid layer of caviar. Chill. Serve with Bremner wafers or Carr's Table Water Crackers.
NOTE: This recipe is to die for; expensive, but worth it.

CHRISTMAS CRACKER SPREAD

1 envelope unflavored
  gelatin
½ cup cold water
1 (11 oz.) can tomato soup
2 (3 oz.) packages cream
  cheese, softened
1 cup mayonnaise
1 cup (about 3 ribs) finely
  chopped celery

2 tablespoons finely
  chopped bell pepper
1 tablespoon finely
  chopped onion
½ cup sliced green olives
  with pimientos

Soften gelatin in cold water. Heat soup without water. Add softened gelatin; stir to melt. Cool tomato soup mixture. Blend cream cheese, tomato soup and mayonnaise until smooth (a food processor is ideal for this), stir in rest of ingredients, pour into a small glass bowl or soufflé dish and chill. Decorate before serving with slices of olive. Serve on crackers or party rye or pumpernickel.
NOTE: A tasty, inexpensive alternative to shrimp mold.

Henry Gaede

PECAN CRISPS

1 recipe Bleu Cheese
  Dressing, see Index
Chopped pecans

Melba toast rounds or Ritz
  crackers

Lay toast rounds or crackers out on a baking sheet. Spoon bleu cheese dressing on each—not enough to drip over edge. Sprinkle with nuts. Bake at 350° for 15 minutes, or until golden brown and bubbly.
NOTE: Do not assemble too far in advance—they get soggy quickly.

NEW DELHI CHICKEN

4 whole chicken breasts (8
  halves), skinned and
  boned
2 tablespoons butter
1 cup sour cream
½ cup mayonnaise
¼ cup chili sauce
2 tablespoons horseradish

1 tablespoon
  Worcestershire sauce
Juice of 1 lemon
¼ teaspoon Tabasco
1 teaspoon curry powder
2 tablespoons Major Grey's
  chutney, finely chopped
Paprika for garnish

Preheat oven to 400°. Cut each chicken breast half into 8 to 10 pieces. Place in buttered baking pan, dot with butter, and cover with wax paper. Bake for 6 to 8 minutes—do not overcook. Separate chicken pieces while still warm. Mix everything but chicken and paprika together, stir in chicken, cover tightly and refrigerate overnight. To serve, pile in center of a serving dish lined with lettuce leaves. Sprinkle lightly with paprika. Serve with toothpicks.

NOTE: Makes a good chicken salad for a summer luncheon.

CAVIAR MOLD

2 (8 oz.) packages cream
  cheese, softened
1 small onion, grated
½ cup sour cream
4 hard-boiled eggs, sieved

1 small jar red or black
  caviar
1 lemon, sliced thin or cut
  in wedges
Melba toast rounds

Combine cream cheese, onion, and sour cream in electric mixer or by hand. Do not use food processor. Refrigerate overnight. Pile on serving plate in a round shape (sort of what you would get if you unmolded it from a pie plate). Sprinkle sieved egg over cream cheese; top with caviar. Garnish with lemon. Spread on melba rounds and squeeze lemon over, if desired.

Cathy Solomons

CRAB CANAPES

1 recipe Crab Stuffing, see index
Melba toast rounds or homemade toast rounds
Freshly grated Parmesan cheese

Lay toast rounds out on cookie sheet. Mound crab stuffing on rounds. Sprinkle with cheese. Bake at 350° until hot and cheese is browned; about 15 minutes.

CAULIFLOWER DIP

1 cup mayonnaise
2 tablespoons grated onion
2 tablespoons Worcestershire sauce
3 tablespoons lemon juice
2 tablespoons light brown sugar
2 tablespoons prepared mustard
Salt to taste
Paprika to taste

Combine ingredients. Refrigerate at least 8 hours before serving. Serve with raw cauliflower—good with other vegetables too.

CURRY DIP

1 cup mayonnaise
1 teaspoon curry powder
1 teaspoon lemon juice
1 tablespoon grated onion

Combine ingredients. Refrigerate at least 8 hours before serving. Serve with raw vegetables—cauliflower, carrots, celery, squash, etc.

DILL DIP

1 cup mayonnaise
½ cup sour cream
1 tablespoon dill weed
1 tablespoon chopped
   green onion
1 tablespoon chopped
   fresh parsley

1 tablespoon seasoned
   salt
Dash Worcestershire
   sauce
Dash garlic powder

Mix together until smooth. Refrigerate at least 8 hours before serving.

DUDLEY'S DIP

1 (8 oz.) package cream
   cheese, softened
⅓ cup crumbled bleu
   cheese

½ cup catsup
½ small onion
1 tablespoon horseradish
5 to 8 drops Tabasco

Combine in food processor until smooth, or grate onion and mix well by hand. Refrigerate overnight before serving.

Dudley Taft

KARI'S DIP

1 cup mayonnaise
2 tablespoons tarragon
   vinegar
1 tablespoon anchovy
   paste
½ teaspoon dry mustard
½ teaspoon Tabasco

5 sprigs parsley, without
   stems
½ small onion
1 small clove garlic
3 hard-boiled eggs, peeled,
   of course

Toss everything in the food processor and let it rip. Or chop solid ingredients fine and blend well. Refrigerate a few hours or overnight before serving.

Stephen Traub

MEXICAN CHEESE DIP

2 tablespoons butter
1 medium onion, finely
  chopped
1 (4 oz.) can green chili
  peppers, chopped

1 (2 lb.) box Velveeta
  cheese

Sauté onion and peppers in butter over medium heat until onions are translucent. Add cheese and melt over very low heat. Place in fondue pot or chafing dish and serve with corn chips or chunks of homemade bread.

Sheron George

EGGS EVERGLADE

2 envelopes unflavored
  gelatin
1 (13¾ oz.) can chicken
  broth diluted with water
  to make 2 cups liquid

6 hard-boiled eggs, peeled
2 cups mayonnaise
2 tablespoons curry
  powder

Sprinkle gelatin over cold chicken broth in a small saucepan. Heat, stirring constantly, until gelatin dissolves, about 3 minutes. Remove from heat. Combine broth mixture, eggs, mayonnaise and curry powder in a food processor or blender until very smooth. Pour into a well-oiled 8-cup ring mold and chill for at least 12 hours. Better made a day ahead. Unmold and serve with cherry tomatoes, Major Grey's chutney, black olives stuffed with bleu cheese or bits of cold, freshly cooked salmon in center of ring. Serves 8 as a salad or more as an appetizer.

Susan Patterson

PIRATES' HOUSE ESCARGOTS

2 dozen snails (2 cans)
24 mushroom caps

1 recipe Snail Butter, see
below

Melt half the snail butter in a skillet and sauté mushroom caps until tender. Remove from skillet and place in 4 individual casserole dishes. Prepare snails for cooking according to instructions on can. Place a snail in each mushroom cap. Cover each snail with about 1 teaspoon snail butter. Broil until butter melts and snails are hot. Serve with lots of crusty French bread. Serves 4.

SNAIL BUTTER

1 cup butter, softened
2 tablespoons minced
   shallots

2 cloves garlic, crushed
1 tablespoon finely
   chopped fresh parsley

Combine in bowl or food processor until well-blended.

STUFFED MUSHROOMS FLORENTINE

Large mushrooms, stems
   removed, about 4 to 6
   per person
½ cup melted butter
1 recipe Spinach Balls, see
   Index (do not make into
   balls)

Freshly grated Parmesan
   cheese

Dip mushroom caps in melted butter. Lay out on baking sheet. Stuff with spinach ball mixture. Sprinkle with Parmesan cheese and bake at 350° until brown, about 15 to 20 minutes.
NOTE: Make leftover spinach ball mixture into balls and freeze for another time. Chop mushroom stems, sauté in butter and use in omelets or scrambled eggs.

SAUSAGE STUFFED MUSHROOMS

1 pound mushrooms,
   preferably all the same
   size
3 ounces summer sausage
2 (3 oz.) packages cream
   cheese, softened

1 tablespoon
   Worcestershire sauce
1 tablespoon dill weed
1 teaspoon salt
1 teaspoon Tabasco

Chop summer sausage fine in food processor or meat grinder. Add remaining ingredients; process or beat until smooth. Remove stems from mushrooms. Wipe caps clean with a damp paper towel. Lay out stem-side up on a jelly roll pan. Fill a piping bag fitted with a large star tip with stuffing. Pipe into mushroom caps. Mushrooms may be refrigerated at this point. To bake, preheat oven to 350°. Bake until brown and bubbly, 10 to 15 minutes. Serve hot.

NOTE: How many mushrooms this recipe will fill depends entirely on their size—could be anywhere from 32 to 72. The smaller mushrooms are good for hors d'oeuvres, the larger ones nice for an appetizer. If you don't have a piping bag, use a teaspoon. Save the stems for stock or soup.

CHICKEN LIVER PÂTÉ

½ pound chicken livers
½ cup butter
2 tablespoons finely
   chopped onion
1 large clove garlic,
   crushed

½ teaspoon salt
1 teaspoon dry mustard
¼ teaspoon nutmeg
⅛ teaspoon ground cloves
Pinch cayenne pepper

Barely cover chicken livers with water and bring to a boil. Reduce heat, cover and simmer 15 to 20 minutes. Drain well. Put livers in blender or food processor and purée. Add remaining ingredients and blend well. Taste and adjust seasonings. Pack in crock or jar and refrigerate at least 24 hours before serving. Remove from refrigerator 1 hour before serving. Serve with crackers or French bread—rye crisps are especially good.
NOTE: Pâté freezes well.

Edith Rhodes

DUCK LIVER PÂTÉ

Livers from 2 ducks
All available fat from inside
ducks
1 tablespoon chopped
shallot
1 clove garlic, crushed

⅛ teaspoon dried thyme
½ bay leaf, crumbled
1 tablespoon unsalted
butter, softened
1 tablespoon cognac
Salt and pepper to taste

Cut livers and fat separately into ¼-inch pieces. Place fat, shallot, garlic, thyme and bay leaf in a heavy skillet and cook, stirring constantly, for 2 minutes. Add livers; cook 2 to 3 minutes, until done. Remove from heat and let stand about 10 to 15 minutes. Place in food processor or blender and purée until smooth. Add remaining ingredients and blend well. Taste for seasonings and adjust. Do not underseason, as flavors will mellow when pâté cools. Pack into a 1-cup soufflé mold or crock, cover and refrigerate overnight. Keeps a minimum of 1 week in the refrigerator, and freezes great. Serve with crackers or homemade melba toast.
NOTE: Even liver haters love this pâté.

A good way to crush garlic—peel, pour about 1 teaspoon of salt on a chopping board, and use the tip of a table knife or spatula to make a paste of salt and garlic. The salt acts as an abrasive. Adjust salt measurement in recipe accordingly.

PHILIP'S OYSTERS

Rock salt
Shell oysters
Bottled Italian dressing
(you can use homemade)
1 (10 oz.) package frozen
spinach

Extra-sharp Cheddar
cheese
Sliced bacon

Cover the bottom of a shallow baking dish with rock salt. Open oysters, place in the half shell on salt. Sprinkle dressing over oysters. Grate *frozen* spinach, sprinkle over oysters. Grate cheese, sprinkle over spinach. Cut bacon slices in fourths, place ¼ slice on top of each oyster. Preheat broiler; broil oysters close to heat until bacon is crisp, about 5 minutes. Serve hot. Allow 3 to 4 oysters per person as an appetizer.

NOTE: A mouli grater is ideal for this. First grate a block of spinach over oysters, then a block of cheese. It's much quicker.

Philip A. Rhodes

OYSTERS SAVANNAH

Topping

1 bell pepper
2 ribs celery
½ pound raw bacon
1 (2 oz.) jar pimientos

1 teaspoon black pepper
1 teaspoon salt
¾ teaspoon Tabasco

Chop everything fine in a food processor. Process until topping is well-blended and holds together.

2 dozen shell oysters or
1 pint oysters, drained

Rock salt

Preheat oven to Broil. Lay oysters on the half shell on a bed of rock salt on a metal baking sheet. Cover each oyster with 1 tablespoon topping. Or spread drained oysters in 1 layer in a shallow casserole dish, or place several in individual casseroles, scallop shells, or metal crab shells. Spread a layer of topping over oysters. Broil 4 to 5 inches from heat until topping is browned and bubbling, 7 to 8 minutes. Drain off any grease. Serve immediately.

NOTE: We have tried several different presentations for this famous dish. Besides natural oyster shells, metal crab shells work best. The topping sits above the edge of the shell and as it cooks, the accumulated fat runs off into the rock salt. If the sides of the baking dish are too high, the grease pools on top of the oysters and the topping will not get crisp.

PELICAN GOODIES

1 pound lean ground beef
1 pound hot pork sausage
2 medium onions, chopped
2 to 3 cloves garlic, crushed, or garlic powder to taste
1 tablespoon Worcestershire sauce

2 pounds Velveeta or mild Cheddar cheese, cut in chunks or grated
3 loaves party rye or pumpernickel bread

Brown beef and sausage in a large skillet. Drain well. Add onions, garlic and Worcestershire sauce; cook 5 more minutes. Lower heat, add cheese and stir until melted. Mixture will be gloppy. Drop by spoonfuls onto party rye or pumpernickel. Broil until cheese bubbles.

NOTE: Make up hors d'oeuvres, freeze on baking sheets and transfer to Zip-loc bags. Broil from a frozen state as needed.

Gail Brickley

MUSHROOM STRUDEL

4 tablespoons butter
1½ pounds mushrooms, finely chopped
2 tablespoons finely chopped shallots
1 teaspoon salt
¼ teaspoon pepper
1 tablespoon curry powder
1 tablespoon sherry

1 cup sour cream
2 tablespoons fine dry breadcrumbs
1 (1 lb.) package filo dough, thawed
½ cup butter, melted
1 cup fine dry breadcrumbs

Sauté mushrooms, shallots, salt, pepper, curry powder, and sherry in 4 tablespoons butter in a heavy skillet. Cook until mixture is soft and all liquid disappears, about 15 to 20 minutes. Mixture must be *dry,* but do not let it brown. Set mixture aside until cool, then stir in sour cream and 2 tablespoons bread crumbs. To assemble: Spread out a cool, damp dish towel. Unwrap dough very carefully. Have another damp dish towel ready to cover dough to keep it from drying out. Separate 2 pieces of dough and lay on dish towel, 1 on top of the other. Brush with melted butter and sprinkle with bread crumbs. Repeat twice until you have 3 double layers of dough. Carefully spread half the mushroom mixture over dough, leaving a 1-inch margin on both sides and top edge. Turn the long sides of the dough over the filling. Roll up from the short end. Brush top edge with butter to seal. Place on greased baking sheet and brush with melted butter. Repeat with other half of filling. Bake on a greased cookie sheet at 375° for 25 to 30 minutes, or until golden. Transfer to platter or board and slice for serving.
NOTE: May be frozen before baking. Bake frozen at 375° for 35 to 40 minutes. Makes 2 strudels, each serving 8.

Sally-Byrd Newton Combs

NEW POTATOES WITH SOUR CREAM AND CAVIAR

New red potatoes, 1 inch in   **Sour cream**
  diameter   **Red lumpfish caviar**

Scrub potatoes but do not peel. Place in saucepan; cover with cold, lightly salted water. Bring to a boil, lower heat, cover, and simmer until just tender. Drain and rinse in cold water. With a small knife, cut a cone-shaped piece out of each potato. Spoon in a blob of sour cream; sprinkle caviar on top. You may have to shave a small piece off the bottom of some potatoes for them to stand up. Serve chilled.

SOUFFLÉ CRACKERS

Saltines   **Melted butter**
Ice water

Preheat oven to 400°. Brush baking sheet with melted butter. Fill a 9x13-inch pan or large bowl with ice water. Add 8 to 10 crackers at a time. Let float to absorb as much water as possible, turning once, about 1 minute. Fish out with fingers and place on baking sheet, leaving about ½ inch between crackers. Carefully brush tops with melted butter, covering crackers completely. Be careful not to squash crackers. Bake 15 minutes. Reduce heat to 300° and continue baking until golden brown and crisp, about 25 minutes. Cool on wire racks. Store in airtight container.
NOTE: A 1½-inch polyester brush from the hardware store works great. Eat crackers plain, or serve with pâté, artichoke dip, or whatever strikes your fancy.

SEVICHE

1 pound bay scallops, or
   sea scallops cut in
   fourths, or
1 pound flounder fillets,
   cut into bite-size pieces
   (remove skin)
Juice of 3 or 4 limes,
   enough to cover fish
1 teaspoon salt
½ teaspoon pepper
2 cloves garlic, crushed

¾ teaspoon tarragon
2 tablespoons finely
   chopped fresh parsley
1 tablespoon chopped
   chives
5 tablespoons canned
   green chili peppers,
   optional
½ teaspoon dry mustard
6 tablespoons olive oil

Arrange scallops or fish pieces in 1 layer in a shallow glass dish. Pour lime juice over fish, so that every piece is moistened and juice covers bottom of dish. Cover and refrigerate at least 10 hours or overnight, turning often. Meanwhile, combine remaining ingredients. Drain scallops, pour sauce over and serve.

NOTE: If you wish, and if they are in season, slice 3 peeled avocados into bite-size pieces and combine with seviche and sauce before serving, or cut avocados in half and stuff with seviche and sauce for an appetizer. Garnish with salad greens and onion rings.

Bailee Kronowitz

Use wax paper for sifting and grating onto, wrapping pre-measured ingredients in, pounding meat between—the uses are endless, it's more economical than aluminum foil or plastic wrap, and biodegradable besides. Don't use to wrap meat or to freeze in.

SHRIMP DIP

1 pound raw shrimp,
  cooked and peeled
1 (8 oz.) package cream
  cheese, softened
1 cup mayonnaise
1 small onion, or 2
  tablespoons grated
  onion

1 teaspoon Worcestershire
  sauce
½ teaspoon salt

Toss everything in food processor and process until well-blended. Or, grate onion, chop shrimp fine, and mix all ingredients well. Refrigerate at least 2 hours before serving for flavors to blend.

Mincy Peterson

SHRIMP PASTE

3 pounds raw shrimp,
  cooked and peeled
Juice of 1 lemon
2 teaspoons
  Worcestershire sauce

1 tablespoon grated onion
Salt, red pepper and
  Tabasco to taste
Good quality mayonnaise

Chop shrimp in food processor until very fine, or grind in meat grinder. Mix with seasonings and enough mayonnaise to give desired consistency. Serve on crackers or use as sandwich spread.

NOTE: Good with homemade mayonnaise, but be very careful to keep shrimp and mayonnaise cold. Bought mayonnaise acts as a preservative, and shrimp will keep longer.

Flora Undercoffler

SHRIMP MOLD

2 pounds raw shrimp, unpeeled
1 envelope unflavored gelatin
Juice of 1 lemon
2 tablespoons cold water
1 cup sour cream
1 (8 oz.) package cream cheese, softened
½ cup mayonnaise
¼ cup finely chopped bell pepper
¼ cup finely chopped celery
¼ cup finely chopped green onions
2 tablespoons finely chopped pimientos
¼ cup chili sauce
Few drops Tabasco
½ teaspoon salt
1½ teaspoons Worcestershire sauce

To cook shrimp: Bring a large pot of water to a boil. Add 2 bay leaves, 1 tablespoon salt, 1 small onion, peeled and cut in half, 6 peppercorns, and the rind of the juiced lemon. Add shrimp; cook until pink, about 2 minutes. Do not overcook. Drain immediately and rinse in cold water. Peel while still warm; chop fine—use your food processor or blender. You should have approximately 3 cups of chopped shrimp. Soften gelatin in lemon juice and cold water. Beat together cream cheese, sour cream and mayonnaise until smooth. Add remaining ingredients and beat until well-blended. Melt gelatin and fold into shrimp mixture. Pour into a well-oiled 1-quart ring mold or fish mold. Cover and refrigerate 8 hours or overnight. Turn out onto serving platter, garnish with watercress and serve with crackers. **NOTE:** This recipe doubles easily, especially if you've just come back from shrimping and have an extra five pounds! Use a 2-quart ring mold.

MARINATED SHRIMP

4 pounds unpeeled raw
  shrimp (medium or large
  work best)
1 (11 oz.) can tomato soup
1½ cups vegetable oil
¾ cup white wine vinegar
¼ cup sugar
½ teaspoon paprika

1 tablespoon dry mustard
1 tablespoon
  Worcestershire sauce
2 teaspoons salt
1½ teaspoons Tabasco
2 medium onions, thinly
  sliced
4 lemons, thinly sliced

Bring a large pot of salted water to a boil. Add shrimp, return water quickly to a boil (check shrimp for doneness after 2 minutes) and drain. *Do not overcook.* Peel, leaving tails on. Whisk marinade ingredients together until well-blended, adding onions and lemons last. Stir in shrimp. Marinate in a plastic container in refrigerator at least 24 hours, stirring occasionally. Remove from marinade with a slotted spoon and serve in a glass bowl or lettuce-lined metal bowl.

CHINESE PEANUTS

Raw shelled peanuts

1 tablespoon soy sauce

Place peanuts 1 inch thick in cast iron skillet. Toss with soy sauce. Preheat oven to 350° and bake 15 minutes, stirring often, until peanuts are brown and dry. Do not burn.

Ivan Bailey

SPINACH BALLS

2 (10 oz.) boxes frozen chopped spinach
2 large onions, finely chopped
2 cups Pepperidge Farm Herb Dressing
6 eggs
¾ cup margarine, melted
½ cup freshly grated Parmesan cheese

1 large clove garlic, crushed
1½ teaspoons thyme
1½ teaspoons pepper
2 cups freshly grated Parmesan cheese, optional

Bring a pot of water to a boil. Drop in frozen spinach, remove from heat and let spinach sit until thawed. Drain. Squeeze spinach a handful at a time to get as dry as possible. Do not omit this step—it's tedious, but necessary. Mix all ingredients, except the 2 cups Parmesan cheese, together with your hands. Refrigerate 2 to 3 hours or overnight so mixture will handle better. Roll into balls, using approximately 1 teaspoon mixture per ball. You may leave balls plain or roll in extra Parmesan cheese. Place on cookie sheets; bake at 375° for 20 minutes or until brown. Serve hot in chafing dish or on warming tray, or pass on a tray—they'll disappear quickly.

NOTE: To freeze, lay out on cookie sheets; place in freezer. When frozen, remove from cookie sheets and store in Zip-loc bags. Bake frozen on cookie sheets at 375°. Makes between 125 and 150. Recipe doubles easily.

Good knives are a cook's best friend, and well worth the expense. Don't buy knives in sets. If your funds are limited, you should be able to get by with a chef's knife, chosen to fit your hand, a utility knife, and a serrated bread knife.

BEVERAGES

BLOODY MARYS FOR A CROWD

2 (46 oz.) cans tomato juice
1 teaspoon black pepper
1 tablespoon salt
1 teaspoon Tabasco
1 tablespoon
  Worcestershire sauce
1 fifth vodka

Mix well and chill. Serve over ice with celery sticks and lime wedges.

A BAR FOR 50

2 bottles each: Scotch, gin, rum, vodka, bourbon and blended whiskey
1 bottle each: sweet and dry vermouth (for martinis and Manhattans)
4 liters white wine
½ to 1 case beer, optional
3 liters each: Coke, Sprite or 7-Up, ginger ale, tonic and club soda
2 quarts each: orange and grapefruit juice
Water in a pitcher
Maraschino cherries, lime wedges and olives in bowls (orange slices look pretty, but no one uses them)
Lemon twists (cut top and bottom off lemon, cut peel in narrow strips almost to bottom, tear off when needed)

Bar munchies—pretzels, peanuts or whatever you like
Paper napkins
Stirrers
Glasses
Corkscrew
Jigger
Dish towel
8 pour spouts
50 pounds ice
Ice scoop
Ice chest
2 large bowls
Plastic bucket for used ice and trash
A good bartender

Figure on 3 drinks per person per hour for the first hour of a bar, pouring 25 drinks per bottle. This is a safe 2 hour bar with the addition of an extra bottle of whatever your friends drink most of. Set up a long table against a wall with room behind for the bartender. Set up liquor, mixers and glasses in an arrangement that makes sense to you. Ice down wine (and beer) in a large bowl. Fill another large bowl with ice for drinks. Leave majority of ice in ice chest under bar. Put napkins, stirrers and garnishes in front where people can reach them. Lay dish towel on table where you will be pouring to catch drips. Pour spouts and a jigger greatly simplify mixing of drinks.

NOTE: For a morning or luncheon bar, make up a batch or 2 of Bloody Marys (see Index.) You'll save yourself a lot of time and trouble if you will hire a knowledgeable college student (male or female) to set up, pour, and break down bar. Fifty dollars is a fair price. Consider renting glasses—you'll need about 25 wine glasses and 50 highball glasses, and a few rocks glasses.

WHITE SANGRIA

1 large orange, thinly sliced and seeded
1 large lemon, thinly sliced and seeded
1 large lime, thinly sliced and seeded
1 cup triple sec
½ cup sugar
2 fifths (2 liters) dry white wine, chilled
1 liter club soda, chilled

At least eight hours before serving, mix fruit and Triple Sec in a plastic bag or container. Refrigerate until serving. Before serving, mix fruit and sugar in punch bowl or large pitcher. Add wine and club soda. Do not add ice. Serves 20.

CHATHAM ARTILLERY PUNCH

8 liters white rum
4 liters gin
4 liters rye
4 liters brandy
3 gallons rosé or Catawba
  wine
1 pound green tea, steeped
  overnight in 2 gallons
  cold water and strained

2 quarts maraschino
  cherries, drained
2 pounds pineapple
  chunks—fresh is best
5 pounds light brown
  sugar
Juice of 3 dozen lemons
Champagne

Mix all ingredients except champagne in a large, clean plastic trash can with lid. Cover and store in a cool place for a minimum of 2 months—it only improves with age. Serve in a punch bowl with a large block of ice. Add champagne to taste; 1 to 2 bottles per punch bowl. Also good mixed with orange juice and/or club soda for a lighter drink, or sipped straight as a liqueur. Make sure each cup contains some fruit, but by no means feed it to your children. This is the most subtly lethal punch you will ever drink. Three glasses and you're out!

NOTE: Perhaps you could make this a neighborhood project, or save your old wine bottles, bottle it, and give as Christmas presents. You say you don't want to make 10 gallons of punch? Oh, all right, here's a reduced version—

2 liters rum
1 liter gin
1 liter rye
1 liter brandy
3 bottles rosé or Catawba
  wine
¼ pound green tea in 2
  quarts cold water

2 cups maraschino
  cherries
½ pound pineapple
2½ cups firmly packed
  light brown sugar
Juice of 9 lemons

PIRATES' HOUSE PUNCH

1 (46 oz.) can grapefruit
 juice
2 (46 oz.) cans pineapple
 juice
3 quarts orange juice
¾ cup maraschino cherry
 juice—or just enough to
 make a pinky-orange
 color

Ginger ale and/or orange
 sherbet to taste, optional
Orange, lemon and lime
 slices for garnish

Mix first 4 ingredients together and chill. When ready to serve, add ginger ale and/or sherbet balls if desired. Garnish with sliced fruit.

NOTE: Freeze punch mixture in a ring mold and use instead of ice in a punch bowl. Serve unspiked to the kiddies and make yours into Pirates' Punch, see Index. Makes approximately 2 gallons.

WATERMELON PUNCH

1 ripe, juicy watermelon
2 cups rosé wine

Juice of ½ lemon
1 to 1¼ cups sugar

Cut watermelon in half. Cut out heart of watermelon and chop coarsely for garnish, or use melon baller. Toss with approximately ¼ cup sugar; freeze. Scoop pulp from watermelon. Squish through fingers into a metal sieve. Push through sieve with a ladle or wooden spoon into a large bowl, stopping occasionally to remove seeds and fibers. Stir in ¾ to 1 cup sugar, lemon juice and rosé. Chill at least 3 hours or overnight. Pour into tall glasses, stir in watermelon balls or pieces, and garnish with fresh mint, if available.

NOTE: May also be served as a cold soup. Serves 8 to 10.

Kit Traub

EGGNOG I

12 eggs, separated
1½ cups confectioners'
  sugar
1 quart milk
1 cup cognac

1 cup dark rum
1 large orange
1 lemon
1 quart heavy cream
Grated nutmeg

Beat egg yolks and sugar until thick. Stir in milk, cognac, and rum. Beat egg whites until they just hold a soft peak and fold in. Refrigerate several hours. With a vegetable peeler or sharp knife, cut off only the orange part of the orange rind, being careful not to get any white. Cut into very thin strips about 1½ inches long. Grate the lemon rind. Whip the cream until it just begins to thicken—not so that it actually holds peaks. Stir half-whipped cream into egg and milk mixture and whisk a few times. Stir in lemon rind and half the orange rind. Pour into serving bowl. Sprinkle remaining orange rind and nutmeg over top. Serves 24.

Henry Gaede

EGGNOG II

24 eggs, separated
2 cups sugar
1 pint bourbon

½ pint rum
2 quarts whipping cream

Beat egg yolks until light. Gradually add sugar; beat until light and fluffy. Gradually beat in bourbon and rum. Let stand several hours or overnight in the refrigerator. Whip cream stiff and fold into egg mixture. Before serving, whip egg whites until stiff but not dry and fold into egg-cream mixture. Sprinkle nutmeg over top before serving.
NOTE: Refrigerate egg whites until 1 hour before whipping. Serves 30.

Herb Traub

JUNGLE DRINKS FROM THE TREASURE ISLAND BAR

Blue Lagoon

½ ounce gin
½ ounce rum
½ ounce vodka

½ ounce tequila
¾ ounce blue curaçao
5 ounces Collins mix

Blend well. Serve over ice in a tall glass.

Jungle Rot

½ ounce gin
½ ounce rum
½ ounce vodka
½ ounce tequila

½ ounce triple sec
1 ounce Collins mix
1½ ounces Coke
Splash ginger ale

Blend well. Serve over ice in a tall glass. Garnish with lime.

Pagan Pleasure

1 ounce dark rum
½ ounce orange curaçao
¼ ounce crème de noyaux
½ ounce lime juice
¼ ounce grenadine

2½ ounces pineapple juice
Orange slice, optional
1 sugar cube soaked in 151
   rum, optional

Blend well; serve in a glass packed with enough ice to support orange slice and sugar cube. Flame sugar cube before serving.

Tiki Mongo

1 ounce light rum
1 ounce dark rum
1 ounce 151 rum
1 ounce orange curaçao

2 ounces Collins mix
2 ounces orange juice
½ ounce lime juice
½ ounce grenadine

Mix well and serve over ice in a *large* glass, or divide between 2 glasses. In any case, share with a friend.

HARD-HEARTED HANNAH
(THE VAMP OF SAVANNAH, G.A.)

1 ounce brandy
½ ounce orange curaçao
2 ounces orange juice

Dash grenadine
Champagne

Zip first 4 ingredients with ice in blender; strain into champagne glass and top with champagne.

MINT JULEP

6 tender mint leaves
1 ounce simple syrup, see
  Index

2 ounces bourbon
Crushed ice
Mint for garnish

Muddle mint leaves and simple syrup together in a julep cup or metal glass. Fill with crushed ice. Add bourbon. Stir with an up-and-down motion until glass frosts on the outside. Garnish with mint and serve with straws. Serve on the porch when it's too hot to do anything else but sit and drink juleps. The ritual of the Mint Julep and the drink itself make for GREAT parties, especially on Kentucky Derby day.
NOTE: If you don't have an ice crusher, wrap ice in a *clean* burlap sack or heavy towel and pound with a mallet.

 # PIRATES' PUNCH, a.k.a. SKULL CRUSHER

1 ounce rum
1 ounce 151 rum
½ ounce grenadine

Pirates' House Punch, see
  Index

Pour first 3 ingredients in large ice-filled glass or mug—a skull mug is ideal. Top with punch. Stir. Garnish with orange, lime and cherry if desired.

FLAVORED VODKA

Orange or Lemon Vodka

Cut the peel of 1 orange or lemon in a long strip. Put peel in 1 fifth vodka and refrigerate for at least 24 hours. Remove peel and serve.

Pepper Vodka

Proceed as above, using a strip or two of hot red pepper.

NOTE: Vodka is traditionally served with zakusky, Russian hors d'oeuvres, but many people continue drinking vodka throughout the meal. Vodka is served ice cold in small shot-size glasses. The glass is supposed to be drained in one gulp, preceded by a toast and followed by a bite of food.

Olga Shishkevish

HOT MULLED WINE

4 cups sugar
6 cinnamon sticks
1 teaspoon ground cloves
3 navel oranges, thinly
   sliced
1 lemon, thinly sliced
2 cups water
1 gallon dry red wine

About 30 minutes before serving, heat all ingredients but wine in an 8-quart pot. Bring to a boil and simmer 5 minutes, stirring occasionally. Pour in wine and heat until piping hot but not boiling, stirring occasionally. Serve hot. Makes 18 cups or 36 1/2-cup servings.

HOT BUTTERED RUM

2¼ ounces rum
5 cloves
1 cinnamon stick

Apple cider
1 tablespoon butter,
  softened

Place rum, cloves and cinnamon stick in a large mug. Fill with cider. Heat in microwave oven. Or pour contents of mug into saucepan and heat gently on top of stove. Do not boil. Top with butter and serve hot.

PIRATES' HOUSE SPECIAL COFFEE DRINKS

Café Jackson

1 ounce Grand Marnier
½ ounce Tia Maria

Hot coffee
Sweetened whipped cream

Dip the edge of a mug or heat-proof wine glass in simple syrup (see Index), then in cinnamon sugar. Pour liqueurs in mug or glass, fill with coffee and top with whipped cream.

David Jackson

Café Vandermint

1 ounce Vandermint
½ ounce dark crème de
  cacao

Hot coffee
Sweetened whipped cream

Pour liqueurs in a mug or heat-proof wine glass. Fill with coffee. Top with whipped cream.

PIRATES' HOUSE SPECIAL ICE CREAM DRINKS

Bermuda Triangle

1 ounce Kahlua
½ ounce green crème de menthe

1 heaping cup good quality vanilla ice cream

Bird of Paradise

1½ ounces Cointreau
½ orange slice, optional (goes in blender)

⅔ cup good quality vanilla ice cream
⅔ cup orange sherbet

Frozen Brandy Alexander

¾ ounce brandy
¾ ounce dark crème de cacao

1 heaping cup good quality vanilla ice cream
Nutmeg to sprinkle on top

Godsend

¾ ounce Amaretto di Saronno
¾ ounce Scotch

1 heaping cup good quality vanilla ice cream
Nutmeg to sprinkle on top

Mix well in blender and serve in a tall glass—a pilsner glass is ideal. Makes 1 big (and fattening) drink.

SIMPLE SYRUP

2 cups sugar   1 cup water

Heat in a saucepan and boil for 5 minutes. Keep in a bottle in the refrigerator and use as needed.

SOUPS
AND
SANDWICHES

BEEF-BARLEY SOUP

1½ to 2 pounds stew beef
   or meaty soup bones
2 quarts water
1 large onion, chopped
2 teaspoons instant beef
   broth
1 cup barley
4 medium carrots, peeled
   and chopped

4 ribs celery, chopped
1 cup canned tomatoes,
   chopped
1½ tablespoons salt
½ teaspoon pepper
¼ teaspoon oregano

Bring beef, water, onion and beef broth to a boil. Lower heat and simmer covered 1½ to 2 hours, until meat is tender. Add remaining ingredients and cook until vegetables are tender, 30 to 40 minutes. Serves 6 to 8.

Kat Cohen

CREAM OF CAULIFLOWER SOUP

1 cup cooked, chopped
   cauliflower, or 1 (10 oz.)
   package frozen
   cauliflower, cooked,
   drained and chopped
2 tablespoons butter
¼ cup chopped onion
2 small ribs celery with
   leaves, chopped

1½ cups or 1 (13¾ oz.) can
   chicken broth
1 cup whipping cream
1 tablespoon chopped
   fresh parsley
Salt and pepper to taste
Chopped fresh coriander
   or freshly ground
   nutmeg for garnish

Heat butter in a heavy saucepan. Cook onions and celery until onions are translucent. Add chicken broth and cauliflower and bring to a boil. Simmer until vegetables are soft. Purée in a food processor, blender or food mill. Return to saucepan, add cream and heat gently. Add parsley and salt and pepper to taste. Garnish with coriander or nutmeg if desired. Serves 4.

Sally-Byrd Newton Combs

BRUNSWICK STEW

3½ pound frying chicken
1 pound lean boneless
  pork chops, trimmed of
  fat
1½ pounds lean ground
  beef
3 large onions, chopped
1 quart chicken stock
  (from cooking chicken)
1 (14 oz.) bottle catsup
2 (1 lb.) cans tomatoes,
  mashed, with juice

3 (1 lb. 1 oz.) cans creamed
  corn
2 pounds potatoes, peeled
  and diced (optional)
3 teaspoons salt
1 teaspoon black pepper
¼ teaspoon cayenne
  pepper, or to taste
1 tablespoon
  Worcestershire sauce
¼ teaspoon Tabasco, or to
  taste

Place chicken and pork chops in a large pot, cover with salted water, bring to a boil, lower heat, cover and simmer until chicken is tender, about 30 minutes. Remove chicken and pork from stock and cool. Strain stock and reserve. When chicken is cool enough to handle, remove skin, remove chicken from bones and chop fine—a food processor works great, but don't overprocess. Grind pork, using meat grinder or food processor. Meanwhile, cook beef and onion in 1 quart chicken stock until beef loses pink color, about 20 minutes. In your largest, heaviest pot combine all ingredients, bring to a boil, lower to heat and simmer 1½ to 2 hours, stirring frequently, as it burns easily. Taste for seasonings.
NOTE: This freezes well, but omit potatoes. Some people prefer their Brunswick stew without potatoes in any case. Makes approximately 1 gallon.

Sprinkle a little flour on the lid of a hot pot as a reminder not to touch.

FRENCH ONION SOUP

2 pounds onions, thinly
  sliced
4 tablespoons butter
1 teaspoon salt
1 tablespoon flour
3 (11 oz.) cans Campbell's
  beef bouillon plus 3 cans
  water, or

1 can beef bouillon, 1 (13¾
  oz.) can chicken stock,
  plus 1 can each water
½ to 1 cup white wine or
  vermouth (to taste)
Black pepper

Melt the butter over moderate heat in a heavy Dutch oven. When butter is foaming, add onions and salt. Fry for 20 to 30 minutes, stirring occasionally, letting the onions become a deep rich brown. Be careful not to burn onions, or you will have a bitter taste. When onions are done, stir in flour off the heat; return to heat, stirring constantly for a minute or two, then pour in the bouillon and/or broth and water. Bring liquid to a boil, reduce heat to a simmer, add wine, and simmer for 30 minutes. Taste for seasoning.

6 to 8 1-inch slices good
  quality French bread
½ cup grated Swiss
  cheese

½ cup freshly grated
  Parmesan cheese
Oil

Preheat oven to 325°. Arrange the slices of bread on a baking sheet, brush with oil, and toast for about 15 minutes. When you are ready to serve the soup, preheat oven to 375°. Arrange the bread side by side on top of the soup, and sprinkle with the cheese. (You may ladle the soup into individual oven-proof bowls, add a bread slice to each, and sprinkle with cheese.) Bake the soup in the middle of the oven for 10 to 15 minutes, or until the cheese has melted and formed a light brown crust. If it is not brown enough, brown under the broiler for a minute. Serve at once. Serves 6 to 8.

GREEK LEMON SOUP

½ cup heavy cream, whipped
2 tablespoons grated lemon peel
1 tablespoon freshly grated Parmesan cheese
4 cans (13¾ oz.) chicken broth

½ cup raw rice
2 egg yolks
¼ cup fresh lemon juice
Snipped fresh chives, if desired
1 peeled lemon, cut in paper-thin slices, if desired

Stir lemon peel and Parmesan cheese into whipped cream; refrigerate. Heat broth to boiling; stir in rice. Simmer uncovered until rice is soft, stirring occasionally, about 15 minutes. Whisk egg yolks and lemon juice until light. Gradually whisk 1 cup hot broth into egg yolk mixture. Remove broth from heat; slowly stir egg yolk mixture into broth. Pour soup into bowls, add a blob of whipped cream to each, and garnish with chopped chives and/or lemon slices if desired.

NOTE: Can also be served cold (refrigerate at least 5 hours) but is more scrumptious hot. Reheats well and freezes well, but be careful not to boil when reheating. Serves 6.

Franklin Traub

ZUCCHINI SOUP

4 small zucchini, washed and sliced
3 tablespoons butter
2 medium onions, finely chopped
1 clove garlic, crushed
2 (13¾ oz.) cans chicken broth, or 3½ cups homemade chicken stock

1 to 2 tablespoons finely chopped fresh parsley
1 teaspoon lemon juice
Freshly ground black pepper
⅓ cup heavy cream

Place sliced zucchini in a colander, sprinkle with salt, and let stand 30 minutes. Heat the butter in a heavy pot. Add the onion and garlic and cook over low heat for 5 minutes, until translucent. Do not brown. Rinse and dry zucchini. Add to pot and continue cooking for 5 minutes. Add the stock, bring to a boil, lower heat, and simmer for 15 minutes. Remove from heat and purée solids in food processor or blender, adding liquid only as needed. Add parsley, lemon juice, and cream; whisk until well-blended. Add pepper to taste, and salt if needed. Reheat and serve hot, or chill and serve cold. Serves 4 to 6.

GAZPACHO

2 bell peppers, seeded
4 medium tomatoes,
  peeled and seeded
2 cucumbers, peeled and
  seeded
½ cup bread crumbs
6 tablespoons red wine
  vinegar

1 medium onion
1 to 2 cloves garlic
5 tablespoons good quality
  olive oil
4 cups tomato juice
Salt
Pepper

Dice half a pepper, half a tomato and half a cucumber by hand for garnish. Place in separate bowls and reserve. Soak bread crumbs in vinegar. Drop peeled garlic onto running blade of food processor or blender. Add peppers and onion and purée. Add tomatoes and cucumbers. Purée. Pour in olive oil while machine is running and process until emulsified. Pour into 2-quart pitcher, stir in tomato juice, and season with salt and pepper to taste. Stir in bread crumbs and vinegar. Chill well. To serve, stir well and pour into bowls. Garnish with diced pepper, tomato and cucumber.
NOTE: Theoretically, the little pieces of vegetables used as a garnish prevent indigestion. Removing the seeds from the tomatoes and cucumbers doesn't hurt, either. To seed cucumbers, peel, cut in half lengthwise, and scoop out seeds with a teaspoon. Serves 6.

ICED LEBANESE SOUP

2 cucumbers
1 cup tomato juice
1 cup chicken stock
3 cups plain yogurt
1 cup heavy cream
2 cloves garlic, crushed

4 ounces fresh small
   shrimp, cooked and
   peeled
1 hard-boiled egg, grated
Fresh mint to garnish

Peel cucumbers; cut in half lengthwise. Scoop out seeds with a teaspoon. Dice cucumbers; place in colander, sprinkle with salt, and let stand for 30 minutes. Rinse with cold water. Mix liquid ingredients, yogurt, cucumber, garlic, shrimp and egg. Chill well. Garnish with fresh mint. Serves 6.

POTATO-CHEESE SOUP

3 cups peeled, diced
   potatoes
1 medium onion, chopped
1 cup potato water
2 tablespoons butter
1 teaspoon salt
¼ teaspoon pepper
½ teaspoon celery salt

3 cups milk
10 slices American cheese
Garnish:
4 to 6 slices bacon, fried
   until crisp, drained and
   crumbled
1 to 2 green onions,
   chopped

Place potatoes and onion in saucepan; cover with cold water. Bring to a boil, lower heat, cover and simmer until soft, about 20 minutes. Drain, reserving 1 cup of potato water. Place potatoes, onion, butter and potato water in blender or food processor. Process until smooth. Return to saucepan; whisk in milk and seasonings. Add cheese and heat, whisking occasionally, until cheese melts. Taste and adjust seasonings. Serve with bacon and green onions sprinkled on top. Serves 4.

Kathi Williams

ROOT SOUP!

1 large or 2 small carrots, peeled
1 medium turnip or parsnip, peeled
1 medium yellow or white onion, peeled
1 medium boiling potato, peeled
1 clove garlic, crushed
4 tablespoons butter

2 cups chicken stock, or
1 can chicken broth plus water to make 2 cups
2 tablespoons vodka
Salt
Freshly ground pepper
Whipped cream or yogurt, optional
Finely chopped fresh ginger, optional

Slice vegetables thin. Melt butter in skillet. Add the vegetables and sauté until onions are transparent, about 10 minutes. Do not brown. Meanwhile, heat chicken stock in large saucepan. Add vegetables to stock, cover, and simmer until vegetables are soft, about 15 minutes. Remove from heat, add vodka, and purée in food processor or food mill. Taste for seasonings; add salt and pepper as needed. Pour into soup bowls. Top with a blob of lightly salted whipped cream or yogurt and sprinkle with ginger root.

NOTE: May be made in advance and reheated. Do try this recipe—despite the unglamorous name, it is absolutely delicious! Serves 4.

SEAFOOD GUMBO

1 recipe Okra Gumbo Soup, see Index
1½ cups cooked and peeled baby shrimp (frozen are fine, but thaw them)

1 pound crabmeat, picked over for shells

5 minutes before serving, add seafood and heat through.

FILÉ GUMBO

⅓ cup vegetable oil
⅓ cup all-purpose flour
¼ pound mild or hot
    smoked sausage
1 large onion, chopped
1 large clove garlic,
    crushed
1 tablespoon finely
    chopped fresh parsley
1½ teaspoons salt
¾ teaspoon black pepper
2 bay leaves

½ teaspoon thyme
Cayenne pepper to taste
¼ teaspoon Creole
    Seasoning, optional, see
    Index
1 quart cold water
1 pound raw shrimp,
    peeled
1 (12 oz.) can fresh
    oysters, drained
    (optional)
2 tablespoons filé powder

Heat the oil in a heavy pot. Gradually add the flour. Cook over medium heat for about 15 minutes, stirring constantly, until roux is dark mahogany brown. Do not burn. A good roux is the secret of success. Add remaining ingredients except seafood and filé. Bring mixture to a boil, lower heat and simmer, covered, for about 45 minutes. Remove cover and add shrimp and oysters. Simmer uncovered about 5 minutes, or until just cooked. Remove pot from heat and stir in filé. Cover pot and let sit 5 minutes. Serve in bowls over white rice.

NOTE: Substitute cooked and drained mild or hot Italian sausage for smoked sausage. Serves 4.

 ## MISS EDNA'S SEAFOOD BISQUE

1 (11 oz.) can tomato
    soup
1 (11 oz.) can split pea
    soup
1½ soup cans milk
½ pound crabmeat, picked
    over for shells

½ pound cooked and
    peeled baby shrimp
    (frozen are fine, but thaw
    them)
Dry sherry
Lemon sliced in thin
    rounds

Combine soups in heavy saucepan. Whisk in milk, making sure mixture is smooth. Bring to a boil, whisking occasionally to keep from scorching. Reduce heat to low, stir in crabmeat and shrimp. Be careful not to scorch soup. Before serving, add 1 tablespoon sherry (or to taste) to each soup bowl and stir to blend. Float a thin slice of lemon on top to garnish.

SPLIT PEA SOUP

1 (1 lb.) meaty ham bone or ham hock
4 cups water
1 (13¾ oz.) can chicken broth, or
2 cups homemade chicken stock
2 cups (12 oz.) dried split peas, rinsed
⅔ cup finely chopped green onions
⅓ cup finely chopped carrots
⅓ cup finely chopped celery
1 teaspoon sugar
½ teaspoon marjoram
¼ teaspoon freshly ground pepper
2½ cups milk
1 cup heavy cream
Dry sherry

Place ham bone in large heavy pot. Add water, chicken broth and peas. Bring to a boil. Skim. Reduce heat, cover, and simmer, stirring occasionally, for 30 minutes. Add vegetables and seasonings and continue to simmer gently, stirring occasionally, for 30 to 40 minutes, or until peas are very soft and mixture is thick. Remove ham bone. Purée soup in food processor, or mash against sides of pot with a wooden spoon. When ham bone is cool enough to handle, remove meat from bone, chop and reserve. 30 minutes before serving, heat soup. Whisk in milk and cream. Add ham. Bring to a boil, lower heat, and simmer very gently, whisking occasionally, for 10 to 15 minutes. This soup burns easily, so watch carefully. Correct seasoning—you will probably need to add salt. After serving soup, stir in sherry to taste.

NOTE: Even better the second day—and it freezes well.

NAVY BEAN SOUP

1 pound navy beans,
  soaked overnight and
  drained
8 cups water
Ham bone or 2 ham hocks
1 medium onion, chopped
2 ribs celery, chopped
1 carrot, peeled and
  chopped

2 cloves garlic, crushed
3 medium potatoes,
  peeled, cooked and
  mashed, or
1 packet instant mashed
  potatoes, cooked
  according to package
  directions
Salt and pepper to taste

Combine ingredients in a large pot and cook until beans are tender. Add water if necessary. Season to taste and purée in food processor or food mill—remove ham bone or ham hocks first! Cut meat off bones and return to pot. Serves 6.

Suzanne D. Peterson

OKRA GUMBO SOUP

2 (1 lb.) cans tomatoes,
  coarsely chopped
1 tablespoon tomato paste
1 medium onion, coarsely
  chopped
1 small bell pepper,
  coarsely chopped
2 ribs celery, coarsely
  chopped

3 ounces ham, diced
5 cups water
1 teaspoon salt
½ teaspoon pepper
¾ teaspoon Angostura
  bitters, optional
1 pound frozen okra

Combine all ingredients except okra in a soup pot. Bring to a boil, lower heat, and simmer 1 hour. Add okra and simmer for 20 minutes more.

NOTE: Angostura bitters add a certain something, but don't go out and buy a bottle just for this recipe.

RUSSIAN SOUP

2 pounds beef short ribs
12 cups water
10 peppercorns
2 tablespoons butter
1 large onion, chopped
2 carrots, peeled and
  chopped
2 medium potatoes, peeled
  and diced

2 small turnips, peeled and
  diced
½ small cabbage,
  shredded
1 (8 oz.) can sauerkraut,
  drained
Salt
1 tablespoon dillweed
Sour cream

Bring beef ribs, water, and peppercorns to a boil in a large pot. Lower heat to a simmer, cover, and cook 2 hours, or until meat is tender. Remove meat; cover and refrigerate. Refrigerate stock overnight; fat will rise to top and congeal. Remove fat and peppercorns and discard. Cut meat into bite-size pieces and add to stock. Sauté onions and carrots in butter until onions are translucent. Add to stock and bring to a boil. Lower to a simmer and cook, covered, until vegetables are tender. Add cabbage, sauerkraut, dillweed, and salt to taste. Continue cooking until cabbage is tender, about 15 minutes. Taste and correct seasoning. Add a big blob of sour cream to each soup bowl after serving.

NOTE: If you have a piece of Polish sausage, slice it thin and add with the cabbage and sauerkraut. Serves 8.

 Stock up on wooden spoons. Stirring with wooden utensils is gentler on your pots and your ears, and the handles don't get hot and burn your fingers.

VEGETABLE SOUP

1½ pounds stew beef
1 quart water
1 teaspoon salt
1 large onion, chopped
5 to 6 fresh tomatoes,
  peeled and quartered
2 ears corn, cut off the cob
¼ pound okra, sliced
½ pound butter beans,
  shelled
1 medium potato, peeled
  and diced

1 rib celery, chopped, or
1 (1 pound 12 oz.) can
  tomatoes
1 (1 lb.) bag frozen
  vegetable soup mix
1 (8 oz.) can tomato sauce,
  optional
Salt and black pepper to
  taste

Bring meat, water, onion and salt to a boil in a heavy pot. Simmer covered for 1 hour. Add vegetables. Cook for another hour.
Adjust seasonings. For a stronger tomato flavor, add the tomato sauce with the vegetables. This gives the soup a thicker
consistency.
NOTE: When beautiful fresh vegetables are not in season,
vegetable soup mix is easy to use and the end product is just
as good. Serves 6.

Martha Summerour

 A piece of paper towel in a recycled glass jar soaks up the smell
of whatever was in there before—and always remove the card-
board lid liner. Of course, your friends may think that your paper
towel collection is a little odd.

GRILLED HAM AND CHEESE

2 slices white bread
1 slice mozzarella cheese
2 thin slices ham
1 tablespoon Parmesan
   cheese

Salt and pepper
Melted butter or margarine

Place ham and mozzarella on 1 slice of bread. Sprinkle with Parmesan cheese and salt and pepper. Close sandwich. Brush with melted butter on both sides and grill until golden brown and cheese has melted, turning once. Trim crusts for a classy presentation. Serves 1.

CRABMEAT SANDWICH

1 (8 oz.) package cream
   cheese, softened
1 small onion
1 egg yolk
1 (6 oz.) can crabmeat,
   rinsed, drained and
   picked through for shells

1 large tomato, sliced
6 Holland rusks or 3
   English muffins, split
   and toasted
Grated sharp Cheddar
   cheese

Combine cream cheese and onion in food processor until well-blended. Or, grate onion and mix well with cream cheese. Add egg yolk; mix well. Add crabmeat. Refrigerate 1 hour to stiffen and combine flavors. Preheat oven to 350°. Place Holland rusks or toasted English muffins on baking sheet. Place a slice of tomato on each, top with crab mixture and grated cheese. Bake 15 minutes. Serves 3 to 6.

Edith Rhodes

HOSTESS CITY SANDWICH

1 cup (approximately)
  Salad Sauce, see Index
1 pound raw shrimp,
  cooked, peeled and
  chopped
1 tablespoon grated onion
Tabasco to taste

4 slices firm white bread,
  lightly toasted
16 delicatessen-style
  Kosher dill pickle slices
Mild Cheddar cheese, cut
  in thin slices

Mix salad sauce, shrimp, onion and Tabasco and refrigerate 1 hour for flavors to blend. Preheat oven to Broil. Lay out bread on baking sheet. Divide shrimp salad among 4 slices of bread and spread to edges. Top each sandwich with 4 pickle slices, then cover completely with cheese. Broil until cheese melts and bubbles. Serve hot. Serves 4.

SOUTH-OF-THE-BORDER SANDWICH

½ pound Monterey Jack
  cheese, grated
4 slices bacon, cooked and
  crumbled
2 tablespoons minced
  onion
3 tablespoons canned
  chopped green chilies,
  or to taste

3 tablespoons mayonnaise
1 large tomato, sliced thin
8 slices firm white bread
  (Vienna bread is good)
Butter

Mix together cheese, bacon, onion, chilies and mayonnaise. Make 4 sandwiches, spreading insides of bread with more mayonnaise. Place 2 slices tomato in each sandwich. Grill sandwiches in butter over medium heat until golden brown on both sides—if you do them 1 at a time, keep the others warm in a 200° oven. Makes 4 sandwiches.

Mary Louise Mathers

SALADS
AND
SALAD DRESSINGS

BING CHERRY MOLD

1 (16 oz.) can bing cherries
1 (8¼ oz.) can crushed
   pineapple
1 (6 oz.) package cherry
   gelatin

2 cups boiling water
⅔ cup pineapple juice
½ cup cherry juice
1 tablespoon lemon juice
¼ cup chopped pecans

Drain bing cherries, reserving ½ cup juice. Drain pineapple, reserving juice. Add water to pineapple juice if necessary to make ⅔ cup. Dissolve gelatin in boiling water, add pineapple juice, cherry juice and lemon juice. Stir gelatin (in a bowl) over ice until slightly thickened. Add cherries, pineapple and pecans. Mix well. Pour into well-oiled 6-cup mold. Refrigerate until set.

CRANBERRY-ORANGE-PECAN MOLD

1 pound cranberries
1 small orange, peel and
   all, cut in 8 pieces
2 ribs celery, cut in 2-inch
   lengths
1 cup sugar

½ cup pecans
¼ cup cold water
1 (6 oz.) box lemon or
   strawberry gelatin
2 cups boiling water

Chop cranberries, orange and celery in food processor—you may need to do it in 2 batches. Add sugar and nuts and chop until fine but not mushy. Dissolve lemon or strawberry gelatin in boiling water. Stir cranberry mixture into gelatin and pour into well-oiled mold. Refrigerate until set; unmold. Serve plain or with Orange-Cream Cheese-Pecan Dressing, see Index.
NOTE: Strawberry gelatin gives the mold a redder color, but lemon lets more of the natural cranberry flavor through. If you don't have a mold, use a bundt pan.

LIME-CREAM CHEESE-PECAN MOLD

1 (3 oz.) package lime
  gelatin
1½ cups boiling water
1 (3 oz.) package cream
  cheese, softened

⅔ cup mayonnaise
⅔ cup chopped pecans
Grated rind of 2 lemons

Dissolve gelatin in boiling water. Beat the cheese until smooth. Whisk into hot gelatin until well-blended. Stir mixture in bowl over ice until slightly thickened. Whisk in mayonnaise, pecans and lemon rind. Pour into a well-oiled 3 to 4-cup mold. Refrigerate until set.

STRAWBERRY-ORANGE-PECAN MOLD

1 pound frozen
  strawberries, thawed
1 small orange (peel and
  all), cut in 8 pieces
2 ribs celery, cut in 2-inch
  lengths

½ cup chopped pecans
1 (6 oz.) package
  strawberry gelatin

Drain strawberries and reserve juice. Chop orange and celery in food processor or blender until fine but not mushy. Add enough water to the strawberry juice to make 2 cups. Bring to a boil, add to gelatin, and stir to dissolve. Stir gelatin in a bowl over ice until slightly thickened. Stir in strawberries, chopped orange and celery, and pecans. Pour into a well-oiled 5½ to 6 cup mold or individual molds. Refrigerate until set. Serve with Orange-Cream Cheese-Pecan Dressing, see Index.

LEMON MOLD

1 (6 oz.) box lemon gelatin
2 cups boiling water
¼ cup mayonnaise
1 cup heavy cream,
  whipped

1 small can crushed or
  chunk pineapple, fruit
  cocktail, peaches or
  whatever you have on
  hand, drained

Dissolve gelatin in boiling water. Whisk in mayonnaise. Stir in bowl over ice until slightly thickened. Fold in whipped cream and fruit. Pour into a well-oiled 6-cup mold. Refrigerate until set.

FRUIT SALAD

1 cup miniature
  marshmallows
1 (8 oz.) can pineapple
  chunks, drained (reserve
  juice)

1 (11 oz.) can mandarin
  oranges, drained
1 cup coconut flakes
1 cup sour cream
½ cup chopped pecans

Mix together well and chill. You may want to add some pineapple juice.
NOTE: You may add ½ cup chopped grapes and/or ½ cup maraschino cherries if desired.

Sheron George

5-CUP SALAD

1 cup miniature
  marshmallows
1 (8 oz.) can pineapple
  chunks, drained
1 (11 oz.) can mandarin
  oranges, drained

1 cup Thompson seedless
  grape halves
1 cup sour cream

Mix together well and chill. Best made 6 to 8 hours in advance. Serves 4 to 6.

WATERGATE SALAD

1 (3¾ oz.) package
  pistachio pudding
1 (20 oz.) can pineapple
  chunks, drained
1 (8 oz.) container Cool
  Whip, thawed

1 cup chopped nuts
1 cup sliced fresh
  strawberries
1 cup miniature
  marshmallows

Mix pudding with pineapple. Mix in Cool Whip until no green streaks show. Add rest of ingredients and chill. Serves 6.

Susan Provost

CUCUMBER SALAD

4 medium cucumbers
1 large sweet onion,
  preferably Vidalia, sliced
1 cup sugar

1 cup water
½ cup cider vinegar
½ cup oil
Celery seed

Peel cucumbers. Score lengthwise with tines of fork. Slice cucumbers thin. Place cucumbers and onion in salted ice water; let stand 1 to 2 hours. Cook sugar and water over low heat until sugar is dissolved. Cool. Add vinegar and oil to cooled sugar syrup; mix well. Drain and rinse cucumber and onion slices. Pour vinegar and oil mixture over them to cover. Sprinkle with celery seed to taste. Refrigerate overnight.
NOTE: A big Zip-loc bag works well to marinate salad in. Just make sure it is properly sealed, and put it on a tray for back-up (or you may be bailing out the bottom of your refrigerator the next day!); or store in a big jar or crock. Serves 8 to 10.

REFRIGERATOR SLAW

1 medium cabbage,
  shredded
1 bell pepper, chopped
1 large onion, chopped
¾ to 1 cup sugar

¾ cup vegetable oil
1 cup cider vinegar
1 teaspoon dry mustard
1 teaspoon salt
1 teaspoon celery seed

Layer cabbage, bell pepper and onion in a large bowl. Do not mix. Pour sugar over top. Bring dressing ingredients just to a boil and pour slowly over cabbage while hot. Do not mix. Cover tightly and refrigerate 24 hours before serving. Keeps at least a week in the refrigerator. Serves 8 to 10.

May DeMaurice

HEARTS OF PALM SALAD

1 can hearts of palm,
  drained and sliced
1 small red onion, sliced
  in rings
1 (2 oz.) jar chopped
  pimientos, drained
1 head romaine lettuce,
  washed and torn in bite-
  size pieces
1 head iceberg lettuce,
  washed and torn in bite-
  size pieces

¼ cup olive oil
¼ cup red wine vinegar
1 clove garlic, crushed
¼ teaspoon salt
¾ cup freshly grated
  Parmesan cheese
  (*not* from a can)

Mix oil, wine vinegar, garlic, salt and Parmesan cheese. Line a large salad bowl with lettuce. Top with hearts of palm, red onions and pimientos. Pour dressing over all and toss.
NOTE: The recipe originally called for 2 cans hearts of palm, but who can afford it? Serves 8.

Sally-Byrd Newton Combs

SAVANNAH SALAD

¼ cup olive oil
¼ cup vegetable oil
¼ cup wine vinegar
1 large clove garlic,
   crushed
1 small sweet onion,
   sliced thin

1 teaspoon salt
½ teaspoon pepper
1 teaspoon crushed
   oregano
1 teaspoon freshly grated
   Parmesan cheese
1 tablespoon water

Place in a jar with a tight-fitting lid and shake to combine—best made early in day.

4 hard-boiled eggs
4 heads Bibb, Boston and
   leaf lettuce (4 heads
   total)

Croutons, see below
¼ cup chopped toasted
   pecans

Sieve egg yolks and whites separately. Wash lettuce and dry well. Reserve 6 Bibb lettuce leaves to line 6 cold salad plates. Tear remaining lettuce into bite-size pieces and divide evenly among plates. Sprinkle croutons, sieved egg and pecans over salads. Just before serving, spoon dressing generously over each salad.

NOTE: To make croutons, trim crusts from 4 pieces of stale white bread. Cut into tiny cubes. Fry in a mixture of 4 table-spoons olive oil, 4 tablespoons butter, and 1 crushed clove garlic. Drain on paper towels and store tightly covered until ready to use. Serves 6.

Bailee Kronowitz

VIDALIA ONION RELISH

**3 to 4 Vidalia onions,
thinly sliced (use a food
processor if you have one)**

Marinade:

1 cup sugar   **2 cups water**
**½ cup red wine vinegar or
cider vinegar**

Dressing:

**½ cup good quality
mayonnaise**   **1 teaspoon celery salt**

Marinate onions in marinade for at least 2 hours in refrigerator. Drain well and mix with dressing. For easier serving, chop onions coarsely with knife or food processor. Serve as an hors d'oeuvre on saltines or as a substitute for coleslaw. Good the next day, too.

NOTE: You must use *sweet* onions for this recipe. Westerners can substitute Walla Walla Sweets, although they aren't quite as good as our own Georgia Vidalias or Glennville Sweets (at least, we like to think so!). At any rate, this is a spring dish—something to look forward to all year.

Martha Summerour

WILTED CUCUMBERS

**1 burpless cucumber,
washed and unpeeled, or
2 small cucumbers,
peeled
Salt**

**¼ cup sour cream
1 tablespoon lemon juice
1 teaspoon sugar, or to
taste**

Slice cucumbers very thin and layer in a dish (such as a soufflé dish), sprinkling each layer with salt. Place plastic wrap directly on cucumbers and weight down with a full half gallon wine bottle, a full liter Coke bottle or something similar. Let stand at room temperature for about 2 hours. Remove weight, pour off juice, rinse well in colander with cold water, then wrap cucumbers in a tea towel and squeeze until dry. Combine sour cream, lemon juice and sugar; toss with cucumbers and chill.

NOTE: Good served in tomato cups. Cut a slice off the top of each tomato. Remove the seeds carefully with a teaspoon. Sprinkle with salt, turn upside down, and leave to drain on paper towels.

24-HOUR SALAD

Layer in a large bowl:

1 head iceberg lettuce, chopped

1 raw cauliflower, cut into bite-size flowerets

1 bunch green onions, chopped

8 ounces mozzarella cheese, grated

1 pound bacon, cooked until crisp and crumbled

1 bunch broccoli, cut into bite-size flowerets (slice stems thin)

Spread on top:
1 cup mayonnaise

Sprinkle over mayonnaise:
1 tablespoon sugar

Cover tightly and refrigerate 24 hours. Mix well and serve. Keeps well for days in refrigerator. Serves 8 to 10.

Susan Provost

MARINATED VEGETABLE SALAD

1 (1 lb.) can French-cut green beans, drained
1 (17 oz.) can Leseur green peas, drained
1 (12 oz.) can whole-kernel corn, drained

1 (2 oz.) jar chopped pimientos, drained
1 cup chopped celery
1 bell pepper, chopped
1 bunch green onions, chopped

Marinade

¾ cup vinegar
½ cup vegetable oil
½ cup sugar

1 teaspoon salt
1 teaspoon pepper

Combine vegetables in large bowl. Bring marinade ingredients to a boil in saucepan. Cool. Combine with vegetables. Cover and refrigerate 12 hours or overnight, stirring occasionally.
NOTE: A nice change from 3-bean salad, and a good winter salad. Serves 8 to 10.

Lisa Bonfield

SALADE MIXT

¼ red cabbage, grated
2 carrots, peeled and grated
1 small cucumber, sliced
4 white radishes, grated
6 to 8 red radishes, grated

1 turnip, peeled and grated
¼ cauliflower, broken into flowerets
4 large mushrooms, sliced
Boston or Bibb lettuce

Choose 4 or 5 of the above vegetables, not counting lettuce. Place lettuce leaves on individual salad plates. Arrange piles of vegetables on lettuce, keeping individual vegetables separate. Spoon vinaigrette over vegetables.

Vinaigrette

1 tablespoon Dijon mustard	Pinch of sugar
3 tablespoons *fresh* lemon juice	¾ cup vegetable oil
Salt and freshly ground pepper	Mixed fresh herbs, finely chopped (parsley is fine)

Mix together mustard, lemon juice, salt, pepper and sugar in a small bowl. Gradually whisk in oil until dressing is slightly thickened and creamy. *Taste!* Correct seasonings. Stir in herbs before serving.

NOTE: A good recipe to practice with a new food processor.

RUSSIAN SALAD

4 medium potatoes, boiled, peeled and cubed	3 green onions or 1 medium onion, chopped
2 (1 lb.) cans navy beans, rinsed and drained, or	1 (10 oz.) jar dill pickle salad cubes, drained
2 cups (12 oz. bag) dried navy beans, cooked in salted water	¼ cup vinegar
	¾ cup salad oil
1 (8 oz.) can sliced beets, drained and cubed	Salt and pepper to taste

Mix potatoes, beans, beets, onion and pickles. Whisk oil and vinegar, salt and pepper together until blended. Pour over vegetables and toss. Taste for seasonings. Cover and refrigerate 8 hours or overnight before serving.

NOTE: Some people prefer a mayonnaise and sour cream dressing (half and half), with salt and pepper to taste, instead of the oil and vinegar. Serves 6 to 8.

Olga Shishkevish

SPINACH SALAD

½ pound spinach
1 head lettuce (Romaine,
   Boston, iceberg,
   whatever)
2 hard-boiled eggs,
   chopped

1 (8 oz.) can sliced water
   chestnuts, drained
1 cup alfalfa or bean
   sprouts
5 slices bacon, cooked
   crisp and crumbled

Dressing

1 cup salad oil
⅓ cup catsup
2 teaspoons
   Worcestershire sauce
¼ cup cider vinegar

¼ cup sugar
¼ teaspoon salt
1 small onion, chopped
   fine

Wash spinach well, remove stems and dry. Wash and dry lettuce; tear into bite-size pieces. Combine salad ingredients in large bowl. Whisk together all dressing ingredients except onion until smooth and well-blended. Stir in onion. Pour over salad and toss—you will probably not need to use all the dressing. Leftover dressing will keep indefinitely in the refrigerator. **NOTE:** If you have fresh mushrooms on hand, slice a few and toss them in too. Serves 6.

Suzanne W. Peterson

 What to do with leftover tomato paste? Line a plate or baking sheet with wax paper; drop tomato paste in 1 tablespoon blobs onto plate. Freeze, then store in Zip-loc bag—premeasured and ready to use!

GOLDEN MACARONI SALAD

2 cups uncooked elbow
  macaroni
1 to 1½ teaspoons yellow
  food coloring, optional,
  depending on how
  golden you want it to be
6 hard-boiled eggs,
  chopped
1 medium bell pepper,
  diced
1 (2 oz.) jar diced pimiento

1 cup (4 oz.) sharp
  Cheddar cheese, diced
½ cup finely chopped
  onion
2 teaspoons prepared
  mustard
2 teaspoons salt
Mayonnaise to moisten
  well

Add food coloring to boiling salted water. Add macaroni; cook until tender. Rinse in cold water; drain. Combine eggs with macaroni, add remaining ingredients and mix well. Chill thoroughly. Serves 6 to 8.

MOM'S MACARONI SALAD

4 cups (8 oz. dry)
  macaroni, cooked
1 cup sour cream
½ cup mayonnaise
2 teaspoons prepared
  yellow mustard
1 teaspoon salt

½ to ¾ pound cubed ham
1 cup cubed Cheddar
  cheese
¾ cup chopped radishes
2 cups chopped celery
¼ cup finely chopped
  onion

Cook macaroni according to package directions; drain and rinse with cold water. Add all other ingredients, mix well, and chill for at least 6 hours before serving. Serves 6 to 8.
NOTE: Substitute cooked chicken or turkey for ham if desired.

Jean Roche

PIRATES' HOUSE POTATO SALAD

2 pounds potatoes,
  cooked, peeled and
  cubed
2 cups Salad Sauce, see
  Index
¼ to ½ teaspoon Tabasco,
  or to taste
1 tablespoon grated onion

1½ teaspoons salt
⅓ cup sweet pickle relish
5 hard-boiled eggs,
  chopped fine
1 hard-boiled egg, sliced
  or cut in wedges (for
  garnish)

Mix well and refrigerate. Better made a few hours in advance to develop flavor.

POTATO SALAD

6 medium Idaho potatoes
1 small onion, finely
  chopped
2 to 3 ribs celery, chopped
4 hard-boiled eggs,
  chopped
½ cup sweet pickle salad
  cubes
1 (2 oz.) jar chopped
  pimientos, drained

Salt and pepper, seasoned
  salt and celery salt to
  taste
Mayonnaise
1 tablespoon yellow
  mustard
½ capful apple cider
  vinegar

Boil potatoes, drain, peel and cut into cubes. Mix with onion, celery, eggs, salad cubes, pimientos and seasonings. Let sit 45 to 60 minutes. Mix in mayonnaise, mustard and vinegar. Refrigerate at least 2 hours before serving. Tastes great the next day. Serves at least 10 to 12.

Suzanne D. Peterson

CHICKEN SALAD

2 whole chicken breasts
(4 halves)
1 cup water
1 cup dry white wine or
vermouth
1 medium onion
2 ribs celery

3 tablespoons sweet pickle
relish
Juice of ½ lemon
½ cup mayonnaise
¼ teaspoon curry powder
Salt and pepper to taste

Simmer chicken in water and wine until done, 20 to 25 minutes.
Cool, skin and bone. Chop fine in food processor, meat grinder,
or by hand. Chop onion and celery until fine. Combine ingredients. Refrigerate at least 2 hours before serving.
NOTE: Great on crackers or for sandwiches.

Sally-Byrd Newton Combs

HOT CHICKEN, SHRIMP OR CRAB SALAD

1 cooked chicken, boned
and cut up, or
1 pound raw shrimp,
cooked and peeled, or
1 pound crabmeat
2 cups thinly sliced celery
½ cup cashews

½ teaspoon salt
1 small onion, grated
1 cup mayonnaise
2 tablespoons lemon juice
½ cup grated cheese
½ cup crushed potato
chips

Combine all ingredients except cheese and potato chips; put
in casserole. Combine cheese and potato chips and sprinkle
on top. Bake at 350° until hot, 25 to 30 minutes. Serves 4 to 6.

Susan Provost

SHRIMP SEASHELL SALAD

1 pound raw medium-size
   shrimp, cooked and
   peeled
2 cups (4 oz. dry) cooked
   shell macaroni
1 cup sliced celery
¼ cup finely chopped
   fresh parsley
¼ cup sweet pickle relish
1 cup raw cauliflower,
   broken into bite-size
   flowerets

½ cup mayonnaise
3 tablespoons garlic
   French dressing, or
   1 teaspoon powdered
   Good Seasons garlic
   dressing
1 tablespoon fresh lemon
   juice
1 teaspoon grated onion
1 teaspoon salt
1 teaspoon pepper
Salad greens

Cut cooked shrimp into 2 or 3 pieces. Combine shrimp, macaroni, celery, parsley, pickle relish and cauliflower in large bowl. Combine mayonnaise, garlic dressing, lemon juice, onion and seasonings; blend well. Add mayonnaise mixture to shrimp mixture and toss lightly. Chill. Serve on salad greens.

NOTE: Don't overcook shrimp or macaroni. Best made 8 hours in advance or the day before so flavors can mellow. Serves 4 to 6.

Sally-Byrd Newton Combs

ORANGE-CREAM CHEESE-PECAN DRESSING

1 (8 oz.) package cream
  cheese, softened
1 (6 oz.) can concentrated
  orange juice, thawed
  (not diluted)

2 tablespoons milk
1½ teaspoons sugar
¼ teaspoon salt
¼ cup chopped pecans

Beat cream cheese until smooth. Add orange juice, milk, sugar
and salt; beat until smooth. Stir in pecans. Refrigerate 8 hours
or overnight to blend flavors. Remove from refrigerator an hour
before serving to soften. Use on fruit salads.

POPPY SEED DRESSING

⅔ cup white wine vinegar
¼ cup fresh lemon juice
1½ cups sugar
2 teaspoons salt
3 tablespoons poppy
  seeds

2 teaspoons dry mustard
1 teaspoon paprika
1 small onion, cut in
  quarters
2 cups vegetable oil

Heat vinegar, lemon juice, sugar, and salt until sugar dissolves.
Place poppy seeds, mustard, paprika, onion and hot liquids in
blender or food processor. Process for 30 seconds. With motor
running, add oil very slowly until mixture is creamy and smooth.
Can be stored in refrigerator in a jar for at least 4 weeks. If it
separates just shake it up. Serve over fresh fruit or spinach
salad, or mix with mayonnaise half and half and use on cole
slaw. Makes 1 quart.

BLEU CHEESE DRESSING

2 cups mayonnaise
¼ cup buttermilk
2 tablespoons milk
4 ounces bleu cheese,
  crumbled

½ teaspoon lemon juice
Dash Worcestershire
  sauce
Dash Tabasco
Dash pepper

Mix well with a whisk (do not use food processor). Add more milk if dressing is too thick. Refrigerate. Keeps indefinitely. Makes about 3 cups.

THOUSAND ISLAND DRESSING

1 cup mayonnaise
2 tablespoons milk
⅓ cup chili sauce
1 hard-boiled egg,
  chopped fine
1 tablespoon finely
  chopped fresh parsley

1 tablespoon finely
  chopped green olives
1 tablespoon sweet pickle
  relish
1 tablespoon finely
  chopped onion

Combine and refrigerate for at least 2 hours before serving.

TARTARE SAUCE

2 cups mayonnaise
¼ cup sweet pickle relish
1 teaspoon finely chopped
  fresh parsley
1 tablespoon chopped
  pimientos

1 tablespoon finely
  chopped onion
1½ teaspoons Dijon
  mustard

Mix well and refrigerate. Serve with fried seafood. Makes about 2½ cups.

COCKTAIL SAUCE

1 (12 oz.) bottle chili sauce
¾ cup catsup
¼ cup horseradish
½ cup (2 ribs) finely
   chopped celery

¼ cup fresh lemon juice
1 tablespoon
   Worcestershire sauce

Mix together well and refrigerate. Keeps indefinitely. Makes about 3 cups.

REMOULADE SAUCE

1 cup mayonnaise
1 hard-boiled egg,
   chopped
1 tablespoon finely
   chopped fresh parsley
1 tablespoon finely
   chopped green pepper
1 tablespoon grated onion
2 tablespoons chopped
   green olives

2 tablespoons finely
   chopped celery
1 tablespoon chopped
   capers
1 tablespoon dry mustard
Dash Worcestershire
   sauce
Dash Tabasco
Pinch salt
⅛ teaspoon black pepper

Combine and refrigerate at least 2 hours before serving. Especially good with cold seafood.

SALAD SAUCE

2 cups mayonnaise
1 cup finely chopped
  celery
¼ cup finely chopped bell
  pepper
1 (2 oz.) jar pimientos,
  drained

½ teaspoon salt
Dash pepper
1 teaspoon fresh lemon
  juice

Mix well and refrigerate. Makes about 4 cups.

SPICY MAYONNAISE

3 egg yolks
1 teaspoon salt
1 teaspoon cayenne
  pepper
1 teaspoon celery seed
1 medium onion, grated

2 tablespoons vinegar or
  lemon juice, or 1
  tablespoon each vinegar
  and lemon juice
2 cups salad oil

Mix everything together except oil. Beat in oil very slowly with electric mixer or whisk. Beat at least 5 minutes after all oil is in. Taste. You may want to add more vinegar or lemon juice. Refrigerate immediately. Keeps 3 or 4 days in refrigerator. Excellent with artichokes or on bacon, lettuce and tomato sandwiches.
NOTE: The easiest way to make mayonnaise is in a food processor. Use 1 whole egg and 2 egg yolks, and pour the oil in slowly through the feed tube while the machine is running. You must still grate the onion by hand.

Suzanne D. Peterson

SEAFOOD

FLOUNDER AMANDINE

2 pounds flounder fillets
¼ cup flour
1 tablespoon paprika
1½ teaspoons salt
2 tablespoons salad oil
¼ cup butter
2 tablespoons fresh lemon
  juice

¼ teaspoon Tabasco
½ cup toasted slivered
  almonds, see Index
2 tablespoons freshly
  chopped parsley
Lemon Rice, see Index

Preheat oven to Broil. Rinse fillets and dry with paper towels. Mix flour, paprika and salt; coat fillets on both sides with flour mixture. Butter a shallow baking pan and arrange fillets close together. Brush with oil. Melt butter in saucepan; add lemon juice and Tabasco. Broil fillets 2 to 3 inches from heat for 5 to 8 minutes, or until a light crust forms on surface. Do not turn while broiling, and do not overcook. Transfer to a warm platter and pour butter sauce over top. Sprinkle with toasted almonds and chopped parsley. Serve with Lemon Rice. Serves 4.

Fay Wiggers

 ## FLOUNDER BELLE FRANKLIN

For each serving:

2 tablespoons (1 oz.)
  crabmeat
5 raw shrimp, peeled
¼ cup grated Swiss
  cheese
1 (¼ to ⅓ lb.) flounder fillet
1 tablespoon Scampi
  Butter, see Index

¼ cup Belle Sauce, see
  below
¼ cup grated mild Cheddar
  cheese
1 tablespoon toasted
  almonds, see Index

Preheat oven to 375°. Place crabmeat, shrimp and Swiss cheese in individual au gratin dishes. Place flounder fillet on top, tucking edges under. Drizzle scampi butter over fish. Pour Belle Sauce over fish to cover. Bake for 20 minutes. Remove from oven, sprinkle Cheddar cheese on top to cover, sprinkle almonds on top of cheese, and return to oven for 5 minutes to melt cheese.

NOTE: If you don't have individual casserole dishes, use a shallow baking dish, make individual piles of crabmeat, shrimp, and cheese and lay fillets over each. Sprinkle butter over fillets, coat each with sauce and bake as above.

BELLE SAUCE

4 tablespoons butter
4 tablespoons flour
2 cups Fish Stock, see below

1 tablespoon white wine

Melt butter in saucepan. Add flour off heat and stir until smooth. Add fish stock and return to heat. Bring to a boil over medium heat, stirring constantly. When sauce boils and has thickened, lower heat and simmer for 20 minutes, stirring occasionally. Remove from heat and stir in wine.

Fish Stock

1 (8 oz.) bottle clam juice
1 cup water
1 cup dry white wine or vermouth

1 medium onion, peeled and sliced
6 parsley stems

Bring to a boil in a non-aluminum saucepan, lower heat, and simmer for 20 minutes. Strain.

FLOUNDER STUFFED
WITH SHRIMP AND MUSHROOMS

1 large (3 lb.) flounder or 4
  flounder or sole fillets
4 ounces (unpeeled) raw
  shrimp, peeled
4 ounces mushrooms,
  sliced
4 tablespoons butter

1 tablespoon butter
1 tablespoon flour
½ cup milk
¼ cup heavy cream
Salt and pepper to taste
6 tablespoons bread
  crumbs

Have your fishperson clean, bone and skin your flounder, then put the fillets back together the way they came off the fish. Preheat oven to 425°. Sauté mushrooms quickly in the 4 tablespoons butter. Remove from skillet, drain well, and reserve butter. Melt the 1 tablespoon butter in a saucepan, add flour and blend. Stir in milk. Bring to a boil, stirring constantly. Boil for 2 minutes. Remove from heat, stir in cream, and season to taste. Stir in shrimp and mushrooms—the shrimp are uncooked at this point. Lay out 2 bottom fillets in a buttered baking dish. Spoon shrimp filling onto fish. Lay remaining 2 fillets on top. Pour reserved mushroom butter over fish and sprinkle with bread crumbs. Bake for 15 to 20 minutes, until fish flakes easily but is not dry. Garnish with lemon slices. Serves 4.

FLOUNDER POACHED IN CIDER

4 to 6 (6 oz.) flounder fillets
1 teaspoon butter
4 green onions, finely
  chopped
½ teaspoon salt
Freshly ground black
  pepper
1 tablespoon lemon juice

2 tablespoons apple
  brandy or applejack
1 cup apple cider
2 tablespoons butter
2 tablespoons flour
⅓ cup heavy cream
4 tablespoons freshly
  grated Parmesan cheese

Preheat oven to 400°. Butter a large baking dish with 1 teaspoon butter and sprinkle with green onions. Arrange fillets in a single layer in the dish. Sprinkle with salt and pepper, lemon juice and brandy. Heat cider almost to boiling, pour over fish, cover dish tightly with aluminum foil and bake for 12 minutes, until barely cooked. Remove dish from oven and turn to Broil. Pour off liquid carefully, strain and reserve. Melt 2 tablespoons butter in a saucepan, stir in flour and cook for 1 minute. Add strained liquid and cream and bring to a boil. Pour sauce over fish. Sprinkle with cheese and brown under broiler for 3 minutes.
NOTE: If you don't have apple brandy, regular brandy will do. Serves 4 to 6.

Paula Sullivan

CHINESE STEAMED FISH

2 to 2½ pound whole fresh or salt water fish (red snapper, bass, bluefish, grouper), cleaned
2 green onions
3 slices fresh ginger the size of quarters, peeled
½ teaspoon salt
¼ cup vegetable oil
¼ cup soy sauce

Shred green onions lengthwise and cut into 1-inch lengths. Sliver ginger. Sprinkle fish with salt and place in a wide, shallow dish with a rim about 1 inch high, such as a pie plate. Place a steaming rack in a wok and fill bottom of wok with water. Bring water to a boil. Place dish on rack, cover, and steam fish for 15 to 20 minutes. When fish is almost done, heat ¼ cup oil in small sauce pan until sizzling hot. Remove fish from wok; transfer carefully to serving platter. Spread green onions and ginger over fish. Pour hot oil over fish; pour soy sauce over fish.
NOTE: If you don't have a wok, use a big pot or fish steamer.

FLOUNDER IN FOIL

6 flounder or sole fillets
(about ⅓ pound each)
½ pound crab meat
½ pound (unpeeled
weight) raw shrimp,
peeled
½ pound fresh
mushrooms, sliced
2 tablespoons butter
Fresh parsley, finely
chopped

Thyme and marjoram to
taste
Salt and pepper
6 tablespoons sour cream
6 tablespoons dry
vermouth
6 pieces heavy duty foil,
12 inches square

Preheat oven to 350°. Sauté mushrooms in butter until just
tender; set aside. Lay out foil. In center of each square, lay a
fish fillet. Divide crab, mushrooms and shrimp 6 ways and lay
out on top of fish. Place 1 tablespoon sour cream on top of
each and sprinkle 1 tablespoon vermouth over each. Sprinkle
parsley, herbs and salt and pepper over all to taste. Seal each
packet by drawing up all four corners, sealing edges and twist-
ing top. Allow a little air space, but make sure seams are tight.
Bake on jelly roll pan for 20 to 25 minutes. Serve in foil with
tossed salad and garlic French bread.
NOTE: You can, of course, make this for as many as you like.
Adjust amounts of crab, shrimp and mushrooms accordingly.
If you can't find the right size fillets, just cut big ones up.
Serves 6.

Henry Gaede

MEXICAN FISH

1 (1 lb.) package frozen
flounder fillets
1½ cups mayonnaise
¾ cup half-and-half

½ cup freshly grated
Parmesan cheese
(*not* out of a can)
¼ cup taco sauce

Thaw fish for baking according to package directions—fish should not be completely thawed. Preheat oven to 400°. Lay out fillets in a shallow baking dish. Mix sauce ingredients and pour over fish. Sprinkle more Parmesan cheese on top. Bake for 20 to 25 minutes, or until fish is just cooked but not dry. Serve with rice.

NOTE: Easy and good! Serves 4.

Susan Provost

BAKED TROUT WITH DILL AND LEMON

4 small fresh-water trout, cleaned and scaled, with heads left on
Salt
Freshly ground pepper
4 large sprigs fresh dill, or 1 tablespoon dried
1 shallot, peeled and minced, or white part of 2 green onions, minced

4 teaspoons dry sherry
4 tablespoons bottled clam juice
2 teaspoons olive oil
1 lemon, peeled so that all the white is cut away; thinly sliced

Preheat oven to 450°. Cut 4 circles of aluminum foil with a diameter 2 inches larger than length of fish. Place fish in middle of aluminum foil. Season insides of fish with salt and pepper and put a sprig of dill in each, or divide dried dill among fish. Divide shallot evenly among the fish. Sprinkle 1 teaspoon sherry, 1 tablespoon clam juice and ½ teaspoon olive oil over each fish. Cover with lemon slices. Bring edges of foil together, fold over and pinch together securely. Place foil packages in a baking dish and bake for 10 to 15 minutes. To serve, put foil packages on heated plates. Carefully cut all around top side of foil with scissors so it can be opened easily at the table.

NOTE: This is a delicious diet recipe—you won't feel deprived at all. Serves 4.

STUFFED CREOLE TROUT

**1 recipe Creole Sauce,
see Index**

For each serving:

**4 ounce sea trout fillet
½ cup Crab Stuffing,
see Index
4 to 5 medium peeled raw
shrimp**

**3 tablespoons sautéed
sliced mushrooms
(fresh only)**

In individual casseroles, spread out crab filling. Spread mushrooms and shrimp over crab. Top with trout. If fillets are very thick, cut almost in half horizontally and spread out to cover stuffing. Spread ½ cup creole sauce over trout, or enough to cover. May be made a few hours in advance up to this point, covered and refrigerated. Bake at 375° for 20 to 25 minutes, or until fish and shrimp are just cooked. Serve with red rice.
NOTE: If you don't have individual baking dishes, arrange fish in mounds in a large baking dish. Tuck the trout around the stuffing so it won't escape. Make sure fish is completely covered with sauce. You may substitute flounder for trout.

FRIED CATFISH

**4 to 5 *small* catfish per
person
Salt and pepper**

**Plain cornmeal
(preferably yellow)
Oil**

Heat oil to 375° in an electric skillet or deep fat fryer. Salt and pepper fish generously. Roll fish in cornmeal or place cornmeal in paper bag and shake fish with meal. Place in hot fat and fry until golden brown, turning once. Serve with hushpuppies and coleslaw.

FISH STEW

½ pound slab bacon or fat back, skin removed, and diced
3 large onions, chopped
2 (8 oz.) cans tomato sauce
1 (11 oz.) can tomato soup
1 (12 oz.) bottle hot catsup
Worcestershire sauce, Tabasco, salt and pepper to taste
1 tablespoon sugar
3 pounds firm flat fish (flounder, bream, crappie) or shrimp

Fry bacon or fat back until very crisp in a heavy pot. Remove meat. Sauté onions in fat until translucent. Add meat, tomato sauce, soup and catsup, ½ catsup bottle water and enough water to rinse out cans. Season to taste—you should be able to see specks of pepper. Simmer covered for 3 to 4 hours. 10 minutes before serving, add fish or peeled shrimp and simmer until just cooked. Serve in bowls with thick light bread.
NOTE: Don't throw out leftover sauce. Heat and serve over rice. Serves 6.

Suzanne D. Peterson

SHAD ROE

Shad roe
All-purpose flour seasoned with salt and pepper
Bacon

Fry bacon in heavy skillet until crisp. Remove bacon from pan. Coat roe with flour, place gently in hot bacon grease and brown on medium heat. Turn, cover skillet and brown other side. Drain on paper towels. Serve with bacon strips and tartare sauce.
NOTE: After you turn roe and cover skillet, it will sound like the War of 1812 is taking place on your stove. Do not be alarmed, just keep the lid on. You may need to cover skillet when you are browning the first side if roe starts popping.

Conway Harvard

SALLY'S STUFFED SNAPPER

3 to 4 pound red snapper, cleaned (with head left on)
1½ cups fine, fresh bread crumbs
½ cup finely chopped onion
½ cup finely chopped celery
¼ cup finely chopped bell pepper

1 apple, cored but not peeled, finely chopped
2 tablespoons finely chopped fresh parsley
⅛ teaspoon paprika
⅛ teaspoon nutmeg
Salt and pepper to taste
¼ cup butter, melted
2 tablespoons butter, softened

Mix stuffing ingredients together. Preheat oven to 400°. Grease a large baking pan. Place fish in pan; stuff cavity behind head. Dot with softened butter. Measure thickness of fish—it will probably be 2½ to 3 inches thick at the thickest point. Bake 10 minutes to an inch of thickness, or about 25 to 30 minutes. Serve immediately on a warm platter.

NOTE: The fish will be done to perfection if you follow the above instructions. There is nothing nastier than overcooked snapper. If you can get your fishperson to bone your fish, great. Stuff the whole body cavity. Serves 4 to 6.

Sally-Byrd Newton Combs

BAKED POTATOES STUFFED WITH CRABMEAT

6 baking potatoes, washed
2 tablespoons butter, softened
1 cup sour cream
1 small onion, grated
1 teaspoon salt
¼ teaspoon cayenne pepper

8 ounces crabmeat
Paprika
½ cup grated sharp Cheddar, Swiss or mozzarella cheese
3 green onions, chopped

Bake potatoes at 400° for 1 hour, or until done, poking with a fork after 30 minutes to allow steam to escape. While potatoes are still warm, cut in half lengthwise and scoop out insides, being careful not to tear skin. Mash potato, butter, sour cream, onion and seasonings until smooth. Stir in crabmeat. Lay potato skins out on baking sheet and fill. Sprinkle with paprika and bake for 15 to 20 minutes at 375°, until hot. Remove from oven, turn oven to Broil, sprinkle with cheese and run under broiler until cheese melts. Sprinkle with green onions before serving.

NOTE: Try using only 10 skins and pile the filling high. Serves 5 to 6.

MRS. TRAUB'S CRAB CASSEROLE

3 tablespoons butter
3 tablespoons flour
1½ cups milk
1 tablespoon chopped
  fresh parsley
Grated rind of 1 lemon
Juice of 1 lemon
2 tablespoons Durkee's
  Famous Sauce
1 tablespoon
  Worcestershire sauce

¼ teaspoon salt
Dash pepper
½ teaspoon nutmeg
1 pound crabmeat
3 tablespoons sherry
1 egg, lightly beaten
2 slices bread, crumbed
2 tablespoons butter,
  melted

Preheat oven to 350°. Melt 3 tablespoons butter; stir in flour. Remove from heat, whisk in milk. Cook over medium heat until thick and boiling, stirring constantly. Stir in remaining ingredients (down to nutmeg) and whisk until well-blended. Combine crabmeat, sherry and egg. Pour sauce over crabmeat; mix well. Pour into casserole. Combine bread crumbs and butter and sprinkle over casserole. Bake for 30 minutes. Serves 4, doubles easily.

Franklin Traub

DEVILED CRAB

1 pound fresh crabmeat
1 individual package
   saltines, crushed
4 hard-boiled eggs,
   mashed
¾ cup mayonnaise

¼ cup butter, melted
2 teaspoons
   Worcestershire sauce
1 teaspoon Tabasco
½ teaspoon dry mustard
Salt and pepper to taste

Combine crabmeat, cracker crumbs and eggs in a large bowl. Beat remaining ingredients together until smooth. Mix well with crab. Pack into a shallow baking dish—a quiche dish is ideal. Bake at 350° until hot, about 30 minutes.

NOTE: If you don't like bell pepper, this is the deviled crab for you. It's different and quite tasty.

Suzanne D. Peterson

 ## PIRATES' HOUSE DEVILED CRAB

1 pound fresh crabmeat
¾ cup cornbread crumbs
¾ cup white bread crumbs
1 medium onion, finely
   chopped
1 bell pepper, finely
   chopped
2 ribs celery, finely
   chopped
2 eggs

⅓ cup mayonnaise
1 tablespoon Dijon
   mustard
1 tablespoon lemon juice
2 tablespoons
   Worcestershire sauce
½ teaspoon salt
½ teaspoon pepper
Dash Tabasco

Combine crabmeat, bread crumbs, onion, pepper and celery in large bowl. Beat together remaining ingredients until smooth. Mix well with crab. Pack into a shallow baking dish—a quiche dish is perfect. Bake at 350° until hot, about 30 minutes.

NOTE: Spare yourself and give your food processor a workout with crumbs, onion, pepper and celery. You may substitute white bread crumbs for cornbread. Serves 6.

CRAB IMPERIAL

2 teaspoons butter,
  softened
1 egg
2 tablespoons mayonnaise
2 teaspoons
  Worcestershire sauce
½ teaspoon salt
¼ teaspoon pepper

1 pound crabmeat
¼ cup finely chopped
  green pepper
¼ cup finely chopped red
  pepper or pimiento
2 tablespoons butter, cut
  into small pieces

Preheat oven to 375°. Spread the softened butter over 4 medium-sized natural or ceramic scallop shells. Beat the egg lightly with a wire whisk. Add the mayonnaise, Worcestershire sauce, salt and pepper and whisk until smooth. Add the crabmeat and green and red pepper and toss together gently but thoroughly with a rubber spatula. Spoon the crab mixture into the buttered shells, dividing evenly and mounding slightly. Dot the tops with pieces of butter. Bake in upper third of oven for 15 to 20 minutes, then brown under broiler for 30 seconds if desired. Serve at once. Serves 4.

DONNA KAY'S CRAB AND RICE CASSEROLE

1 pound crabmeat, picked
  for shells
1 cup raw rice, cooked
5 hard-boiled eggs,
  chopped
½ cup chopped celery
¼ cup chopped onion
¼ cup finely chopped
  parsley

1½ cups mayonnaise
½ teaspoon salt
½ teaspoon pepper
Cayenne pepper to taste,
  optional
4 cups total grated
  Cheddar, Monterey Jack,
  and/or Swiss cheese

Preheat oven to 350°. Mix all ingredients except 2 cups cheese together. Consistency should be like tuna salad; add more mayonnaise if too dry. Put in large casserole dish, top with remaining 2 cups cheese, and bake for 30 minutes or until bubbly. Serves 6.

Donna Kay McLaurin

CRAB STUFFING

1 pound crabmeat
½ cup mayonnaise
3 tablespoons fresh lemon
  juice
3 tablespoons
  Worcestershire sauce

2 tablespoons Dijon
  mustard
½ teaspoon salt
1 teaspoon black pepper

Mix well. Use for stuffed shrimp, stuffed creole trout and crab canapés.

STUFFED AVOCADOS

3 large, ripe avocados,
  cut in half
½ pound raw shrimp
½ pound bay or sea
  scallops
1 cup mayonnaise
1 tablespoon Dijon
  mustard

1 egg
1 small bell pepper,
  chopped fine
½ teaspoon salt
¼ teaspoon pepper

Cook shrimp in boiling salted water until barely done, about 2 minutes. Simmer scallops in salted water until barely done. Peel shrimp and cut into bite-size pieces. Cut sea scallops in bite-size pieces; leave bay scallops whole. Preheat oven to 350°. Combine mayonnaise, mustard, egg, bell pepper, salt and pepper. Fold in seafood gently. Hollow out avocados enough to hold seafood, leaving about ½ inch of avocado all around. Mound filling as high as you can, and spread sauce to cover edges of avocado. Place on a baking sheet and bake about 25 minutes, until puffed and brown. Serve immediately. **NOTE:** Makes a good luncheon dish or appetizer for an elegant meal. Serves 6.

Henry Gaede

SEAFOOD AU GRATIN

1 pound crabmeat
1 pound cooked and peeled
   baby shrimp, (frozen are
   fine, but thaw them)
Casserole Sauce
   see below

½ to 1 cup grated Cheddar
   cheese

Preheat oven to 350°. Combine crabmeat, shrimp and casserole sauce. Pour into casserole dish. Top with grated cheese and bake until bubbly and cheese is melted, about 30 minutes. **NOTE:** You may bake this in individual casseroles. Good with Red Rice, see Index. Serves 4 to 6.

CASSEROLE SAUCE

2 cups milk, divided
¼ cup all-purpose flour
½ cup Cheez Whiz
½ cup grated Cheddar
   cheese

½ teaspoon salt
Dash black pepper

Mix 1½ cups milk with cheese, Cheez Whiz, salt and pepper in a heavy saucepan. Cook, stirring constantly, over medium heat until cheese melts and mixture boils. Mix ¼ cup flour with ½ cup milk until smooth. Stir into cheese mixture until thickened. Simmer for 20 minutes. If not using right away, place a piece of plastic wrap directly on surface of sauce to prevent a skin from forming.
NOTE: We use this in our seafood au gratin, potatoes au gratin and as a sauce for broccoli.

SHRIMP AND CRAB CASSEROLE

1 pound crabmeat
1 pound raw shrimp, peeled
½ small green pepper, chopped
⅓ cup chopped fresh parsley

2 cups cooked rice
1½ cups good quality mayonnaise
2 (10 oz.) packages frozen peas, thawed but not cooked
Salt and pepper to taste

Preheat oven to 350°. Mix all ingredients together lightly. Place in buttered casserole and bake, covered, for 1 hour, or until shrimp are done.

NOTE: May be made ahead of time and refrigerated before baking. If the shrimp are unusually large, cut them in half or they will take too long to cook. Good served with spiced peaches. Serves 8.

Franklin Traub

SCALLOPS STEFANINI

2 (10 oz.) packages frozen chopped spinach
1 to 2 tablespoons Snail Butter, see Index
1 to 2 tablespoons Major Grey's chutney, chopped
2 tablespoons heavy cream
Salt to taste

Nutmeg to taste—should not be overpowering
1 pound bay or sea scallops—cut large sea scallops in half
1 recipe Belle Sauce, see Index
Toasted Almonds, see Index

Cook spinach according to package directions. Drain, rinse with cold water and squeeze out 1 handful at a time until as dry as possible—no short cuts allowed. Combine spinach with snail butter, chutney, cream, salt and nutmeg. Divide spinach among 4 individual casserole dishes, or place in 1 big dish. Divide scallops among casseroles. Top with Belle Sauce to cover. Bake at 350° until scallops are done; 25 to 30 minutes. Do not overcook—bay scallops may take less time. Sprinkle with almonds and serve.

NOTE: Freeze leftover snail butter for another time. It's good on steak, hamburgers and French bread, as well as snails. Serves 4.

JAMBALAYA

1 recipe Red Rice, see Index

4 tablespoons bacon grease or margarine

1 medium onion, chopped

2 ribs celery, chopped

1 medium bell pepper, chopped

¼ to ½ pound Polish sausage, sliced thin

½ pound bay or sea scallops

½ pound raw shrimp, peeled

Salt, pepper and Tabasco to taste

Melt bacon grease in large skillet. Sauté onion, bell pepper, celery and sausage until onion is translucent. Add seafood, cover, and cook over low heat until just done, 4 to 5 minutes. Stir ingredients into red rice—either just cooked or reheated—season to taste and serve.

NOTE: Leftover chicken and/or ham cut in cubes make a nice addition. If you are feeling extravagant, oysters are good too—drain a pint and add with seafood.

HOW TO GIVE AN OYSTER ROAST

1 bushel oysters for every   **Cocktail sauce, see Index**
15 people   **Beer**

For a traditional oyster roaster, you need a metal plate, like a boiler plate, which can be found in a junkyard. Look for ¼-inch thick black iron about 3 feet by 4 feet. 12-gauge steel is an alternative. To suspend the plate the desired 15 inches over the heat, you can use concrete blocks (cheap and portable) or you can have an iron or metal shop build a stand with a rectangular frame set on 15-inch legs. If you don't want to chop wood and keep a fire going, go to a butane gas supplier and buy a burner and tank set with a 20-pound tank. The burner comes with its own stand, so make sure the heating unit is short enough to fit under the boiler plate.

If you use pine logs, as do most people, the fire should be very hot and flaming; you don't want coals. The plate should be set over the fire as soon as possible so it will get red hot. Keep the fire stoked the entire cooking time. Have a garden hose nearby. (Do not attempt to chop fire wood right next to the hose—rubber is easily severed with an ax.) Scrounge some clean burlap sacks from a grocery store or feed-and-seed purveyor. Rinse them out. They must be clean or the oysters will get gritty when they open.

To cook oysters, rinse off well with your handy hose. Spread by the shovelful in a layer 1 shell deep on top of the plate. Throw the soaking wet sacks over the oysters in a double layer. Spray as needed, making sure the sacks do not dry out. Do not add too much water, or the oysters will sit in a foamy puddle and boil rather than roast. It takes about 5 minutes to cook the oysters. You can remove the sacks about 2 minutes after starting and rotate the shells, but different people prefer oysters in different stages of doneness, so it's not really necessary. You will know when they are ready either by tasting or waiting for several to open.

An ideal oyster serving table has a hole in the middle to toss shells through. Whatever you use, cover with lots of newspapers, put out lots of paper napkins, oyster knives and gloves. Have a large garbage can under the hole or nearby for shells.

Hard as it may be to believe, some people do not like oysters. Toss some hot dogs on the edge of the boiler plate for them, or send out for fried chicken. Other traditional accompaniments are red rice, coleslaw, potato salad and saltines. Some people serve melted butter with their oysters, but as oyster roasts are held outside during the cooler months, the butter has a tendency to congeal rapidly.

NOTE: If you have total oyster fanatics on hand, the kind who stand rooted to one spot and stuff down oysters until they drop, you may want to figure 10 people per bushel.

OYSTER PERLOO

1 quart oysters, drained (reserve juice)
4 slices bacon
1 medium onion, chopped
2 ribs celery, chopped
1 small bell pepper, chopped
2 cups raw rice
Salt and pepper to taste

Fry bacon in heavy Dutch oven until crisp. Remove bacon. Sauté onions, celery and pepper in bacon grease until onions are translucent. Crumble bacon and return to pot. Add drained oysters and cook until they release juice, 1 to 2 minutes. Add rice; add water to reserved oyster juice to make 2 cups liquid. Stir liquid into rice, bring to a boil, lower to a simmer, cover and cook exactly 20 minutes. Remove pot from heat and let sit 20 minutes without peeking. Fluff up rice with a fork, correct seasonings, and serve. Serves 4.

Queenie Mae Boyd

BARBECUED SHRIMP

½ cup butter
½ cup vegetable oil
2 cloves garlic, crushed
3 bay leaves, crumbled
2 teaspoons rosemary,
   crushed
½ teaspoon basil
½ teaspoon oregano

½ teaspoon cayenne
   pepper
1 tablespoon paprika
½ teaspoon freshly ground
   pepper
1 teaspoon lemon juice
2 pounds fresh shrimp in
   the shell

Melt butter in a heavy oven-proof pot. Add oil, mixing well. Add all other ingredients except shrimp and place over medium heat. Stir constantly until sauce boils. Simmer for 10 minutes, stirring frequently. Remove pan and let stand uncovered at least 30 minutes to mellow. Preheat oven to 450°. Add shrimp to sauce, mix thoroughly and return to heat. Cook over medium heat for 6 to 8 minutes, or until shrimp start to turn pink. Transfer to oven and bake 5 to 10 minutes. Do not overcook shrimp. Serve in bowls with sauce, French bread, and lots of napkins. Serves 4.

GARIDES ME SALTSA (SHRIMP IN TOMATO, WINE, AND FETA CHEESE SAUCE)

2 tablespoons olive oil
¼ cup chopped onions
4 ripe tomatoes, peeled,
   seeded and chopped, or
1 (1 lb.) can tomatoes,
   drained, seeded and
   chopped
½ teaspoon oregano
Salt and pepper

½ cup dry white wine or
   vermouth
1½ pounds raw shrimp,
   peeled
2 ounces feta cheese,
   crumbled
2 tablespoons chopped
   fresh parsley

Heat olive oil in a large heavy skillet. Sauté onions until translucent. Add tomatoes, seasonings, wine and shrimp. Cook, stirring, until shrimp are pink and cooked through, about 5 minutes. If sauce is thin, remove shrimp to serving platter and reduce sauce to desired consistency. Stir in cheese and pour over shrimp. Sprinkle with parsley and serve over rice. Serves 4.

Shirley Corriher

CREOLE SHRIMP

**1 recipe Creole Sauce,
  see below**

**1 to 2 pounds raw shrimp,
  peeled**

When Creole Sauce is desired thickness, add shrimp and simmer until just cooked, about 5 minutes. Do not overcook shrimp. Serve on white rice or Red Rice (see index). Serves 4 to 8.

CREOLE SAUCE

**¼ pound bacon, chopped
1 medium onion, chopped
3 ribs celery, chopped
1 clove garlic, crushed
1 bell pepper, chopped
1 (8 oz.) bottle clam juice
1 cup chicken broth
1 (1 lb.) can tomato purée
1 tablespoon finely
  chopped fresh parsley**

**1 tablespoon freeze-dried
  chives
1 bay leaf
1 teaspoon brown sugar
½ teaspoon black pepper
1 teaspoon Tabasco
1 teaspoon lemon juice
Dash Worcestershire
  sauce**

Fry bacon in a heavy pot. Add onion, garlic, celery and bell pepper and cook until onion is translucent. Add remaining ingredients, bring to a boil, lower heat and simmer uncovered, stirring occasionally, until sauce is thickened, 30 to 45 minutes.

SHRIMP ETOUFFÉE

1 pound raw shrimp,
  peeled
½ cup butter
¾ cup finely chopped
  onion
¾ cup finely chopped
  celery, with some leaves

¼ cup finely chopped
  green onions
¼ cup finely chopped
  fresh parsley
1 tablespoon Creole
  Seasoning, see below

Melt butter in a heavy skillet. Cook onion and celery over medium heat until translucent, about 20 minutes. Add green onions and parsley. Cook 10 minutes. Stir in creole seasoning. Add shrimp and cook, covered, stirring 3 or 4 times, until just done, about 5 minutes. Serve over white rice.
NOTE: This is a spicy dish—not for finicky eaters, but very tasty. Serves 3 to 4.

Martha Summerour

CREOLE SEASONING

3 tablespoons salt
3 tablespoons paprika
2½ tablespoons cayenne
  pepper
2 tablespoons black
  pepper
2 tablespoons garlic
  powder

1½ tablespoons onion
  powder
1 tablespoon powdered
  thyme
1 tablespoon powdered
  oregano

Mix well and store in a glass jar. Keeps indefinitely. Use to spice up shrimp, fish and chicken.

Martha Summerour

STUFFED SHRIMP

2 pounds fresh unpeeled
jumbo shrimp
1 recipe Crab Stuffing,
see Index

1 recipe Scampi Butter,
see below

Peel shrimp, leaving tails on. Devein if desired. Cut open on underside of shrimp to butterfly. Stuff each shrimp with 1 tablespoon stuffing and fold tail up over stuffing. Place shrimp in casserole dish; drizzle scampi butter over and around shrimp (you won't need the whole quart). Preheat broiler and broil shrimp 4 inches from heat for 7 to 8 minutes, until shrimp are cooked through and tails blacken. Serves 4 to 6.

SCAMPI BUTTER

1 cup butter
2 cups margarine
1 tablespoon finely
chopped fresh parsley
1 tablespoon basil
1 tablespoon tarragon
1 tablespoon capers

3 drops Tabasco
2 tablespoons paprika
6 tablespoons garlic
powder
2 tablespoons freshly
squeezed lemon juice
4 tablespoons sherry

Melt butter and margarine, add remaining ingredients, and whisk to combine. Mixture will separate when cool, so stir or shake well before using. OR, you can cream butter and margarine together, beat in remaining ingredients, freeze in ice cube trays and store in Zip-loc bags to use as needed. Melt before using. Makes approximately 1 quart.

SWEET AND SOUR SHRIMP

1 pound raw shrimp,
  peeled
1 tablespoon dry sherry
1 tablespoon soy sauce
½ teaspoon salt
2 cups vegetable or
  peanut oil
⅔ cup sugar
¼ cup catsup
⅓ cup pineapple juice from
  pineapple chunks (add
  water if not enough
  juice)

½ cup cider vinegar
2 tablespoons soy sauce
1 clove garlic, peeled
2 tablespoons cornstarch
  dissolved in ⅓ cup water
1 (8 oz.) can pineapple
  chunks, drained—
  reserve juice

Mix cornstarch, sherry, soy sauce and salt. Add shrimp. Heat oil to 375° in a skillet or wok. Separate shrimp and fry until done and crisp on the edges, about 3 minutes. Don't crowd pan. Keep shrimp warm. Pour off all but 1 tablespoon oil. Combine sugar, catsup, pineapple juice, vinegar and soy sauce. Brown garlic in oil and discard. Add catsup mixture, stirring until sugar melts. Bring to a boil, add cornstarch and water and cook until thickened, stirring constantly. Add pineapple chunks and heat thoroughly. Add shrimp, mix well with sauce, and serve at once over white rice. Serves 4.

Bailee Kronowitz

 Buy leaf herbs instead of ground. They have more flavor and stay fresher longer.

POULTRY

CLAIRE'S FRIED CHICKEN

3 to 3½ pound frying
　chicken, cut up, or
Your favorite chicken
　parts
Buttermilk

All-purpose flour well-
　seasoned with salt and
　pepper
Crisco
½ cup butter

Wash chicken and drain. Soak in buttermilk to cover for at least 30 minutes. Heat Crisco and butter in an electric skillet to 375° or in a cast-iron skillet until smoking. You will have to eye-ball the amount of Crisco. Hot fat should come just a little over half-way up the chicken when it's all in the skillet. Meanwhile, place seasoned flour in a paper bag. Shake excess buttermilk off chicken and drop in bag 1 or 2 pieces at a time. Shake to coat with flour, remove with tongs and place in hot fat. When all chicken is in skillet, lower heat (325° on electric skillet), cover, leaving a crack for steam to escape, and cook 10 minutes. Turn chicken with tongs, cover, again leaving a crack, and cook 10 minutes more. If chicken pieces are very large you may need to cook them a bit longer. Drain on paper towels and serve.
NOTE: Claire likes lots of crust. She shakes her chicken in flour, then puts it back in the buttermilk and again in flour. Unless you are very experienced or lucky, this can create a gloppy mess, but if you like lots of crust it's worth experimenting with.

Claire Gale

GUSSIE'S FRIED CHICKEN

3 to 3½-pound frying
　chicken, cut up, or
Your favorite chicken parts
2 eggs

Salt, pepper and garlic
　powder
Self-rising flour
Crisco

Wash chicken and drain. Beat eggs in a 9x13-inch dish. Lay chicken pieces out in dish, sprinkle with salt, pepper and garlic powder, turn, season other side, then slosh around in egg until well-coated. Heat enough Crisco in a cast-iron skillet or electric skillet to come just over halfway up sides of chicken, until smoking or 375°. Place self-rising flour in a paper bag, shake chicken to coat well, remove with tongs and place in hot fat. Cover, leaving a crack for steam to escape, lower heat (to 325° for electric skillet) and cook 10 minutes. Turn chicken with tongs, cover, leaving a crack, and cook 10 minutes longer. Very large pieces may need to be cooked a little longer. Drain on paper towels.

NOTE: We use deep-fat fryers at the Pirates' House. If you have one at home, by all means use it.

Gussie Stoney

CHICKEN CASSEROLE

3 to 3½ pound chicken, cooked, boned and cut up
2 (1 lb.) cans whole green beans, rinsed and drained
1 (8 oz.) can sliced water chestnuts, rinsed and drained

2 (11 oz.) cans cream of chicken soup
¾ cup mayonnaise
2 teaspoons fresh lemon juice
½ teaspoon curry powder
1 cup grated Cheddar cheese

Preheat oven to 350°. Arrange beans in a buttered 9x13-inch baking dish. Spread water chestnuts over, spread chicken over vegetables, then mix soup, mayonnaise, lemon juice and curry powder and pour over chicken. Sprinkle cheese on top. Bake 30 minutes. Serves 8.

Martha Summerour

APRICOT CHICKEN

3 to 3½ pound frying
  chicken, cut up
2 tablespoons mayonnaise
1 envelope Lipton's onion
  soup mix
¼ cup bottled Russian
  dressing
½ cup apricot preserves

Combine sauce ingredients. Spread half on bottom of a 9x13-inch baking dish. Lay out chicken, spread remaining sauce over chicken, cover and refrigerate at least 4 hours or overnight, turning chicken at least once. Bake uncovered at 350° for 50 to 60 minutes.

Frances Donahue
Sally-Byrd Newton Combs

CHICKEN SPAGHETTI

6 chicken thighs and 2
  whole breasts (4 halves)
  cooked, boned and cut
  up
½ cup minced onion
½ cup minced bell pepper
1½ cups chicken stock,
  from chicken
1½ cups (12-ounce can)
  tomato juice
4 tablespoons flour
1½ teaspoons salt
¼ teaspoon pepper
2 tablespoons prepared
  mustard
1 (8 oz.) package
  vermicelli, cooked
  according to package
  directions for use in
  casseroles
½ cup grated Cheddar
  cheese

Combine onion, bell pepper, chicken stock, tomato juice, flour, salt and pepper and cook until thick and smooth. Stir in mustard. Mix chicken, spaghetti and sauce. Place in buttered 9x13-inch baking dish, sprinkle with cheese, and bake at 350° for 30 minutes. Serves 6 to 8.

Suzanne D. Peterson

CHICKEN AND DRIED BEEF CASSEROLE

6 chicken breasts (3 whole breasts) skinned and boned
6 slices bacon

1 (2½ oz.) jar dried beef
1 (11 oz.) can cream of mushroom soup
1 cup sour cream

Preheat oven to 300°. Line bottom of a 9x13-inch baking dish with 12 slices dried beef. Wrap bacon around chicken lengthwise. Place in dish. Slice remaining beef in thin strips and sprinkle over chicken. Mix soup and sour cream together; spread over chicken. Bake for 1½ hours.
NOTE: You may want to partially cook the bacon before wrapping around chicken. Do not cook chicken until it is completely dried out—1½ hours is long enough. Serves 6.

CHICKEN MARENGO

3 to 3½ pound frying chicken, cut up
¼ cup olive oil
1 large onion, sliced
2 cloves garlic, crushed
1 cup dry white wine
1 cup chicken stock
1 (1 lb.) can Italian-style tomatoes, drained, seeded and chopped

½ teaspoon thyme
1 bay leaf
Salt and pepper to taste
2 tablespoons butter
½ pound mushrooms, sliced
½ to 1 cup Greek olives or pitted black olives

Heat olive oil in a heavy pot. Dry chicken with paper towels; brown well on both sides. Remove from pot. Sauté onions and garlic until onions are translucent but not brown. Add wine, stock, tomatoes and seasonings, bring to a boil, lower heat, cover and simmer until tender, about 30 to 45 minutes. Meanwhile, sauté mushrooms in butter. When chicken is tender, remove to a platter and keep warm. Reduce sauce until desired thickness. Taste for seasonings. Stir in mushrooms and olives and pour over chicken. Serves 4.

CHICKEN PIE

3 to 3½ pound frying chicken, cooked, boned and cut in bite-size pieces
4 tablespoons butter or margarine
4 tablespoons all-purpose flour
2 cups strong chicken stock from chicken
Salt and pepper to taste
1 (10 oz.) package frozen mixed vegetables, cooked according to package directions until barely tender
Pie crust or biscuit dough

Melt butter in saucepan. Stir in flour off heat until smooth. Pour in chicken stock; whisk until smooth. Cook, stirring constantly, until sauce thickens and comes to a boil. Mix with chicken and vegetables. Pour into a 9x13-inch baking dish. Top with pie crust strips, solid pie crust with holes cut for steam to escape, or biscuits. Bake at 400° until crust or biscuits are brown, about 30 minutes.

NOTE: Cook chicken the day before, remove chicken from bones, and simmer carcass a few more hours. Refrigerate stock overnight so fat will rise to top. Remove fat. If stock is not flavorful enough, boil to reduce and strengthen. Use your favorite crust or biscuit recipe, or even pie crust mix, biscuit mix or refrigerated biscuits.

PAPRIKA CHICKEN

6 chicken breasts (3 whole breasts), skinned and boned
All-purpose flour seasoned with salt and pepper
4 tablespoons butter
½ cup finely chopped onion
1 cup sliced fresh mushrooms
1 tablespoon paprika
2 tablespoons dry sherry
1½ cups sour cream
¼ cup water
1 tablespoon all-purpose flour

Pound chicken breasts between sheets of wax paper to flatten slightly. Coat both sides lightly with seasoned flour. Melt butter in a heavy skillet until sizzling. Add chicken breasts; cook 3 minutes on each side, turning with tongs. Remove to oven to keep warm. Sauté onion and mushrooms until soft. Stir in paprika, pour in sherry and stir to deglaze pan. Combine sour cream, water and flour. Add to pan and heat. *Do not boil.* When sauce is hot, return chicken to pan and turn to coat with sauce. Serve immediately. Serves 6.

CHICKEN À LA LOWELL

4 large chicken breast halves (2 whole breasts) boned and skinned
4 teaspoons Dijon mustard
Salt and pepper to taste
Italian seasoning to taste
4 slices mozzarella cheese
Olive oil
1 bunch green onions, chopped
½ pound mushrooms, sliced
3 tomatoes, peeled, seeded and chopped
½ cup dry white wine or vermouth
White rice

Pound chicken breasts until thin between 2 pieces of wax paper. Spread 1 teaspoon mustard on each breast. Sprinkle salt, pepper, and herbs on chicken to taste. Lay 1 slice of cheese on each breast; roll chicken up lengthwise and pinch ends to seal. Do not use toothpicks. Refrigerate until chilled. Cover the bottom of a skillet with olive oil. Heat oil, place chicken rolls in pan and sauté until brown on all sides. Remove chicken from pan and keep warm. Make sure you have 2 tablespoons oil in pan; either pour off or add more as the case may be. Add green onions, mushrooms, and tomatoes to pan. Sauté until mushrooms are done. Add wine and cook until sauce is thick, scraping pan to get up all browned bits. To serve, place chicken rolls on bed of rice; pour sauce over chicken. Serves 4.

B. Lowell Kronowitz

GARLIC CHICKEN

3½ pound frying chicken,
  cut up
2 tablespoons olive oil
½ cup finely chopped
  fresh parsley
Peeled whole cloves from
  1 bulb garlic (use entire
  bulb)

Salt and pepper
½ cup dry white wine or
  vermouth

Preheat oven to 375°. Pour oil into a heavy casserole with a lid. Sprinkle chicken with salt and pepper and layer in casserole with parsley and garlic, putting white meat on top. Pour wine over chicken. Cover casserole with foil; seal tightly. Place lid over foil. Bake for 1 to 1½ hours, until chicken is done. Serve with lots of good French bread to soak up sauce—spread garlic on bread. Also good sliced cold for sandwiches.
NOTE: To peel garlic easily, break bulb by pounding with fist and separate cloves. Drop in boiling water for 1 minute, drain and peel. Serves 4 to 6.

Mary Louise Mathers

PARMESAN CHICKEN

3 to 3½ pound frying
  chicken, cut up
⅓ cup butter or margarine,
  melted
1½ cups (3 slices) soft
  white bread crumbs

⅓ cup freshly grated
  Parmesan cheese
1 clove garlic, crushed
1 teaspoon salt
⅛ teaspoon black pepper

Preheat oven to 350°. Mix together bread crumbs, cheese, garlic, salt and pepper. Dip chicken in melted butter, then roll in bread crumb mixture to coat well. Place skin-side up in cast iron skillet or foil-lined baking pan. Drizzle remaining butter over chicken. Bake uncovered for 1 hour until tender and golden brown. Serve hot or cold. Serves 4 to 6.

COUNTRY CAPTAIN

3½ to 4 pound frying chicken, cut up
Crisco
Flour, salt and pepper
2 onions, chopped
2 bell peppers, chopped
1 clove garlic, crushed
3 teaspoons curry powder
2 (1 lb.) cans tomatoes, drained and coarsely chopped
1 tablespoon chopped fresh parsley
1 teaspoon thyme
1 teaspoon salt
½ teaspoon freshly ground pepper
⅓ cup currants or raisins, plumped in 1 cup hot water for 30 minutes, then drained
1 cup almonds, toasted (see *Note*)
2 tablespoons chopped fresh parsley for garnish
2 cups uncooked rice, cooked

Melt enough Crisco to come ½ inch up side of electric skillet or heavy frying pan. Heat to 375°. While Crisco is melting, roll chicken in seasoned flour. Shake off excess. Brown chicken, remove from pan and keep warm. Browning the chicken well is the secret of this dish's success. Drain all but 4 tablespoons fat from pan. Sauté onions, bell pepper and garlic until soft but not brown. Stir in curry powder; cook for 1 minute. Add tomatoes, parsley, thyme, salt and pepper. Add chicken and stir to combine. Cover skillet. Simmer for 30 to 45 minutes or until chicken is tender. Remove chicken from sauce and arrange on platter. Add currants to sauce. Spoon sauce over chicken and garnish with almonds and parsley. Serve over rice.

NOTE: Toast sliced blanched almonds on a baking sheet at 325° for 8 to 10 minutes, or until golden brown. Watch carefully! Serves 4.

CHICKEN TETRAZZINI

3½ to 4 pound frying
　chicken
Bouquet garni (6 pepper-
　corns, 2 parsley stems,
　1 rib celery, 1 carrot, 1
　small onion cut in half,
　bay leaf, pinch of thyme)
Salt
Water to cover
½ pound mushrooms,
　sliced
3 tablespoons butter

½ pound thin spaghetti
3 tablespoons butter
3 tablespoons flour
2 cups chicken stock
　(from chicken)
1 cup heavy cream
¼ cup sherry
Salt and pepper
Nutmeg
½ cup freshly grated
　Parmesan cheese

Cover chicken with water, add seasonings, bring to a boil, cover, reduce heat and simmer until tender. Remove chicken from stock. When chicken is cool enough to handle, remove meat from bones and cut into chunks. Return skin and bones to stock; reduce to 2 cups. Strain. Either skim off fat while hot or refrigerate until fat solidifies and remove. Sauté mushrooms in 3 tablespoons butter until soft. Cook spaghetti in boiling salted water until barely tender, about 7 minutes. Rinse under hot water and drain. Melt 3 tablespoons butter; stir in flour until smooth. Add stock, whisk until smooth and cook, stirring constantly, until boiling. Whisk in cream and sherry. Add salt, pepper and nutmeg to taste. Lower heat and simmer for 10 minutes, stirring occasionally. Mix chicken, mushrooms, spaghetti and sauce. Pour into buttered casserole. Sprinkle Parmesan cheese over top. Bake at 350° for 30 minutes, until heated through and cheese is melted.

NOTE: Use 3 to 4 cups leftover turkey instead of chicken. Use 1 (13¾ oz.) can chicken broth diluted with water to make 2 cups, or make stock from turkey carcass. This casserole freezes well. Serves 4 to 6.

Edith Rhodes

HURRY CURRY

1 turkey breast
2 medium eggplants,
  peeled and cut into
  ½-inch cubes
¼ cup vegetable oil
¼ cup olive oil
1 cup water
½ teaspoon salt
¼ cup butter
4 medium onions, chopped
¼ cup chopped fresh
  parsley
4 large tart apples, peeled
  and chopped

1 cup chicken broth,
  canned or homemade
1 cup dry white wine
1 tablespoon powdered
  ginger
3 tablespoons curry
  powder
Salt and pepper to taste
5 cups raw rice, cooked
  (see Index for Fool-proof
  Rice)

Roast turkey breast; cool. Remove skin; cut meat into bite-size chunks. Heat vegetable and olive oil in a deep pot and sauté cubed eggplant for 5 minutes, stirring frequently. Add water and salt and simmer covered over low heat, stirring occasionally, until tender, about 30 minutes. In a separate pan, melt butter, add parsley and onions and sauté until onion is translucent. Add apples, cover, and simmer 30 minutes, stirring occasionally. Combine eggplant, onions and apples, and turkey. Add wine and chicken broth, ginger and curry powder. Add salt and pepper to taste. Simmer 20 to 30 minutes, then set aside until 20 minutes before serving time. Reheat over low heat before serving—make sure it's hot! If too thick, add wine.

Side Dishes

The most time-consuming part, yet the most fun, is preparing the side dishes. These may be prepared well ahead of serving time, and stored, covered with plastic wrap, in the refrigerator. Remove an hour before serving to bring to room temperature. Side dishes should be put into small bowls or cups (glass is pretty) with a teaspoon or demitasse spoon to serve. ⟶

Chopped green onion
Chopped hard-boiled
  eggs
Roasted peanuts
Chopped bell pepper
Chopped tomato, peeled
  and seeded
Bacon, fried crisp and
  crumbled
Coconut
Toasted coconut
Sunflower seeds

1 cup raisins soaked in ½
  cup bourbon and ½ cup
  water; drained
Ginger preserve
Major Grey's mango
  chutney
Banana chunks sautéed in
  butter
Pineapple chunks, drained
Mandarin orange slices,
  drained
Chopped pickled peaches

You should have at least 10 to 12 side dishes—the more the merrier. To Serve: Place a mound of rice in the center of a large dinner plate or soup plate and pour curry over. As for the side dishes themselves, your guests will enjoy passing them to each other. If you have a large lazy susan, you may prefer putting the side dishes in the center of your table. Or spread the side dishes out on the table, put the pot of curry and pot of rice on one end, and let your guests serve themselves buffet style. Part of the fun of eating Hurry Curry is the change in flavor of each bite as you work your way around the side dish condiments you have sprinkled around your pile of curry and rice. Even after second helpings, there may be room for this special light dessert:

Hurry Curry Chaser

2 quarts orange sherbet
1 (1 lb.) package
  sweetened frozen
  strawberries, thawed

Cointreau or Grand
  Marnier

Scoop the orange sherbet into serving dishes ahead of time and place in freezer to hold (if you have room—otherwise just dish up after everyone has finished their curry.) When ready to serve, spoon a little of the strawberries over each serving and pour an ounce of liqueur over each. G-r-r-eat!

NOTE: Before dinner, Mr. Traub suggests you serve no hors d'oeuvres because Hurry Curry is delicious and very filling. Martinis and mixed drinks are okay, as they seem to sharpen the appetite! Serves 8 to 10 with second helpings.

Stephen Traub

TURKEY OR CHICKEN BASTE

2 cups (1 lb.) butter
⅔ cup finely chopped
   onion
3 cloves garlic, crushed

½ cup finely chopped
   fresh parsley
1 cup dry white wine

Melt butter. Cook onion and garlic in butter until soft. Add remaining ingredients and use to baste turkey or chicken on the grill.
NOTE: Heavenly!

Laurie and Jim Widman

CORNBREAD DRESSING

3 cups cornbread crumbs,
   from your favorite recipe
3 cups white bread crumbs
½ cup chopped celery
½ cup chopped onions
2 eggs

3 cups chicken stock,
   enough to moisten
   crumbs well
½ cup butter
1½ teaspoons salt
1½ teaspoons pepper

Mix all ingredients together well and stuff into turkey, or bake in a covered dish along with turkey or chicken.
NOTE: If you like more celery and onion, add it. You may also want to add some chopped bell pepper.

PIRATES' HOUSE DUCK

2 5-pound Long Island
   ducklings, thawed
Salt and pepper
2 teaspoons rosemary
½ medium onion, peeled
½ apple

½ orange
Soy sauce
¼ cup Grand Marnier or
   brandy
1 recipe Orange Sauce for
   Ducks, see below

Remove insides of ducks. Reserve livers and all available fat for duck liver paté, see Index. Preheat oven to 350°. Sprinkle insides of ducks with salt, pepper and 1 teaspoon rosemary. Place ¼ onion, apple and orange in each cavity. Cut a slit in the tail and stick legs through to help duck hold shape. Fold neck skin under duck. Rub ducks all over with soy sauce. Place ducks breast-side down on a rack on a baking pan. Bake for 1 hour, turn breast-side up, and bake 1½ hours longer, or until skin is crisp and golden. Remove ducks from oven; let sit 15 minutes. Using kitchen shears, cut duck in half lengthwise down breastbone. Turn duck over and cut along each side of backbone. Discard backbone. Remove apple, orange and onion and discard. Place the 4 duck halves on an oven-proof serving platter. Run under broiler until crisp and hot, about 5 minutes. Meanwhile, warm liqueur carefully. Do not boil! Pour over ducks, turn out the lights, ignite, and bring flaming ducks to the table amid oohs and aahs. Serve with Orange Sauce. Serves 4.

Orange Sauce for Ducks

⅓ cup firmly packed light
   brown sugar
⅓ cup sugar
Grated rind of 1 orange
Rind of ½ orange, peeled
   so that no white is on
   rind and cut into very
   fine strips

1 cup orange juice
   (including juice from
   oranges)
¼ teaspoon salt
1 tablespoon cornstarch
1 tablespoon cold water

Combine sugars, grated orange rind and strips, orange juice and salt in a heavy saucepan. Bring to a boil, lower heat and simmer until strips of rind are tender, about 15 minutes. Dissolve cornstarch in cold water and add to sauce. Simmer, stirring constantly, until sauce thickens and becomes clear. May be made ahead and reheated gently.
NOTE: Keeps at least 1 month in the refrigerator.

MOTHER EDEL'S NUT DRESSING

1 cup crushed saltine cracker crumbs
1 cup stale bread crumbs
½ cup butter, softened
1 cup chopped onion
1 tablespoon minced parsley
2 tablespoons finely chopped celery
2 eggs, well-beaten
¼ teaspoon black pepper
2 cups chopped pecans
Water, or chicken or turkey stock

Mix cracker and bread crumbs together; stir in butter. Add remaining ingredients; mix well. Add enough liquid to moisten. Stuff in bird or bake in greased, covered baking dish at 350° for 1 hour, uncovering for the last 5 minutes of baking time.
NOTE: This is a double, turkey size recipe. Half would be plenty for a chicken. If you do bake it outside the bird, chicken or turkey stock instead of water will give it more flavor.

Danyse Edel

 Never, never, never buy boned chicken breasts! Anyone can learn to bone a chicken breast and save lots of money. *From Julia Child's Kitchen* has excellent directions, starting on page 207, about how to do it. Once you figure it out, you should be able to do one in less than a minute, which is certainly worth a savings of 2 dollars a pound.

MEAT

CREOLE STEAK

3 pound boneless chuck
  steak
Salt and pepper
4 ribs celery, chopped
2 large bell peppers,
  chopped

½ cup catsup
½ cup chili sauce
2 tablespoons
  Worcestershire sauce
1 (17 oz.) can Leseur peas
1 (3 oz.) can mushrooms

Remove excess fat from steak. Season steak generously with salt and pepper on both sides. Place in baking dish; cover with celery and bell pepper. Blend catsup, chili sauce and Worcestershire sauce and pour over steak. Cover with plastic wrap and marinate in refrigerator at least 4 hours. Remove from refrigerator 1 hour before time to bake. Preheat oven to 350°. Dot with butter and bake uncovered for 40 to 50 minutes. Steak should be rare, or it will be tough. Remove meat to cutting board. Combine celery, peppers and sauce with peas and mushrooms; heat. Carve meat, place on platter, pour vegetables over meat and serve.
NOTE: You may add another can of peas and mushrooms if you like. Serves 4 to 6.

Edna Traub

KANSAS CITY RIB ROAST

Rib roast
Garlic salt

Pepper

Have roast at room temperature. Preheat oven to 400°. Season with garlic salt and pepper. Place in hot oven at 12 o'clock noon. After 1 hour, turn oven off. DO NOT OPEN OVEN. 1 hour before dinner, turn oven back on to 400°. This roast gives servings of well-done, medium, and rare juicy meat.
NOTE: For a 2-rib roast, cook only 30 minutes the second time.

Danyse Edel

DEVILISH FLANK STEAK

1½ to 2 pound flank steak
1 clove garlic, crushed
1 teaspoon salt
1 teaspoon dried rosemary,
  chopped
¼-inch thick slice fresh
  ginger, peeled and finely
  chopped, or

½ teaspoon ground ginger
½ cup Dijon mustard
2 tablespoons soy sauce

Score the flank steak lightly on both sides. In a small bowl, mash the garlic, salt and spices with the back of a spoon to make a paste. Stir in the mustard and soy sauce. Spread half the mixture on one side of the steak. Grill sauce-side down for 5 minutes. Spread top side of meat with remaining sauce, turn, and grill 5 minutes. Slice against the grain and at an angle. Serve hot or cold.
NOTE: Spread a whole tenderloin with this mixture, cook over charcoal until medium rare, chill and slice thin. Great served on homemade rolls for a party.

BEEF MARINADE

¼ cup light brown sugar
5 ounces soy sauce
1 teaspoon lemon juice

½ cup bourbon
1½ cups water

Combine ingredients. Marinate meat at least 24 hours in refrigerator. Remove meat from refrigerator 4 hours before cooking.
NOTE: Have your butcher roll and tie a sirloin tip roast or rib eye, or use a rump roast, and cook on rotisserie or on a Weber grill according to instruction manual. Good also for steaks.

Suzanne D. Peterson

STEAK MARINADE

½ cup soy sauce
3 tablespoons honey
4 tablespoons cider
  vinegar
1 clove garlic, crushed
1 tablespoon finely
  chopped fresh ginger

1½ cups vegetable oil
4 green onions, chopped,
  or 1 medium onion,
  sliced

Mix together, pour over steak in glass dish or Zip-loc bag and marinate for 6 hours in refrigerator, turning occasionally. Grill steak over charcoal or broil, basting with marinade.
NOTE: Good for less tender cuts of meat, such as chuck, round or flank steak, cooked rare or medium rare.

Sheron George

OVEN ROAST

3 to 4 pound chuck roast
2 tablespoons oil
½ cup Heinz 57 steak
  sauce

1 large onion, chopped
1 (11 oz.) can beef bouillon

Line a 9x13 inch baking dish with heavy-duty aluminum foil. Oil foil with 2 tablespoons oil. Do not pour off excess oil. Place roast on foil, pour steak sauce, onions and beef bouillon over roast and seal foil. Preheat oven to 400°. Bake for 20 minutes. Turn oven down to 325° and bake for 2½ hours.
NOTE: You may substitute 1 envelope Lipton's onion soup mix for onion and beef bouillon. For a really tender roast, after baking at 400° for 20 minutes, lower heat to 275° and bake 5 to 6 hours.

Judy Driggers
Sheron George

BARBECUED BRISKET

3 pound beef brisket or
  lean boneless chuck
  roast, trimmed of fat
1 (11 oz.) can cream of
  mushroom soup

1 envelope Lipton's onion
  soup mix
1 recipe Martha's Barbecue
  Sauce, see below

Preheat oven to 300°. Place a double thickness of heavy-duty aluminum foil in a jelly roll pan or 9x13 inch baking dish. Place meat in pan; mix barbecue sauce, mushroom soup and onion soup mix together. Pour over meat. Seal foil tightly, leaving about 1-inch clearance between foil and meat. Bake for 2½ to 3 hours, or until meat is almost falling apart. Let sit for 10 minutes before slicing. Slice thin and serve with sauce, or cut into bite-size pieces and reheat with sauce.
NOTE: Great with homemade French fries and tossed salad. Serves 4 to 6.

Martha Summerour

MARTHA'S BARBECUE SAUCE

1 cup catsup
2 tablespoons prepared
  yellow mustard
¼ cup cider vinegar
⅓ cup dark brown sugar

2 teaspoons
  Worcestershire sauce
½ teaspoon salt
¼ teaspoon Tabasco or to
  taste

Combine all ingredients in a small saucepan and heat, stirring, to combine flavors. Brush on chicken pieces, spareribs, pork chops or backbone. Good for grilling outdoors, but do not start basting meat with sauce until meat is almost done, as the catsup in the sauce burns quickly.

Martha Summerour

OLD FASHIONED POT ROAST

3 to 4 pound boneless chuck roast
2 tablespoons flour
2 tablespoons vegetable oil
1½ teaspoons salt
¼ teaspoon black pepper
½ teaspoon marjoram
¼ teaspoon thyme
¼ teaspoon basil

1 small onion, sliced
½ cup dry red wine
½ cup water
3 medium onions, cut in sixths
1 pound carrots, peeled and cut in chunks
1 pound small potatoes, peeled

Preheat oven to 350°. Sprinkle meat lightly with flour; rub in. Heat oil in heavy oven-proof Dutch oven and brown meat slowly on all sides, using tongs to turn meat. Drain oil. Season meat with salt, pepper, marjoram, thyme and basil. Add sliced onion, wine and ½ cup water. Cover, place in oven and cook for 2 hours. Add vegetables and another ½ cup water. Cover and continue cooking for 1 to 1½ hours or until tender.

Gravy

Remove vegetables and roast from Dutch oven. Keep warm. Skim fat from pan juices. Add water to juices to make 1½ cups. Combine ¼ cup flour and ½ cup cold water and stir until smooth and well-blended. Stir flour mixture gradually into pan juices until gravy reaches desired thickness. Season with salt and pepper; simmer 2 to 3 minutes.

NOTE: To make a great hash: Cut leftover meat in cubes. Chop a medium onion or 2 shallots and sauté in 2 tablespoons butter until translucent. Pour in a glug of red wine and reduce. Add meat and leftover gravy, and a little more wine if you like. Simmer until heated through, correct seasonings and serve with noodles or rice. Wonderful!

Tom Roche

SWISS STEAK

1½ pounds cube steak
Self-rising flour seasoned
 with salt, pepper and
 garlic powder
Vegetable oil
1 large onion, sliced
1 (1 lb. can) tomatoes

2 tablespoons tomato
 paste
1 bay leaf
Pinch sugar
Salt and pepper to taste
1 cup water, or as needed

Cut steak into serving-size pieces. Coat with seasoned flour. Heat oil in heavy skillet until smoking. Brown meat well on both sides, turning with tongs. Do not crowd pan. Remove meat from pan when brown. Pour off all but 2 tablespoons oil; sauté onion until brown. Squish tomatoes through fingers into pan, adding juice. Add meat and remaining ingredients. Cover and simmer until tender, 1½ to 2 hours, adding water as necessary. Serves 4.

MEAT LOAF

1½ pounds ground beef
½ pound pork sausage
1 cup cracker meal or fine
 bread crumbs
2 tablespoons finely
 chopped onion
¼ cup finely chopped
 celery
1 clove garlic, crushed

2 eggs
1 cup tomato juice
¼ cup catsup
1 tablespoon
 Worcestershire sauce
¼ teaspoon chili powder
2 teaspoons salt
¼ teaspoon pepper

Mix everything together well with hands. Pack into a bread pan and refrigerate 1 hour. Unmold into baking dish and bake at 350° for 1½ hours. Remove from oven, let sit 10 minutes, transfer to platter and serve. Serves 6.

Edna Traub

IONIA'S MEATLOAF

1½ pounds ground beef
½ cup bread crumbs
⅓ cup finely chopped
   celery
⅓ cup finely chopped
   onion
⅓ cup finely chopped bell
   pepper

1 egg
1 tablespoon tomato paste
⅓ cup catsup
3 to 4 tablespoons
   evaporated milk
½ teaspoon salt
Black pepper

Preheat oven to 350°. Combine all ingredients with hands and shape into a loaf. Place in a baking dish and top with Franklin's Sauce, see below. Bake for 1 hour. "Pull from the oven and amaze your friends!!!" Serves 4 to 6.

Ionia Wright

FRANKLIN'S SAUCE

⅔ cup catsup

⅓ cup firmly packed dark
   brown sugar

Mix together until sugar is dissolved and pour over meatloaf.

Franklin Traub

Freeze ground beef, chicken, etc., in flat packages, and it will thaw much quicker.

PEPPER STEAK

1½ pounds boneless beef
  steak, 1-inch thick (rib,
  sirloin, chuck, flank),
  partially frozen
2 tablespoons oil
1 medium onion, sliced
  thin
2 ribs celery, cut in 2-inch
  lengths
1 to 1½ cups beef bouillon
  or water

½ teaspoon
  Worcestershire sauce
¼ cup soy sauce
½ bay leaf, crushed
¼ teaspoon basil
1 large bell pepper, cut in
  strips
1 tablespoon cornstarch,
  mixed with ½ cup water
Salt and pepper to taste
Hot cooked rice

Slice steak in ¼ inch thick slices. Dry on paper towels. In large
skillet sauté onion and celery in oil until onion is translucent.
Add steak and brown over high heat. Stir in bouillon, Worcestershire sauce, soy sauce, bay leaf and basil. Lower heat, cover
and simmer over low heat until meat is almost tender. Add pepper strips and simmer 10 to 15 minutes, stirring occasionally.
Stir in cornstarch and water, cook and stir until mixture thickens. Add salt and pepper to taste. Serve over rice. Serves 4.

Margaret Faulkner

 ## PIRATES' HOUSE PEPPER STEAK

1½ pounds boneless
  chuck steak cut into
  1-inch strips, or
1½ pounds cube steak
All-purpose flour seasoned
  with salt, pepper and
  garlic powder

Vegetable oil
1 large onion, sliced
1 large bell pepper, cut in
  strips
1 (2 oz.) jar chopped
  pimientos, drained
2 cups water or as needed

Roll meat in flour; shake off excess. Heat enough oil to cover bottom of a heavy skillet. Brown meat well, a few pieces at a time. Do not crowd pan. Remove meat from pan when brown. Pour out all but 2 tablespoons oil. Sauté onions until brown. Return meat to pan, add water and simmer until meat is tender, adding water as needed. Cube steak will take longer than chuck. 10 minutes before end of cooking time, add bell pepper strips and pimiento. If sauce is not thick enough, stir in 1 tablespoon flour dissolved in ¼ cup water. Serve over white rice. Serves 4.

COUNTRY-STYLE STEAK AND GRAVY

1 to 2 pounds cube steak
Self-rising flour, salt,
pepper, and garlic
powder
Vegetable oil

1 medium onion, sliced
1 cup water
Salt and pepper to taste

Heat enough oil in a heavy skillet to cover bottom of pan ¼ inch deep. Mix flour, salt, pepper and garlic powder. Coat cube steak with flour, making sure meat is completely coated; shake off excess. Brown meat well on both sides, removing from pan when browned. When all meat is browned, pour all but 2 tablespoons of oil from pan and sauté onions until translucent. Return meat to pan, add 1 cup water, lower heat and cover. Simmer for 2 hours, or until meat is tender, stirring occasionally. You may need to add more water. Gravy should be thick. Before serving, skim fat and taste for seasoning. Great with homemade mashed potatoes. Serves 3 to 6, depending on amount of meat.

BEEF BOURGIGNON

2 to 2½ pounds boneless chuck roast, cut in 2-inch cubes
1 tablespoon olive oil or vegetable oil
¼ pound slab bacon, diced, or
¼ pound sliced bacon
2 medium onions, sliced
2 cloves garlic, crushed
2 carrots, peeled and cut in strips
2 tablespoons all-purpose flour
1 tablespoon tomato paste
2 (10¾ oz.) cans beef bouillon
2 cups Burgundy, or any full-bodied red wine
½ teaspoon thyme
1 bay leaf
Salt and pepper to taste
4 tablespoons butter
½ pound mushrooms, whole, quartered, or sliced, depending on size

In a heavy pot, fry bacon slowly in olive oil until crisp. Remove. If using sliced bacon, crumble. Dry meat on paper towels and brown well on all sides in grease, turning with tongs. A fork will pierce the meat and will let all of the juices out. Do not crowd pan. Remove meat when browned. Pour off all but 2 table-spoons grease. Sauté onions, garlic and carrots until onions are brown. Add flour and stir until smooth. Return meat to pot. Stir in tomato paste, bouillon, wine, thyme, bay leaf and pepper. Do not add salt. Bring to a boil, reduce to a simmer, cover and cook 2 to 2½ hours, or until tender. Meanwhile, sauté mush-rooms in butter until soft. When meat is tender, remove from pot. Reduce sauce until slightly thickened. If you reduce it too much it may be too salty. If this happens, just add water. You probably won't need to add salt, but taste to be sure. Return meat to pot, add mushrooms, and simmer gently until heated through.

NOTE: The secret of this dish is in the browning of the meat. It must be dark brown on all sides. It is a very tedious process, the grease spits all over the place and smells up your hair, but the finished product is worth it. Also, in cooking, be sure to use a wine that you would drink on its own. It doesn't have to be vintage wine, but it should taste good. This is a good dish to make a day ahead, or to freeze, so you won't smell like bacon grease at your dinner party. Serves 4.

SHORT RIBS MARENGO

3 to 4 pounds meaty beef
   short ribs
Oil to cover bottom of
   Dutch oven
2 medium onions, sliced
4 carrots, cut in quarters
   lengthwise
2 tablespoons flour
1 (1 lb.) can tomatoes,
   drained, seeded, and
   coarsely chopped

1 (11 oz.) can beef bouillon
1 soup can water
½ cup dry white wine or
   vermouth
1 bay leaf
½ teaspoon thyme
Salt and pepper to taste

Heat oil in a heavy Dutch oven. Brown meat well on all sides, using tongs to turn. Do not crowd pan. Remove meat as it browns. When all meat is browned, pour off all but 2 table-spoons oil, add onions and carrots and sauté until brown. Stir in flour. Replace meat, add tomatoes, bouillon, water, wine and seasonings. Do not add salt. Bring to a boil, lower heat, cover, and simmer 2 hours, or until meat is tender. Remove meat; boil liquid to reduce to desired thickness. Remove as much fat as possible from surface. Before serving, reheat meat in sauce. Taste for seasonings.

NOTE: It's a good idea to make this the day before serving and refrigerate. The fat hardens and lifts right off. For added flavor, use a combination of vegetable oil and olive oil, or all olive oil.

BARBECUED BEEF SHORT RIBS

2 to 3 pounds meaty beef
   short ribs
1 large onion, peeled and
   cut in fourths
1 rib celery, cut in 2-inch
   lengths
1 large carrot, cut in 2-inch
   lengths

Salt, pepper and garlic
   powder to taste
Water
1 recipe Martha's Barbecue
   Sauce, see Index, or
Your favorite store-bought
   or homemade sauce

Place ribs and vegetables in a large heavy pot; cover with water. Bring to a boil, lower heat, cover and simmer 2 to 3 hours, or until tender. Cool slightly and place entire pot in re-frigerator overnight. Fat will rise to the top and solidify, and will be easy to remove. Discard fat and vegetables, lay ribs out in a baking dish, and cover with barbecue sauce. Bake at 350° for 30 minutes, or until ribs are hot and sauce is bubbly.

MAMA POLSTON'S STEW BEEF

2 pounds stew beef
4 tablespoons oil
Pinch of sage

¼ teaspoon red pepper
Salt to taste

Brown meat in oil in a heavy pot. Pour off excess fat. Add water to barely cover meat; add seasonings. Cover and cook over low heat until tender, 2 to 3 hours. Serve over rice or cook your favorite dumplings with meat before serving. Serves 4 to 6.

Sheron George

MONGOLIAN BEEF

1 pound flank steak,
  partially frozen
1 large bunch green
  onions
2 to 3 cloves garlic,
  crushed

Vegetable or peanut oil
Pinch sugar
Salt
Soy sauce
Rice or rice noodles

Slice meat very thin on the diagonal. Dry on paper towels. Cut onions in thirds; shred. Fill wok ⅓ full of oil. Heat until a drop of water sizzles on the surface. Add half the meat; stir-fry for 20 to 30 seconds until brown. Remove from wok. Wait for oil to heat up again; cook remaining meat. Remove from wok. Pour all but 2 tablespoons oil from wok. Return to heat, add garlic, stir-fry for 30 seconds, add green onions, and stir-fry until slightly limp. Add meat, a pinch of sugar, and salt and soy sauce to taste. Serve on rice or rice noodles.

PIRATES' HOUSE SPAGHETTI SAUCE

1½ pounds ground beef
1 (1 lb.) can tomatoes,
  coarsely chopped
1 tomato can water
1 (6 oz.) can tomato paste
1 bell pepper, chopped
1 medium onion, chopped

2 to 3 ribs celery, chopped
¼ teaspoon garlic powder,
  or 1 clove garlic,
  crushed
½ to 1 teaspoon oregano
½ to 1 teaspoon rosemary
1 bay leaf

Brown meat in large pot. Drain fat. Add garlic, onions, bell pepper and celery. Sauté until tender; add tomatoes. Add remaining ingredients. Simmer on low heat, uncovered, for a maximum of 4 hours, adding water if necessary.
NOTE: The longer it cooks, the better it tastes.

GREENBRIAR BEEF STROGANOFF

1½ pounds sirloin tip
  roast, cut in ¼-inch
  strips
½ cup flour
¼ teaspoon salt
1 tablespoon paprika
2 tablespoons butter
¼ pound mushrooms,
  sliced
1 small onion, chopped

1 clove garlic, crushed
2 tablespoons butter
3 tablespoons flour
2 tablespoons tomato
  paste
1 (11 oz.) can beef bouillon
1 cup sour cream
1 teaspoon lemon juice
2 tablespoons sherry

Combine flour, salt and paprika and dredge meat. Melt 2 tablespoons butter in a large heavy skillet and brown meat quickly. Add mushrooms, onion and garlic and cook until tender. Remove meat and mushrooms from skillet. Add 2 tablespoons butter to pan and blend in 3 tablespoons flour. Stir in tomato paste. Slowly add bouillon and cook, stirring constantly, until thickened. Return meat and mushrooms to skillet. Just before serving, stir in sour cream, lemon juice and sherry. Heat, but *do not boil.* Serve over Parslied Rice, see Index. Serves 6.

SATURDAY NIGHT SPECIAL

½ to 1 pound ground beef
½ cup chopped onion
½ teaspoon salt
1 (11 oz.) can chicken
  gumbo soup

2 tablespoons catsup
2 tablespoons dry mustard
Pepper to taste

Brown meat; drain well. Add remaining ingredients. Simmer 30 to 45 minutes. Spoon onto lightly toasted hamburger buns or English muffins, open-face style. Serves 2 to 4.

Nancy Appun

VEAL SCALLOPINI

1 pound boneless veal
  cutlets
1 tablespoon all-purpose
  flour
½ teaspoon salt
Dash pepper
¼ cup cooking oil
½ medium onion, sliced
  thin
1 (1 lb.) can tomatoes,
  juice and all (Italian plum
  tomatoes are best)

½ pound fresh
  mushrooms, sliced
1 tablespoon finely
  chopped fresh parsley
1 tablespoon capers,
  drained
¼ teaspoon garlic powder
¼ teaspoon oregano
Hot buttered noodles

Pound veal between wax paper as thin as possible without tearing. Combine flour, salt and pepper; dust veal lightly with flour mixture. Heat oil in a heavy skillet and brown veal slowly a few pieces at a time. Remove meat from skillet; sauté onion in oil until soft but not brown. Add meat, tomatoes (squish some and leave some whole), mushrooms, parsley, capers, garlic powder and oregano. Cover and simmer 25 to 30 minutes until veal is tender, stirring occasionally. If sauce is not thick enough, remove veal and reduce sauce to desired consistency. Arrange veal on hot buttered noodles and top with sauce.
NOTE: Mrs. Wiggers has been making this dish for 25 years. She has served it to colonels and generals, and they love it. It doubles easily, and waits well for tardy guests. Serves 4.

Fay Wiggers

Never turn meat with a fork—it lets all the good meat juices out. That's what tongs are for. Besides, if you don't have tongs, how do you retrieve corn on the cob from boiling water?

WIENER SCHNITZEL

½ to 1 pound lean veal
round steak about
½-inch thick
1 cup all-purpose flour
seasoned with salt and
pepper

1 to 2 eggs, well-beaten
2 cups (approximately)
very fine fresh white
bread crumbs
½ cup butter
1 lemon, sliced

A few hours before serving, cut veal in 2x3 inch pieces, cutting along natural divisions of meat and removing fat and membranes. Don't worry if pieces are not evenly shaped. Place pieces of meat 1 at a time between 2 sheets of wax paper and pound flat with a rolling pin, smooth mallet or heavy bottle. Pound meat as thin as possible without tearing. Line up from left to right: flattened meat, seasoned flour on a plate or wax paper, eggs in a pie plate or similar dish, bread crumbs on a plate, and an empty plate. Dip veal in flour on both sides and shake off excess. Dip in egg, then in bread crumbs, pressing to make sure crumbs adhere. Shake off excess and place on empty· plate and refrigerate until time to cook. This is the trick to make the breading stick. Melt butter in a heavy skillet on medium-high heat until bubbly. Place 2 or 3 pieces of veal at a time in skillet, brown on one side, turn with tongs and brown on other side. Remove to a platter set in a warm oven. It should take no more than 2 minutes to cook an entire piece. Repeat with remaining veal. If meat browns too quickly, lower heat. Garnish platter with lemon slices and serve.

NOTE: Veal is already expensive enough without paying premium prices for cutlets. Pounding the veal breaks down the tough fibers, and the meat is tender and tasty. Under no circumstances should you use store-bought breadcrumbs, especially when a blender or food processor turns them out in a flash. If you have leftover crumbs, freeze them. Serves 2 to 4.

FOIE DE VEAU VENETIAN
(SAUTÉED CALVES LIVER)

3 to 4 slices calves liver
All-purpose flour, salt and
  pepper
4 tablespoons butter
1 medium onion, sliced

2 tablespoons white wine
  vinegar
½ cup white wine
1 tablespoon chopped
  fresh parsley

Rinse liver; remove skin and any veins. Cut in ¼ inch strips. Heat butter in a skillet. Sauté onions until golden, remove from pan and keep warm. Add more butter to pan if necessary. Roll liver quickly in seasoned flour, a handful at a time, and sauté immediately. Do not flour liver in advance. Cook liver for 45 to 60 seconds. Remove from pan when done; keep warm with onions. When all the liver is done, pour in vinegar. Add wine and parsley, scrape up browned pieces and stir while boiling until thickened. Add liver and onions, heat thoroughly and serve. **NOTE:** It is the miraculous addition of vinegar that saves this dish from tasting too much like liver! Serves 4.

BUTTERFLIED LEG OF LAMB

1 leg of lamb, domestic or
  New Zealand
1 (8 oz.) jar Dijon mustard
1 teaspoon rosemary

1 teaspoon ginger
1 clove garlic, crushed
2 tablespoons olive oil

Have your butcher bone and butterfly your lamb (tell him not to roll and tie it) or do it yourself. Mix remaining ingredients, spread on both sides of lamb, and let sit 1 hour. Broil in oven or grill over charcoal 10 to 15 minutes on each side. Let sit 5 to 10 minutes, slice, and serve.
NOTE: When the lamb is butterflied it will look lumpy and irregular. Don't worry. When you cook it, you will have pieces ranging from rare to well-done, to suit everyone. A nice change from steak on the grill. Serves 6 to 8.

MARINATED LEG OF LAMB

3 to 4 pound leg of lamb
2 large cloves garlic,
   slivered
¼ cup vegetable oil
¼ cup olive oil
⅓ cup vinegar
½ cup red wine
1 medium onion, chopped
1 large carrot, peeled and
   chopped
2 large cloves garlic,
   crushed
2 tablespoons
   Worcestershire sauce

½ teaspoon thyme
½ teaspoon chervil
1 teaspoon rosemary
1 bay leaf, crushed
1 tablespoon finely
   chopped fresh parsley
1 teaspoon salt
½ teaspoon pepper
2 tablespoons tomato
   paste
1 tablespoon cornstarch
   dissolved in 3
   tablespoons water

Have your butcher bone, roll, and tie your lamb, or bone it yourself. If you do it yourself, don't roll and tie until after inserting
garlic. Make small slits all over lamb with a small, sharp knife
and insert garlic slivers. Combine everything except tomato
paste, cornstarch and water and pour over lamb in a Zip-loc
bag or glass dish. Marinate overnight. Remove meat from marinade, place on baking pan, and roast in a preheated 425° oven
for 30 to 50 minutes, depending on size of roast and desired
degree of doneness. While meat is roasting, put marinade in
saucepan, cook for 15 minutes and strain. Pour off as much oil
as possible. Return to saucepan. Add tomato paste and cook
5 more minutes. If sauce is not thick enough, gradually add
cornstarch and water mixture until desired thickness. Let roast
stand for 10 minutes before carving after removing from oven.
Remove strings, slice, arrange on warm platter and serve on
warm plates. Serve sauce on the side.

NOTE: A 3½ pound (pre-boned weight) butt end portion of lamb takes 30 minutes at 425° for rare, and serves 6. If you've never had rare lamb, try it. It's not nearly "lamby" tasting as well done. Also, make sure you or your butcher remove as much fat as possible before cooking.

Bailee Kronowitz

PORK ROAST LYONNAISE

Boneless pork loin roast
Salt and pepper
1 medium onion, sliced
1 carrot, sliced
¾ cup dry white wine
  or vermouth
2 tablespoons finely
  chopped shallot

1 tablespoon Dijon
  mustard
2 tablespoons heavy
  cream
1 tablespoon butter,
  softened

Preheat oven to 500°. Rub roast all over with salt and pepper. Place in a roasting pan; scatter onion and carrot over and around roast. Place in oven and brown for 20 minutes, then lower heat to 300°. Allow 45 minutes per pound, starting from when you lower heat to 300°. When roast is done, remove to a hot platter. Discard vegetables—don't worry if they are burned. Skim all but 1 tablespoon fat from pan juices and place pan on top of stove. Sauté shallot in fat until translucent. Deglaze pan with wine, stirring with a wooden spoon to get up all browned bits and juices. Strain into a small saucepan; reduce by half. Blend mustard with cream and stir into sauce along with butter. Season with salt and pepper if necessary. If sauce is not smooth, strain it again. Slice pork and serve with sauce on the side.

FRIED PORK CHOPS

Pork chops
1 (13 oz.) can evaporated milk

All-purpose flour seasoned with salt and pepper
¼ cup Crisco

Lay pork chops out in a shallow dish. Cover with evaporated milk. Let soak at room temperature for 1 hour, turning if necessary. Heat Crisco in a heavy skillet. Shake excess milk off pork chops, coat with flour and place in hot fat. Brown well on one side. Turn, cover pan, lower heat and cook until brown on other side. Drain on paper towels and serve hot.

Sheron George

BARBECUED SPARERIBS

4 pounds pork spareribs, cut in 3 to 4 rib pieces
2 teaspoons salt

1 tablespoon cider vinegar
1 recipe Martha's Barbecue Sauce, see Index

Place rib pieces in a large heavy Dutch oven. Cover with water. Add salt and vinegar. Bring water to boil and cover pot. Reduce heat and simmer for 20 minutes. Drain immediately in a colander. Do not overcook. If not barbecuing immediately, spread on a platter to cool and refrigerate. Place ribs on a hot grill or under broiler in oven. Turn every 5 minutes for 15 minutes, then start brushing with sauce. Leave ribs on grill or under broiler on each side until sauce becomes sticky. Watch carefully, as the sauce burns easily.
NOTE: Precooking the ribs ensures that they will be fully cooked (important with pork) and also removes excess fat. Serves 4.

BAKED COUNTRY HAM

**1 Smithfield or any well-
cured country ham**

Soak ham overnight in cold water to cover; scrub well with brush. Place in roasting pan. Add 5 cups water to pan; cover tightly with lid or heavy foil. Place in cold oven. Turn oven on, set at 500°. After temperature is reached (watch oven signal), bake ham for 10 minutes. Turn off heat. DO NOT OPEN OVEN. Let stand 3 hours. Heat oven to 500° again; bake 10 minutes. Turn off heat; leave overnight (or about 10 to 12 hours) WITH-OUT OPENING OVEN DOOR. Next day, remove ham from roasting pan, remove skin and trim fat to desired thickness. Score fat and place on rack in baking pan. Glaze.

Glaze

**1½ cups firmly packed
    light brown sugar**
¼ cup dry mustard

**¼ cup whole cloves,
    optional**

Preheat oven to 350°. Combine sugar with mustard thoroughly—use your fingers. Pat mixture all over ham except bottom. Stud with cloves if desired. Bake for 30 minutes, or until well-glazed and fat is lightly browned. Cool thoroughly and refrigerate until needed; overnight is best—it must be cold in order to be carved to the desired thinness. If you just want to serve a big platter of sliced ham, an electric knife works great. Hold the ham by the shank, rest the butt end on a carving board, and carve off very thin slices down the length of the ham. This method is to be done only in the privacy of your kitchen. Otherwise, sharpen up your carving knife and do an artistic job in full view of your friends.

NOTE: It's a good idea to tape the oven door closed so you won't forget and open it.

Lillian Marshall

ETC., ETC., ETC.

CHEESE AND TOMATO PIE

9-inch pie crust, unbaked (frozen is fine, but make sure it's deep-dish)
3 pounds ripe tomatoes, peeled, seeded and coarsely chopped
3 tablespoons olive oil
1 to 2 cloves garlic, crushed
½ teaspoon salt
2 tablespoons chopped fresh parsley
½ to 1 teaspoon each basil, oregano, marjoram and thyme—to taste

1 tablespoon sugar
Freshly ground black pepper
1 pound onions (use Vidalias if you can get them)
2 tablespoons butter
¼ teaspoon salt
⅓ cup freshly grated Parmesan cheese
½ pound mozzarella cheese
12 cured black Greek olives (buy at delicatessen)

Preheat oven to 375°. Prick pie crust all over with a fork or line with foil and fill with raw rice or beans. Prebake 10 to 15 minutes, until barely browned. Remove from oven. Heat the olive oil in a heavy pan and sauté the garlic until translucent. Do not brown. Add the tomatoes and seasonings. Bring to a boil, lower heat slightly, and simmer uncovered, stirring occasionally, until sauce is thick—it should not be at all runny. Taste and adjust seasonings. This should take 30 to 40 minutes. Peel, halve, and thickly slice the onions. Sauté in butter until soft and translucent. Do not brown. Sprinkle with ¼ teaspoon salt. Sprinkle the Parmesan cheese over bottom of pie shell. Arrange onions over cheese in an even layer. Cover onions with tomato sauce. Slice the mozzarella in thin strips and arrange evenly on top of tomato sauce. The whole top of the pie should be covered with cheese. Slice the olives off their pits and arrange on cheese. Bake for 30 to 35 minutes at 375°, until golden brown. Serve hot. Serves 3 to 4.

NOTE: An all-butter crust is good with this recipe, or use your own favorite, even whole-wheat if you like. If you can get fresh basil, use it in the sauce and omit the dried herbs.

Rafe Harvard

MEXICALI QUICHE

9-inch pie crust (frozen is fine, but use deep-dish)
1 (4 oz.) can green chilies, drained, seeded and chopped
1 (4 oz.) can pitted black olives, drained and chopped
1 (7 oz.) can yellow corn (not creamed), drained
1 (2 oz.) jar chopped pimientos, drained
¾ cup (3 ozs.) grated Cheddar cheese
¾ cup (3 ozs.) grated Monterey Jack cheese
1 cup milk
3 eggs
¼ teaspoon chili powder
¼ teaspoon salt
⅛ teaspoon black pepper
1 bell pepper, seeded and cut in rings

Preheat oven to 375°. Prick bottom and sides of pie crust with fork and prebake for 10 to 15 minutes, until set and lightly browned. Mix chilies, olives, corn and pimientos together. Sprinkle half over the bottom of the pie crust. Combine cheeses and sprinkle half in pie crust. Repeat. Beat together milk, eggs, chili powder, salt and pepper. Pour over filling. Top with green pepper circles. Bake at 375° for 40 to 45 minutes, until set and a knife inserted in the center comes out clean. Let cool about 10 minutes before serving. Serves 3 to 4.

Suzanne W. Peterson

ZUCCHINI QUICHE

9-inch pie crust, unbaked (frozen is fine, but use *deep-dish*)
2 medium zucchini
1 medium onion, sliced
1 tablespoon butter
1 cup grated Swiss or Cheddar cheese
4 eggs
1 cup milk
Salt
Red pepper
Nutmeg

Grate zucchini, place in colander, sprinkle with salt and let stand for 30 minutes. Rinse with cold water and squeeze in a tea towel until dry. Preheat oven to 375°. Prick pie crust all over with a fork and prebake for 10 to 15 minutes, until set and lightly browned. Melt butter in skillet; sauté onion until translucent. Do not brown. Add zucchini to onions; sauté 3 to 4 minutes. Place zucchini and onions in pie crust. Cover with cheese. Mix eggs, milk and seasonings. Pour over filling. Bake for 45 minutes or until puffed and brown, and a knife inserted in the center comes out clean. Let cool about 10 minutes before serving.

NOTE: For a richer (and more caloric!) quiche, use half-and-half or whipping cream. Serves 3 to 4.

PASTA WITH SHRIMP-CRABMEAT SAUCE

2 tablespoons butter
2 tablespoons olive oil
2 tablespoons vegetable oil
2 large cloves garlic, crushed
½ pound medium shrimp, peeled and chopped
½ pound crabmeat, picked over for shells

¼ cup dry white wine or vermouth
1 tablespoon finely chopped parsley
½ to ¾ pound freshly made pasta, cooked just until tender in boiling salted water and drained

Heat butter and oil in skillet. Sauté garlic in oil until brown. Do not burn. Add shrimp and sauté until pink. Add crabmeat and heat thoroughly. Pour in wine and reduce quickly. Add parsley, pour sauce over pasta and toss. Serve hot or at room temperature.

NOTE: Much better with your own homemade pasta, or freshly made pasta from a specialty shop. Serves 4 to 6, depending on whether you serve it for an appetizer or main dish.

Bailee Kronowitz

LASAGNA VERDE

Bolognese Sauce

3 tablespoons olive oil
¼ pound country ham or
   prosciutto, chopped
1 onion, chopped
1 rib celery, chopped
1 carrot, chopped
2 cloves garlic, crushed
½ pound lean ground beef
¼ pound fresh
   mushrooms, chopped
½ cup dry red wine
1 teaspoon chopped fresh
   parsley
½ teaspoon marjoram

½ teaspoon oregano
½ teaspoon thyme
½ teaspoon basil
Freshly ground nutmeg to
   taste
1 teaspoon salt
Freshly ground pepper
1 teaspoon sugar
2 (1 lb. 12 oz.) cans
   tomatoes, preferably
   Italian, peeled, seeded
   and chopped—save juice
1 (6 oz.) can tomato paste

Fry the ham in a heavy pot in 2 tablespoons olive oil until golden. Add the onion, celery, carrot and garlic; continue cooking gently for 10 to 15 minutes, or until the vegetables are soft but not browned. Meanwhile, in a frying pan, brown the ground beef in 1 tablespoon oil. When well browned, drain excess fat, add mushrooms and cook for 5 minutes. Add wine and cook 5 more minutes, scraping the bottom of the pan. Add herbs and seasonings and cook until wine has completely evaporated. Remove from heat; add to ham and vegetables. Add tomatoes and tomato paste, and enough tomato juice to moisten. Bring to a boil, lower heat and simmer uncovered for 1 to 1½ hours, adding more tomato juice if necessary and stirring occasionally.

Béchamel Sauce

3 cups milk
Bouquet garni—6
   peppercorns, parsley
   stalk, bay leaf, small
   piece celery, small piece
   carrot, small unpeeled
   onion cut in half

6 tablespoons butter
6 tablespoons flour
Salt
White pepper

Pour milk into saucepan; add bouquet garni. Heat milk to a simmer, remove from heat and let stand until cool. Strain before using. Melt butter in saucepan. Add flour off heat. Return to heat, whisking until smooth. Add flavored milk and bring to a boil, whisking constantly until thickened. Season to taste. Remove from heat and place a piece of plastic wrap directly on surface of sauce until ready to use, to prevent a skin from forming.

Pasta

1 (10 oz.) box frozen
   spinach, thawed, drained
   well and puréed
3½ cups flour

4 eggs
1 tablespoon olive oil
1 teaspoon salt

Combine ingredients in food processor; process until smooth, adding water if needed to make a smooth, shiny dough. Wrap in plastic and let rest 30 minutes. Roll out ½ recipe pasta in strips as thin as possible. Cut in 24 3-inch squares. Cook the squares, 6 at a time, in a large pot of boiling salted water. When *al dente,* in 2 to 3 minutes, remove with a slotted spoon to a bowl of ice water. Dry pasta squares before using. Use remaining ½ recipe pasta for fettuccine, ravioli, or whatever. →

To Assemble:

**2 cups freshly grated
Parmesan cheese (under
NO circumstances use
the kind in the can)**

¼ cup butter, melted

Butter a 9x13 inch pan. Line bottom with 6 pasta squares. Spoon over pasta ⅓ Bolognese sauce and spread out with spoon. Follow with ¼ Béchamel sauce and ½ cup Parmesan cheese. Continue layering, ending with a top layer of pasta. Cover top layer with remaining Béchamel sauce. Sprinkle remaining ½ cup cheese and melted butter on top. Bake at 350° for 30 minutes. May be made in advance and baked before serving.

NOTE: If you don't have a food processor or pasta machine, or strong arms for kneading and rolling out dough by hand, look for spinach lasagna in the grocery store. Cook whole and cut into squares. However, nothing can replace the tender texture of fresh noodles. This recipe is not as complicated as it looks, and is well worth the effort. Serves 6 to 8.

SPAGHETTI SAUCE

**2 (1 lb. 12 oz.) cans Italian-
style tomatoes with basil**
4 tablespoons olive oil
1 large onion, chopped
**2 large cloves garlic,
crushed**
**2 tablespoons tomato
paste**
**½ teaspoon each oregano,
basil, marjoram and
thyme or to taste**

**½ teaspoon fennel seed,
crushed (use blender,
spice mill or mortar and
pestle**
**Freshly ground black
pepper**
1 teaspoon sugar
**1 pound fresh mushrooms,
sliced**
4 tablespoons olive oil

Drain tomatoes, reserving juice, and remove seeds. Sauté onion and garlic in olive oil in a heavy pot until soft and translucent. Do not brown. Add tomatoes, tomato paste, herbs, pepper and sugar, and about half the reserved tomato juice. Bring to a boil, lower heat, partially cover and simmer about 45 minutes, adding more tomato juice if necessary. Taste for salt—you probably won't need to add any. Purée in food processor or food mill and return to pot. Sauté mushrooms in olive oil until soft. Drain, add to sauce and heat thoroughly. Serve over hot spaghetti.

NOTE: You can use regular American tomatoes in a pinch. For a change, omit the mushrooms, or dice 2 or 3 medium zucchini, add to sauce and cook until tender. Serves 6.

PIZZA FONDUE

½ pound ground beef
1 medium onion, chopped
1 (14½ oz.) jar pizza sauce
1 tablespoon cornstarch
1½ teaspoons fennel seed
1½ teaspoons oregano

½ teaspoon garlic powder
2½ cups (10 ozs.) grated
  Cheddar cheese
1 cup (4 ozs.) grated
  mozzarella cheese

Brown meat and onion in an electric skillet or heavy pot. Drain off fat. Mix cornstarch and seasoning into pizza sauce. Add pizza sauce to meat; stir well. When mixture thickens and comes to a boil, reduce heat to a simmer and add cheeses by thirds, stirring well after each addition. When all the cheese has melted, pour into a fondue pot over low heat. Serve with French bread cubes or over toasted English muffins for a light supper or luncheon dish. Serves 4 to 6 as a main dish, 10 to 12 as an appetizer.

Lisa Bonfield

QUEENIE'S MACARONI AND CHEESE

1 (1 lb.) box elbow
 macaroni
1 pound mild Cheddar
 cheese, grated
½ cup margarine, melted

6 eggs
2 (13 oz.) cans evaporated
 milk
Salt and pepper to taste

Cook macaroni in boiling salted water according to package directions. Drain well and dump into a big bowl. Add grated cheese, reserving ½ cup to sprinkle on top. Stir in cheese until melted. Stir in margarine and eggs—no need to beat first, just stir well to distribute evenly. Add milk. Mixture will be fairly liquid. Pour into a 9x13 inch pan, sprinkle reserved cheese on top and bake at 350° for 45 minutes, until set. Serves 8.

Queenie Mae Boyd

PIZZA

Crust

2 cups warm water
 (110° to 115°)
2 packages yeast
2 teaspoons salt

¼ cup olive oil
5 to 6 cups all-purpose
 flour
Yellow cornmeal

Proof yeast with salt in warm water. Mix yeast, water and olive oil; stir in flour 1 cup at a time. Turn out onto floured counter; knead until smooth, 5 to 7 minutes, adding flour as necessary. Dough will be soft. Place in oiled bowl, turning to coat all sides, cover with plastic wrap and let rise in a warm place until doubled. Punch down and let rest 15 minutes. Divide in half, press out into two 12-inch round pizza pans or 15x10x1 inch pans, or 1 of each, sprinkled with yellow corn meal (prevents crust from sticking.) Divide sauce between crusts, sprinkle on mozzarella and Parmesan cheese, then add toppings of your choice. Bake at 425° for 15 to 20 minutes, or until brown and bubbling.

Sauce

1 (15½ oz.) jar spaghetti
   sauce (Ragu Homestyle
   is good)
1 (8 oz.) can tomato sauce

Garlic powder, basil,
   oregano and hot pepper
   flakes to taste

Mix together and let sit awhile to blend flavors.

Toppings

1 pound mozzarella
   cheese, shredded
1 cup freshly grated
   Parmesan cheese
Sliced onions, sautéed in
   olive oil until tender
Sliced green peppers,
   sautéed in olive oil until
   tender
Sliced mushrooms,
   sautéed in olive oil until
   tender

Italian sausage, removed
   from casing, chopped,
   sautéed until brown and
   drained
Thinly sliced pepperoni
Ground beef, sautéed until
   brown and drained
Anchovies
Sliced green or black
   olives

NOTE: This pizza is absolute perfection! Makes 2 pizzas.

Dede Warren

 In the summer, put bread out in the sun to rise. In the winter, bring a tea kettle filled with water to a boil and place in a cold oven with bread. Don't forget to remove kettle before preheating oven!

CON QUESO RICE

2 cups (12 oz.) dried black
  beans, soaked and
  cooked according to
  package directions
1 cup raw brown rice,
  cooked according to
  package directions
2 tablespoons oil
1 large onion, chopped

2 cloves garlic, crushed
1 (4 oz.) can green chili
  peppers, chopped
4 cups (1 lb.) grated
  Monterey Jack cheese
1 (16 oz.) container ricotta
  cheese
Milk

Preheat oven to 350°. Sauté onions and garlic in oil until soft
but not brown. Mix with beans, rice and chilies. Combine 3½
cups Monterey Jack cheese with ricotta cheese. Add milk if too
stiff to stir easily. Layer rice-bean mixture with cheeses in large
casserole, starting and ending with rice-bean mixture. Bake for
45 minutes. Top with reserved cheese and continue baking
until cheese melts.
NOTE: You can make this in 2 small casserole dishes and
freeze one before baking. Thaw and bake. Serves 8.

RING TUM DITTY

12 ounces bacon, chopped
2 cups onions, chopped
2 (1 lb.) cans tomatoes
1 (1 lb.) can whole kernel
  corn
¾ pound (3 cups) extra
  sharp Cheddar cheese,
  grated

4 to 6 large baking
  potatoes, baked
Basil, salt and pepper to
  taste

Sauté bacon and onions in a heavy pot until bacon is cooked and onion is translucent. Drain well and return to pan. Drain tomato juice into pot; squish tomatoes through fingers into pot. Add corn and seasonings and boil mixture until desired thickness. Add cheese; stir until melted. Spoon over baked potatoes and wait for the compliments. Serves 4 hogolettos or 6 normal people.

Sally-Byrd Newton Combs

BRUNCH CASSEROLE

12 slices extra-thin white
  bread
Butter, softened
1 pound pork sausage
½ pound (2 cups) grated
  Swiss cheese

4 eggs
3 cups milk
1 teaspoon salt
Tabasco to taste

Trim crusts from bread and butter lightly on 1 side. Crumble sausage and cook until lightly browned; drain. Lay out 6 slices bread in a 3-quart casserole, buttered side up. Sprinkle half the sausage and half the cheese over bread. Repeat with bread, sausage and cheese. Beat together eggs and milk until well-blended; beat in salt and Tabasco. Pour over sausage and cheese. Press down on bread until milk comes through. Cover with plastic wrap and refrigerate overnight. Bake at 350° for 1 hour, until puffed and brown. Serves 6.

CHEESE GRITS SOUFFLÉ

4 cups water
2 teaspoons salt
1 cup uncooked grits
2 cups (8 ozs.) grated extra
   sharp Cheddar cheese

½ cup butter or margarine
½ teaspoon
   Worcestershire sauce
4 eggs, separated
Milk

Preheat oven to 350°. Butter a 1½-quart shallow casserole. Bring salted water to a boil. Add grits gradually. Reduce heat and cook until thick, stirring frequently, about 20 to 30 minutes. Add 1½ cups cheese, butter and Worcestershire sauce; stir until cheese and butter are melted. Set aside. Beat egg yolks and add to grits mixture. Beat egg whites until stiff but not dry. Fold grits mixture into egg whites—if grits are too stiff, add milk before folding into egg whites. Pour grits into casserole; top with remaining cheese. Bake for 35 minutes, until puffed and set. Serves 6 to 8.

GARLIC CHEESE GRITS

1 cup uncooked grits
½ cup butter or margarine
1 roll Kraft garlic cheese

2 eggs
Milk

Preheat oven to 350°. Cook grits according to package directions. Stir in butter and garlic cheese; cook until melted. Put eggs in measuring cup and add milk to make 1 cup. Beat well. Add to grits mixture. Bake in a greased 2-quart casserole for 1 hour.

Edith Rhodes

MICROWAVE SCRAMBLED EGGS

4 eggs
½ eggshell full of water
½ cup grated cheese—
  whatever you have

Tabasco
Salt
1 tablespoon butter
  or margarine

Beat eggs and water well with fork; beat in Tabasco and salt to taste. Stir in cheese. Melt butter in au gratin dish or shallow glass or ceramic casserole or pie pan. Pour eggs into dish and microwave for 15 seconds. Stir cooked egg into middle with fork. Continue cooking for 15 seconds at a time and stirring with a fork. Watch carefully. Let uncooked egg run to outside. Do not overcook—stop when eggs are still soft. Serves 3.
NOTE: If you are feeling extravagant, microwave 1 or 2 pieces of bacon and crumble them into the uncooked eggs. Or throw in some chopped green onions, or use Swiss cheese and top with red caviar. Use your imagination!

MINCY'S EGGS

8 eggs
2 half egg shells full
  of water
Salt and pepper to taste
1 pound pork sausage

½ pound fresh
  mushrooms, sliced
1 (3 oz.) package cream
  cheese

Whisk eggs, water, salt and pepper until well-blended. Cook sausage in heavy skillet until brown. Drain in a colander. Return to skillet, add mushrooms and cook until soft. Add cheese, pour in eggs and cook, stirring with a wooden spoon, until eggs are set. Serve immediately. Serves 6.

Mincy Peterson

REBECCA LEFAVE'S
COUNTRY COLLEGE GRANOLA

3 pounds raw rolled oats, or 1 (2 lb. 10 oz.) box old-fashioned oats
½ pound raw sesame seeds
½ pound raw wheat germ
½ pound barley flakes
½ pound raw peanuts
½ pound hazelnuts, walnuts, cashews, brazil nuts, or whatever you like

½ pound raisins
½ pound dried apricots, apples, dates or whatever
½ pound coconut
1 cup oil (anything but olive oil)
1 cup good-quality honey

Mix grains, nuts and fruit together in a *big* bowl or pot. Add oil and honey. Mix thoroughly so that everything is coated and a bit sticky. Preheat oven to 375°. Spread the mixture out on a jelly roll pan (or 2) or any baking sheets with sides. Put in oven and stand by. After 5 minutes, remove sheets from oven, stir the mixture so that the top does not burn, and return to oven. Repeat stirring every 5 minutes for 15 to 20 minutes, until browned to your satisfaction. Continue until all granola is browned. If you stir too infrequently, it will burn, so don't wander off during the toasting procedure. Remove from oven, cool, then store in an airtight container. The toasting can also be done in a pot on top of the stove, but you must stir conscientiously to prevent sticking and burning on the bottom.

NOTE: You will have the best luck finding these ingredients at a health food store. You can put just about anything you want in this concoction. If you like nuts, put more nuts in. If you are fond of fruit, put more fruit in. A *miniscule* amount of salt (sea salt for purists) may be added if desired, especially if granola is to be eaten dry as a snack. A college buddy frequently made this recipe on a hotplate in her room, and gave it by the pound for Christmas presents. The granola is filling and it makes a great dry midnight snack, albeit a fattening one.

Kit Traub

BIRCHERMUESLI

1 cup quick oats,
   uncooked
½ cup nuts
1 can sweetened
   condensed milk

¼ cup lemon juice
3 cups fresh fruit

Mix oats, nuts, milk and lemon juice together. Stir in fruit. Refrigerate 1 hour or overnight before serving.
NOTE: Use any fruit available—strawberries, bananas, peaches, blueberries, apples, even raisins. Use your imagination to make creative combinations.

Suzanne W. Peterson

BLINY

2½ cups milk
4 tablespoons butter
3 cups all-purpose flour
3 tablespoons sugar
1 teaspoon salt
1 package dry yeast
¼ cup warm water
   (110° to 115°)

3 eggs
Melted butter
Sour cream
Caviar
Smoked salmon

Add butter to milk; scald milk. Cool. Dissolve yeast in warm water. Sift flour, sugar and salt together. Beat eggs; stir in cooled milk and butter with wooden spoon. Gradually incorporate dry ingredients. It doesn't matter if batter is somewhat lumpy. Stir in yeast. Cover with plastic wrap and let rise for 1 hour in a warm spot. Beat batter vigorously with wooden spoon, cover and let rise for at least ½ hour or until it reaches its previous height. If you aren't ready to cook bliny, refrigerate batter. Make bliny by dropping batter from a dipper (a ⅓-cup measuring cup works fine) onto a hot, lightly buttered griddle or skillet. Spread out batter slightly with bottom of measuring cup. The surface should be hot enough to brown bliny on 1 side in 50 to 60 seconds. Turn when top is bubbly and dry on the edges, just like pancakes. Bliny should be between 5 and 8 inches in diameter. Keep bliny warm on a towel-lined baking sheet in a 200° oven. Serve hot with melted butter, sour cream, caviar, and/or thin slices of smoked salmon.
NOTE: Russian pancakes are always yeast-raised and always served during Maslyanitsa—the week preceding Lent. The name Maslyanitsa comes from the word maslo, for butter. Traditionally, bliny are spread with melted butter, then red or black caviar or slices of smoked salmon, topped with sour cream and rolled up. Some people like minced hard-boiled egg, minced onion, herring, and always melted butter and sour cream. Serves 4 to 6.

Olga Shishkevish

SWEDISH PANCAKE ROLL-UPS

⅓ cup whole wheat flour 1⅓ cups water
⅔ cup all-purpose flour 1 egg
½ teaspoon salt Butter

Combine dry ingredients and 1 cup water. Add egg and beat until smooth. Let sit 15 minutes. Add more water if necessary to reach consistency of heavy cream. Heat a griddle until a drop of water sizzles. Butter griddle. Pour out batter to make an 8-inch pancake and cook over medium heat until cooked enough to turn, while center is still soft. Turn and cook until other side is done—it will not be brown. Turn twice more to cook out excess moisture. Keep warm in 200° oven. Spread with warmed preserves, warmed mixed fruit and honey, sausage, or whatever you like, and roll up. Top with confectioners' sugar, syrup, honey or whatever. Makes 4 to 5 pancakes.

Henry Gaede

BUTTERED TOAST

1) Take 2 pieces of bread and place in toaster (set medium, light or dark according to taste).
2) When toast is ready, remove and butter.
3) Serve with jam or jelly of your choice.
4) Enjoy!
NOTE: For more toast, use more bread.

Brian Storz—"This is the only thing I know," responded Brian when asked to submit his favorite recipe for the new cookbook.

APRICOT KUGEL

1 (12 oz.) package egg
   noodles, cooked,
   drained and rinsed
1 pint sour cream
½ cup butter, melted
¾ cup sugar
3 eggs
1 (8 oz.) can crushed
   pineapple, drained

1 (6 oz.) package dried
   apricots, snipped
2 to 3 Red or Golden
   Delicious apples, peeled,
   cored, and cut in thin
   slices
1 tablespoon cinnamon
3 tablespoons sugar

Preheat oven to 350°. Butter the bottom of a large casserole.
Spread a layer of apples on the bottom. Combine remaining
ingredients (except cinnamon and sugar), adding noodles last,
and pour on top of apples. Mix cinnamon and sugar and sprinkle on top of noodles. Bake for 45 minutes.

Angela Gale

LUCHEN KUGEL

1 pound egg noodles
1 pint sour cream
1 (8 oz.) package cream
   cheese, softened

½ cup sugar
3 eggs, separated
1 cup raisins

Topping

¼ cup butter, softened
½ cup brown sugar

½ cup chopped walnuts

Cook noodles according to package directions, drain and rinse well. Beat sour cream, cream cheese, sugar and egg yolks together until smooth (a food processor works great). Beat egg whites until stiff but not dry. Fold cheese mixture into egg whites. Fold in noodles and raisins. Pour into large buttered casserole. Mix butter, brown sugar and nuts together with fingers. Sprinkle over noodle mixture. Bake at 350° until set and brown, about 45 minutes. Serves 6.

Angela Gale

CURRIED FRUIT

1 cup firmly packed light
   brown sugar
2 teaspoons curry powder
6 tablespoons butter or
   margarine
1 (29 oz.) can pineapple
   chunks, drained
1 (29 oz.) can pear halves,
   drained

1 (29 oz.) can peach
   halves, drained
1 (17 oz.) can Bing cherries
1 (2 oz.) jar maraschino
   cherries, drained
2 bananas, sliced

Combine sugar, curry powder and butter. Stir over low heat until butter and sugar melt. Drain all fruits. Arrange all fruit except maraschino cherries in a 3-quart glass casserole in 2 layers, pouring half of the brown sugar mixture over each layer. Decorate top with maraschino cherries. If possible, cover and refrigerate at least 8 hours before baking. Bake at 350° for 30 minutes. Serve warm.
NOTE: Wonderful for a winter brunch when fresh fruit is not available.

HOT FRUIT CASSEROLE

1 (14 oz.) can pineapple
chunks, drained
1 (16 oz.) can peach
halves, drained and cut
in half
1 (15 oz.) jar spiced apple
rings, drained

1 (16 oz.) can pear halves,
drained and cut in half
1 (1 lb. 1 oz.) can apricot
halves, drained

Layer fruit in a casserole dish, saving half the apple rings to put on top.

Sauce

½ cup firmly packed light
brown sugar
1 tablespoon flour

1 cup sherry (*not* salty
cooking sherry—ick!)
½ cup butter

Cook until thick. Pour over fruit. Refrigerate overnight. Bake at 350° for 30 minutes, or until bubbly. Serves 6.

Suzanne D. Peterson

CINNAMON-PECAN APPLES

1 (1 lb.) can apples, or
4 medium apples, peeled,
cored and sliced
2 tablespoons butter or
margarine

¼ cup dark brown sugar
¼ cup sugar
¾ teaspoon cinnamon
¼ cup chopped pecans

Melt butter; stir in sugar and cinnamon. Add apples and nuts; stir. Simmer, covered, until apples are soft—fresh apples will take longer to cook than canned. Serve warm or cold.
NOTE: Good at a brunch, with roast pork, or on vanilla ice cream.

PICKLES
AND
PRESERVES

A BRIEF DISCLAIMER—
Most of the recipes in this section were tested in my kitchen, but summer sped by, I bought up every jar in Savannah, and my dining room began to look like the county fair before I could test them all. If there is no yield at the bottom of the recipe, I didn't try it. However, they are all time-tested recipes, and I'm sure they will work for you. If you never process your pickles and preserves in boiling water, I can't make you do it, but I don't want to get in trouble with the USDA, so I will tell you to do it anyway. I for one do not want to risk poisoning my family and friends. **BOTULISM KILLS.**

BREAD AND BUTTER PICKLES

25 fresh, firm, medium-sized unwaxed cucumbers
3 large yellow onions
1 bell pepper
½ cup non-iodized salt
1 quart apple cider vinegar
1 cup honey
1 cup sugar
2 teaspoons mustard seed
1 teaspoon turmeric
2 teaspoons celery seed
3 cinnamon sticks
1 teaspoon powdered alum
2 whole nutmegs
1 teaspoon whole peppercorns
1 tablespoon coriander seed
½ teaspoon salt
1 teaspoon powdered ginger
1 teaspoon curry powder

Scrub cucumbers, rinse and drain. Slice about ¼ inch thick. Chop onions and bell pepper. Add ½ cup salt to a large pot of ice water. Stir to dissolve. Soak cucumbers, onions and bell pepper 3 hours, adding ice as necessary. Make spice bag out of porous cloth, nothing heavier than an old handkerchief (or old drawers?). Into spice bag put freshly grated nutmeg, freshly ground pepper and freshly ground coriander seed, ground in a blender, electric coffee mill or spice mill. Tie with thread. Put in large pot containing vinegar, honey, sugar, mustard seed, salt, turmeric, celery seed, cinnamon sticks and alum. Do *not* add ginger or curry. Scald, but do not boil. Place a bath towel on flat surface. Drain cucumber/onion/bell pepper mixture in colander and spread evenly on towel; cover with a second towel. Roll up both towels, pressing out remaining water. Fill sterilized jars with cucumber/onion/bell pepper, firmly packed but not jammed down. Leave ½-inch space at top. Remove cinnamon sticks from liquid; squeeze out spice bag into the liquid. Stir in ginger and curry. Fill jars almost to brim with liquid, working out air bubbles with a wooden spoon handle. Wipe rim edge with damp cloth. Place lid and rim on jar; *tighten* using moderate strength—if not tight enough, the lid will not seal the vacuum. You may not have enough liquid to fill all the jars, in which case, use your spice bag and cinnamon sticks again, and mix up either a whole or half recipe of pickling juice, depending on how much more you need. Process 15 minutes for pints or quarts, 10 minutes for half pints. Rapidly boiling water should cover jars during processing. After processing, remove jars and let stand to cool. Lids should "snap" in as jars cool off. You may remove the outer rims after jars are cool and wash sticky substances from jar. The lids require strong pull to open and break vacuum. *Do not tighten rim after processing as this may break the vacuum seal.*

NOTE: Of course substitutions are necessary at times, but freshly ground stuff makes a heap of difference. Makes 9 to 12 pints, doubles easily.

Stephen Traub—from an old family recipe created one New Year's morning by Eric's sister

CUCUMBER PICKLES

7 pounds unwaxed
  pickling cucumbers,
  sliced ¼-inch thick
2 gallons water
3 cups pickling lime
6 pounds sugar

3 quarts vinegar
4 tablespoons pickling
  spice tied in cheese
  cloth
3 sticks cinnamon
3 teaspoons turmeric

Dissolve lime in water. Soak cucumbers for 24 hours. Rinse and soak in cold water for 4 hours, changing water every hour. Drain well. Heat sugar, vinegar, pickling spice and cinnamon just until sugar is dissolved. Cool and soak cucumbers in mixture overnight. Simmer gently 3½ hours. Remove spices; pack cucumbers in sterilized pint jars. Stir turmeric into vinegar solution just before pouring over finished pickles. Process in boiling water for 10 minutes.

May DeMaurice

DILL PICKLES

7 pounds unwaxed
  pickling cucumbers (the
  smaller the better)

1 cup non-iodized salt
12 cloves garlic

Wash cucumbers and remove stems. Pour salt over cucumbers. Cover with cold water and ice, and let sit 4 hours. Rinse thoroughly. Place 1 peeled clove garlic in each of 12 sterilized quart jars. Pack cucumbers into jars. (You may not use all 12 jars.)

6 cups white vinegar
3 cups water

½ cup non-iodized salt
2 tablespoons dill seed

Combine and bring almost to a boil. Pour over cucumbers, seal, and process 15 minutes in boiling water.

NOTE: Pickles must be whole or they will not be firm. Do not use apple cider vinegar, as it will turn pickles brown. Makes approximately 12 quarts.

Sheron George

SWEET PICKLES

5 pounds (or however many you want) fresh, firm, medium-sized unwaxed cucumbers

For each quart cucumbers:

1 teaspoon alum (buy at drugstore)

1 tablespoon non-iodized salt

Wash cucumbers and slice ¼ inch thick. Measure cucumbers. 1 quart at a time, rub alum and salt into cucumbers and transfer to a large bowl or pan. Remember how many quarts of cucumbers you have. Let stand 15 to 24 hours, stirring occasionally. Cover cucumbers with ice and leave 3 to 4 hours longer. Rinse well under cold water.

For each quart of cucumbers, heat in a large pot:

**1 cup cider vinegar
1 cup sugar**

1 teaspoon mixed pickling spice

For 5 quarts of pickles you would have 5 cups of vinegar, 5 cups sugar and 5 teaspoons pickling spice. Add cucumbers to liquid and cook, stirring gently, until cucumbers turn a greenish-yellow, about 5 minutes. Pack cucumbers in sterilized pint jars (run through dishwasher or follow directions on box), cover with liquid, seal jars and process in boiling water for 15 minutes.

NOTE: Easy and delicious!

JERUSALEM ARTICHOKE PICKLE I

1 gallon (5 lbs.) Jerusalem
  artichokes (Sunchokes)
1½ quarts onions
1 large bunch celery,
  leaves removed
4 large bell peppers,
  preferably 2 red and 2
  green
⅓ cup salt

2 tablespoons mustard
  seed softened in ½ cup
  hot water
1 pound light brown sugar
1 tablespoon turmeric
1½ tablespoons Tabasco,
  or to taste
1 quart white vinegar
½ cup all-purpose flour

Scrub artichokes and cut off black spots. Chop vegetables by hand (food processor chops too small) and combine in large pot. Add salt, mustard seed and water, brown sugar, turmeric, Tabasco and vinegar. Stir to blend. Bring to a boil and add flour; remove from heat when thickened. Divide vegetables among sterilized jars; pour liquid to within ¼ inch of top. Seal and process in boiling water 10 minutes.
NOTE: These are wonderful served with greens of any kind—turnip, mustard, collards or kale. Also good straight out of the jar. Makes 12 pints.

JERUSALEM ARTICHOKE PICKLE II

1 quart Jerusalem
  artichokes, scrubbed
  and chopped
1 quart chopped green
  cabbage
1 quart chopped green
  tomatoes
1 quart chopped onions
1 stalk celery, chopped
1 quart chopped bell
  peppers

3 gallons water
1 cup salt
½ cup all-purpose flour
5 cups vinegar
3 cups sugar
2 tablespoons turmeric
6 to 8 hot peppers,
  seeded—the long,
  skinny kind
Red pepper flakes if
  necessary

Dissolve salt in 3 gallons water. Soak vegetables in water overnight. Drain. Bring flour, vinegar, sugar, turmeric and peppers to a boil. Add vegetables. Simmer gently for 30 minutes. Put up in sterilized pint or quart jars and process in boiling water 10 to 15 minutes.

NOTE: This should be spicy, so put in hot peppers and pepper flakes to taste.

Suzanne D. Peterson

WHOLE JERUSALEM ARTICHOKE PICKLE

1 peck Jerusalem artichokes, scrubbed
1 gallon vinegar
4 pounds light brown sugar

10-cent box Coleman's mustard
1 quart chopped onions
1 cup salt

Pack whole artichokes in sterilized quart jars—you may have to cut big ones to fit them in. Bring remaining ingredients to a boil and simmer for 5 minutes. Process in boiling water for 15 minutes.

NOTE: This is an old recipe. We assume that a 10 cent box of mustard is a regular small tin of dry mustard.

May DeMaurice

PICKLED OKRA

3 pounds fresh, young
  plump, 2 to 3-inch long
  pods of okra
6 small hot peppers
6 cloves garlic, peeled
6 teaspoons dill seed
12 teaspoons celery seed

12 teaspoons mustard
  seed
2 tablespoons sugar
5 tablespoons salt
2 cups apple cider vinegar
2 cups water

Sterilize 6 pint jars, lids and bands, or run them through the dishwasher. Wash okra in warm, sudsy water (just a squirt of dishwashing detergent), rinse thoroughly under running water and drain. Seed and devein hot peppers under cold running water, being careful not to inhale fumes. Wash hands well with soap and water after handling peppers. In each jar put 1 hot pepper, 1 clove garlic, 1 teaspoon dill seed, and 2 teaspoons each celery and mustard seed. Pack okra in tightly, placing first layer stem-end down and second layer stem-end up. Really jam them in—you should have no trouble getting all the okra in 6 jars. Mix sugar, salt, vinegar and water and bring to a boil. Boil 2 to 3 minutes, making sure sugar and salt are dissolved. Pour boiling solution over okra, filling to within ¼ inch of the rim. Put lids on jars, screw bands tight. Process 10 minutes in boiling water.

NOTE: Tedious though it may be, you need to select each okra individually, squeezing it to make sure it's not woody. You also must get exactly 3 pounds to fill 6 pint jars correctly. Some people can eat a whole jar full at one sitting, they are that good!

PICKLED PEARS

5 pounds hard pears
1 lemon, sliced
1 pint cider vinegar
1 cup water
3 cups sugar

¼-inch thick slice ginger
  root, peeled
1 tablespoon whole cloves
2 sticks cinnamon

Combine vinegar, water, sugar and spices in a large pot. Peel, quarter and core pears and add with lemon to syrup. Bring to a boil, lower heat and simmer until pears can be pierced with a toothpick. Remove from heat. Cover and let stand in syrup overnight. Remove pears from syrup and pack in sterilized quart jars. Bring syrup to a boil; boil until it reaches desired thickness. Pour over pears—you may remove spices from syrup or add to pears in jars. Process for 15 minutes in boiling water. Makes approximately 2 quarts.

PICKLED PEACHES

1 gallon ripe, unblemished
  peaches, peeled
6 cups sugar, divided
2 cups water
3 cups cider vinegar
1 ginger root, peeled and
  cut in half

3 sticks cinnamon
1 tablespoon whole cloves
1 tablespoon whole
  allspice

Boil 3 cups sugar, water, vinegar and spices for 3 minutes. Add 10 to 12 peaches at a time and simmer until tender. Remove cooked peaches and add remaining peaches to syrup. Simmer until tender. Remove pot from heat, return cooked peaches to pot and let stand in syrup 12 to 24 hours. Remove peaches from syrup and pack in sterilized quart jars. Strain syrup and add remaining sugar. Boil until desired thickness. Pour over peaches and seal. Process for 15 minutes in boiling water. Makes approximately 3 quarts.
NOTE: To peel peaches easily, drop in boiling water for 60 seconds, then rinse under cold water. Peels slip right off.

To store leftover ginger root, either freeze in a Zip-loc bag or peel, place in jar, cover with sherry, and refrigerate.

PEPPER RELISH

12 green bell peppers	3 tablespoons salt
12 red bell peppers	2 cups sugar
3 large onions	1 quart cider vinegar

Seed and devein peppers; peel onions. Chop in blender or food processor to about the size of canned chopped pimientos—not too fine. Place in large pot and cover with boiling water. Let stand 10 minutes. Drain. Cover with boiling water and bring to boil. Remove from heat and let stand 10 minutes. Drain as dry as possible. Return to pot, add salt, sugar and vinegar and bring to boil. Lower heat and simmer for 10 minutes, skimming occasionally. Pour into sterilized jars and process in boiling water 10 minutes for pints and 5 minutes for half-pints.
NOTE: Great on meatloaf, hot dogs and ham and cheese sandwiches. Makes approximately 7 pints.

Helen Gaede

CORN RELISH

10 ears corn, cut off cob (do not scrape cobs)	1 pint cider vinegar
	¼ cup flour, dissolved in part of the vinegar
1 small hard head cabbage, chopped	1 cup sugar
2 large onions, chopped	½ teaspoon celery seed
2 red or green bell peppers, chopped	¼ teaspoon turmeric
½ stalk celery, chopped	2 ounces dry mustard

Mix vinegar, flour, sugar and seasonings and bring to a boil. Add vegetables and simmer 30 minutes, being careful not to burn—stir frequently. Taste and add more salt if necessary. Remove vegetables from pot with a slotted spoon and pack into sterilized pint jars. Pour vinegar and spices over, adding more vinegar if necessary. Seal and process for 10 minutes in boiling water.

Edna Traub

HOT PEPPER JELLY

1 cup finely chopped bell
  peppers
½ cup finely chopped hot
  peppers
6½ cups sugar

1½ cups apple cider
  vinegar
1 pouch (½ bottle) Certo
3 to 4 drops red or green
  food coloring, optional

Sterilize jelly jars and lids according to package directions, or wash in dishwasher and do not remove until ready to use. Seed and devein hot peppers under cold running water, being careful not to inhale fumes. Wash hands well with soap and water after handling peppers. Remove seeds and veins from bell peppers and chop all peppers fine in food processor, or chop in blender with part of vinegar. Drain off vinegar before measuring; reserve liquid. Bring peppers, liquid, sugar and vinegar to a boil in a heavy pot. Boil hard for 10 minutes, skimming top occasionally. Remove from heat and let stand 5 minutes. Add Certo and food coloring. Stir well. Pour into jars and seal. Serve with cream cheese or Cheddar cheese and crackers.

NOTE: Try using green bell peppers and green hot peppers, or red bell peppers and red hot peppers. Use a light hand with the food coloring. Add 1 drop at a time and stir well before adding more. The color should be natural-looking. Makes 6 to 7 half-pint jars.

ELDERBERRY JELLY

3 pounds fully ripe
  elderberries
½ cup strained fresh
  lemon juice

7 cups sugar
1 bottle (2 pouches) Certo

Prepare juice: Remove large stems from elderberries. (You can pick off each individual berry, but you'll go nuts doing it.) Place in large, heavy saucepan and crush. Heat gently until juice starts to flow, then simmer, covered, for 15 minutes. Place berries in jelly bag or cheese cloth qnd squeeze out juice. Discard berries. Measure 3 cups juice into a large pot. Add lemon juice and sugar. Mix well. Place over high heat and bring to a boil, stirring constantly. Stir in Certo at once. Bring to a full rolling boil and boil hard 1 minute, stirring constantly. Remove from heat, skim off foam with metal spoon and pour quickly into sterilized jelly jars. Seal with paraffin or lids and bands. Makes 8 to 9 half-pint jars.

PEAR PRESERVES

8 pounds hard pears
1 lemon, thinly sliced

5 pounds sugar

Peel pears. Cut into small pieces about the size of a large pecan half. Mix pears and lemon slices with sugar. Stir to combine. Let stand overnight, stirring occasionally. The next day, bring pears to a boil. Cook over medium heat, stirring often, until pears are translucent and syrup drips in 2 parallel drops from the side of a metal spoon. This may take 2 to 3 hours. Pour into sterilized pint jars and process 10 minutes in boiling water. Makes 6 to 8 pints.

STRAWBERRY PRESERVES

1 quart strawberries
1 tablespoon vinegar

3 cups sugar

Wash and remove stems from strawberries. Put in large heavy pot. Add vinegar; bring to a boil and boil 1 minute. Add sugar and boil briskly for 20 minutes. Pour in shallow pan and let stand 24 hours. Put up in sterilized half-pint jars.

May DeMaurice

PINEAPPLE-PEAR PRESERVES

5 pounds hard pears   **8 cups sugar**
2 cups crushed pineapple

Peel and core pears; chop finely in food processor, blender or food chopper. Combine in large pot with pineapple and sugar; bring to a boil. Simmer, stirring frequently, until pears are translucent and mixture has reached jelling point. This could take 2 hours. Preserves will be thick and sticky. Pour into sterilized half-pint jars and process for 5 minutes in boiling water. Makes 9 to 10 half-pint jars.

Sandy Traub

PEAR MARMALADE

6 pounds hard pears   **1 walnut-size piece ginger**
5 pounds sugar   **root, peeled and cut in 4**
3 oranges   **slices**
1 lemon

Peel and core pears; chop fine in food processor, blender or food chopper. Seed oranges and lemons; chop fine—peel and all. Combine all ingredients in large pot, bring to a boil and cook over medium heat, stirring frequently, until thick; approximately 2 hours. Remove ginger, pour into sterilized half-pint jars and seal. Process 5 minutes in boiling water. Makes 15 to 16 half-pint jars.

VEGETABLES

THE WONDERS OF BACON GREASE

Bacon grease is to Southern cooking what soy sauce is to Chinese. It lends a distinctive sweet-smoky flavor to vegetables and breads that can't be duplicated. And it's free! Just keep a container in the refrigerator (never on top of the stove—bacteria lurk!) and dip into it whenever you cook corn, green beans, butter beans, black-eyed peas, field peas, cabbage, okra, greens, turnips, rutabagas (Yankee turnips) etc. Grease biscuit pans and corn muffin pans with it.

Of course it's not good for you if you follow a restricted fat diet, but a little now and then won't hurt a healthy person. Many Southern vegetables are cooked with little or no water added, so you can tell yourself that the savings on vitamins counteracts the extra fat. You can substitute margarine or vegetable oil, but you won't get the true Southern flavor.

As bacon grease is to soy sauce, so sugar is to MSG. Most Southern cooks toss a pinch of sugar in all their vegetables. It doesn't add sweetness, just improves the flavor. A teaspoon of sugar has only 14 calories, and divided among four people that's not going to ruin your diet. We NEVER use MSG at the Pirates' House. There are enough chemicals in the air already without adding one more to our food!

ASPARAGUS CASSEROLE

Ritz crackers
(approximately 10)
1 (17 oz.) can Leseur peas,
drained
2 (14½ oz.) cans cut
asparagus, drained
(reserve juice)

1 (11 oz.) can cream of
celery, mushroom or
chicken soup
2 tablespoons butter
1 cup grated extra-sharp
Cheddar cheese

Crush enough crackers to cover bottom of a casserole dish. Cover cracker crumbs with half the peas. Cover peas with 1 can asparagus. Layer remaining peas and other can of asparagus. Mix soup with ½ soup can asparagus juice, adding more juice if mixture is too thick. Pour over vegetables. Dot top with butter, cover with grated cheese, and bake at 350° for 30 minutes, or until bubbly.

NOTE: If you like hard-boiled eggs, chop 2 and layer with peas and asparagus. A little cayenne pepper mixed in with the soup adds zip. Serves 6 to 8.

Suzanne D. Peterson

ASPARAGUS-MUSHROOM CASSEROLE

1 (14½ oz.) can asparagus,
drained (reserve juice)
1 (3 oz.) can sliced
mushrooms, drained
(reserve juice)
2 tablespoons butter
2 tablespoons all-purpose
flour
1 cup milk

1 tablespoon asparagus
juice
1 tablespoon mushroom
juice
1 cup grated sharp
Cheddar cheese
½ teaspoon salt
Cayenne pepper to taste
½ cup bread crumbs

Preheat oven to 350°. Melt butter in saucepan; stir in flour off heat until smooth. Combine milk and vegetable juice, stir into flour, return to heat and stir until mixture thickens and comes to a boil. Add cheese; cook until cheese is melted. Season to taste. Combine sauce with vegetables. Pour into small casserole, top with bread crumbs and bake 30 minutes.
NOTE: Can be prepared in advance. Doubles easily. Serves 3 to 4.

Edith Rhodes

CUBAN BLACK BEANS

2 cups (12 ozs.) dried black beans
1 quart boiling water
1 hot pepper, chopped, or 1 teaspoon Tabasco
1 bay leaf
1 tablespoon salt
2 tablespoons olive oil
1 medium onion, chopped
2 bell peppers, chopped
5 cloves garlic, chopped
1 (1 lb.) can whole tomatoes
3 tablespoons powdered cumin

Pour boiling water over dried beans in a heavy pot. Let soak for at least 45 minutes. Add bay leaf, hot pepper and salt. Bring to a boil, lower heat, and simmer, covered, until beans are soft, 1 to 2 hours. Add water as needed. While beans are cooking, sauté onion, bell peppers and garlic in olive oil until vegetables are soft. Add tomatoes and continue cooking until tomatoes are soft and beginning to fall apart. Stir in cumin and pour into the cooked beans. Cook together until flavors are thoroughly blended, ½ to 1 hour. Add water as needed. Serve over white rice. Delicious with roast pork!
NOTE: This may sound like a lot of cumin, but it works just fine.

Luis Maza

GREEN BEANS BONNE FEMME

1 pound green beans
Salt
3 slices bacon
1 tablespoon olive oil
1 clove garlic, peeled
1 medium onion, finely
　 sliced

Freshly ground black
　 pepper
1 tablespoon finely
　 chopped fresh parsley

Wash beans and snap the tips off. Bring salted water to a boil in a large pot. Add the beans, bring the water back to a boil as quickly as possible, and boil uncovered for 10 to 12 minutes, until just tender. Drain the beans in a colander and run them under cold water to stop further cooking. Beans can be done ahead to this point; refrigerate until ready to use. Sauté the bacon in a large frying pan until crisp. Remove and drain on paper towel, then break into pieces. Pour out all but a scant tablespoon of fat from the skillet. Add the olive oil. When it is hot, add the garlic clove and let brown. Discard garlic. Add the onion and cook over medium heat until lightly browned and soft. Add the beans and bacon. Toss gently. Season with salt and pepper and heat through. Transfer beans to a serving dish and sprinkle with parsley. Serves 4.

GREEN BEANS WITH ONIONS

2½ to 3 pounds pole beans
4 slices thick bacon or 4
　 tablespoons bacon
　 grease
1 tablespoon sugar

Salt
Pepper
Small onions, peeled
　 (optional)

With a paring knife or peeler, trim the edges off the beans to remove strings. Do not omit this step—you can do it while watching TV or chatting with a friend. Place bacon in a heavy Dutch oven. Set over low heat and render some of the fat from the meat. Do not brown. Or, melt bacon grease. In the meantime, wash the beans. Then hold a handful at a time under a vigorously running faucet and put beans directly into the Dutch oven. Sprinkle beans with sugar. Do not add any additional water. Heat to boiling, place lid on pot and immediately reduce heat to low. Cook until beans are tender. Depending on the beans, it can take anywhere from 2½ to 4 hours. Add more water if necessary. During last 30 minutes of cooking, place onions around the edge of the pot. Season to taste.

NOTE: Do not add salt at beginning, or beans may be too salty. Serves 6.

BUTTER BEANS

3 pounds (unshelled) butter beans	**Salt**
4 tablespoons bacon grease, smoked neck bone, or ham hock	**Freshly ground pepper**
	1 teaspoon sugar

Shell butter beans. Place in a colander and wash well. Place beans in a saucepan. Cover beans completely with water. Add bacon grease or meat, pepper and sugar. Cook beans until soft, about 45 to 60 minutes. Salt to taste.

NOTE: Butter beans are not the same as coarse lima beans. They are tender and tasty. You may add chopped onion when cooking if you like. Frozen butter beans are cooked the same way.

FRIED CORN

**1 dozen ears corn, husked
  and desilked
4 tablespoons bacon
  grease**

**1 tablespoon sugar
1 teaspoon salt
Pepper to taste
Milk or cream, optional**

Slit each row of kernels down the middle lengthwise before starting to cut the corn off the cob. Cut corn from cob with a very sharp knife into a bowl, cutting as thin as possible and going around each ear of corn at least 2 times. Scrape ears into bowl with edge of knife after cutting off corn to remove all traces of milk. Heat bacon grease in a heavy skillet. Add corn. Rinse bowl with a little water; add water to skillet. Add seasonings and cook until tender, 10 to 15 minutes. Adjust seasoning. If corn dries out, add a little milk or cream.

NOTE: A vegetable brush removes silks from corn easily. Silver Queen makes the best fried corn if you can find it, but whatever kind you use, make sure it's tender. Some people use a vegetable peeler to remove corn from cob, but it must be sharp. If you don't like bacon grease, substitute ½ cup butter, but your corn won't have that authentic Southern taste.

SUCCOTASH

**1 cup shelled butter beans
1 cup raw corn, cut off cob
  in large kernels
2 tablespoons bacon
  grease**

**2 cups water
1 teaspoon salt
⅛ teaspoon pepper**

Place butter beans, bacon grease and water in saucepan, bring to a boil, lower heat and simmer, covered, until almost tender, about 30 minutes. Add raw corn and cook until beans and corn are tender, about 15 minutes. Drain, season to taste and serve. Serves 4.

CABBAGE AU GRATIN

1 small cabbage, shredded
1 cup White Sauce, see
  below

½ cup grated Cheddar
  cheese

Boil cabbage until tender, about 10 minutes, and drain well. Preheat oven to 400°. Layer ½ cabbage, ½ white sauce and ½ cheese in a casserole. Repeat. Bake until bubbly, about 15 minutes.

White Sauce

2 tablespoons butter or
  margarine
2 tablespoons flour

1 cup milk
Salt and pepper to taste

Melt butter until foaming. Stir in flour off heat. Stir in milk. Return to heat, stirring constantly until sauce comes to a boil and has thickened. Season to taste with salt and pepper. Serves 4.

EGGPLANT PIE

1 medium eggplant
2 tablespoons butter
1 cup (4 ozs.) grated extra-
  sharp Cheddar cheese,
  divided
2 slices buttered toast,
  crumbled

2 eggs, slightly beaten
1 teaspoon salt
¼ teaspoon red pepper
  (it must taste)

Peel eggplant, cut into cubes, cover with water and simmer, covered, until tender, about 20 minutes. Drain well and mash with a fork. Mix with butter, ¾ cup cheese, toast, eggs and seasonings. Pour into buttered casserole dish. Top with remaining cheese. Bake at 350° until browned and bubbly, about 40 to 50 minutes. Serves 4.

HERBED EGGPLANT CASSEROLE

1 large or 2 small
   eggplants
1 cup onion-and-garlic
   croutons
1 cup grated Cheddar
   cheese, divided

½ cup milk
1 tablespoon flour
½ teaspoon salt
½ teaspoon pepper
½ teaspoon oregano
1 tablespoon butter

Peel eggplant and cut into ¼ inch cubes. Cook in boiling salted water until tender and drain. Mix with eggplant, croutons, and ½ cup cheese. Put in lightly buttered casserole dish. Combine milk, flour and seasonings and pour over eggplant mixture. Top with remaining cheese and dot with butter. Cover and bake at 350° for 20 minutes. Remove cover and continue baking an additional 10 minutes.

NOTE: Onion-and-garlic croutons come in a box in the grocery store. Try this casserole—it's easy and surprisingly tasty. Serves 4.

Mincy Peterson

 ## SAVANNAH HOPPIN' JOHN

2 cups (12 oz. bag) red
   peas
5 cups water
2 tablespoons bacon
   grease

1 medium onion, chopped
Ham hocks or neckbone
1 cup raw rice
Salt, pepper and Tabasco
   to taste

Wash peas and soak in water 8 hours or overnight. In a heavy pot, sauté onion in bacon grease until soft. Add peas and water, meat, and pepper and Tabasco to taste. Bring to a boil, lower heat, cover and simmer until peas are soft, 1 to 1½ hours. Stir in rice and 1 teaspoon salt, cover and simmer 20 minutes, or until rice is tender. If mixture is too wet, remove lid and simmer until desired consistancy. Taste for seasonings.

NOTE: While the rest of the world makes Hoppin' John with black-eyed peas, people in Savannah insist on red peas. For New Year's day, hog jowl is traditionally used instead of ham hocks or neckbone. In Savannah, we eat Hoppin' John and turnip greens on New Year's Day to bring luck, i.e. money. The peas are for pennies and the greens are for dollars. Believing as fervently as we do in the efficacy of this practice, the Pirates' House serves over 40 gallons of Hoppin' John on New Year's Day. "Even if you don't like it," we say, "eat just a tablespoonful for luck." Serves 6 to 8.

HOPPIN' JOHN

1 pound dried black-eyed
  peas
6 cups cold water
½ pound slab bacon, cut
  into 1-inch cubes

1 teaspoon Tabasco
1 teaspoon salt
2 medium onions, chopped
1 cup raw rice
1½ cups boiling water

Wash peas. Place in a large pot with cold water, bring to a boil, boil 2 minutes, cover, remove from heat and let sit 1 hour. Cook bacon slowly until brown on all sides; use tongs to turn bacon. Reserve grease. Add bacon, Tabasco, and salt to peas. Bring to a boil, lower heat, and simmer covered for 30 minutes. Sauté onion in bacon grease until translucent. Add onions, grease, rice and boiling water to peas. Cover and simmer, stirring occasionally, for 30 minutes, or until rice is tender. It should be moist, but not wet, and most certainly not dry. Taste for seasoning; you will probably need more salt. Serve with cold Stewed Tomatoes, see Index.

NOTE: Hoppin' John is traditionally eaten in the South on New Year's Day to bring luck in the coming year. You may substitute streak o'lean or fatback for the bacon, but the flavor is not as good.

OKRA, CORN, AND TOMATOES

1 pound fresh okra, or 1
  (1 lb.) bag frozen okra
4 to 6 ears fresh corn, or
  1 (10 oz.) box frozen
  corn
1 (1 lb.) can tomatoes

4 slices bacon
1 medium onion, sliced
2 tablespoons bacon
  grease, optional
1 teaspoon sugar
Salt and pepper to taste

Wash okra, cut off stem ends, and slice in ½ inch slices. Cut corn off cobs. Fry bacon in heavy skillet until crisp; remove bacon. Crumble when cool. Fry onions in bacon grease until soft; add okra and cook 2 to 3 minutes, stirring occasionally. You may want to add more bacon grease. Drain tomato juice into pan and squish tomatoes through your fingers into pan. Add corn, crumbled bacon and sugar. Lower heat, cover, and cook until done, 15 to 20 minutes. Season to taste and serve.
NOTE: Good without the corn, served over rice. If you don't want to fry bacon, just use bacon grease.

ONIONS AU GRATIN

4 cups coarsely chopped
  onions
2 tablespoons butter
  or margarine
½ teaspoon salt

½ teaspoon pepper
2 to 3 tablespoons self-
  rising flour
2 cups grated Cheddar
  cheese, divided

Bring chopped onions to a boil with water to cover. Lower heat; simmer until tender, about 20 minutes. Drain well. Combine with butter, salt, pepper and flour. Mixture should not be pasty. Add 1½ cups cheese; mix well. Turn into casserole dish; sprinkle ½ cup cheese on top. Bake at 350° for 20 to 30 minutes, until heated through. Serves 6.

BAKED VIDALIA ONIONS I

1 Vidalia onion per person (or any sweet, yellow onion)	1 tablespoon butter per onion Salt and pepper

Preheat oven to 350°. Place each onion on a square of heavy-duty aluminum foil. Add butter, season generously, and wrap tightly. Bake for 1 hour. Onions may also be cooked, wrapped in foil, on a hot grill for 30 to 45 minutes, or until soft. Turn frequently.

BAKED VIDALIA ONIONS II

Vidalia onions, peeled Instant beef flavor Seasoned salt and pepper	1 teaspoon butter per onion

Preheat oven to 350°. Place 1 to 2 onions per person in a baking dish. Sprinkle with beef flavor flakes, seasoned salt and pepper. Top with butter. Cover tightly with foil and bake for 1 hour.

Suzanne D. Peterson

 Root vegetables (potatoes, carrots, turnips, etc.) should be covered with cold salted water, brought to a boil, covered, and simmered until tender. Green vegetables (green beans, brussels sprouts, asparagus) should be dropped into boiling salted water, cooked uncovered until just tender, and drained immediately.

ONIONS STUFFED WITH RICE

6 large sweet onions, preferably Vidalia or Glennville Sweets
4 tablespoons butter
⅓ cup raw rice
⅓ cup freshly grated Parmesan cheese
¼ cup heavy cream
6 tablespoons dry breadcrumbs
¼ cup finely chopped fresh parsley
¼ cup chopped pecans

2 tablespoons finely chopped fresh basil or 1 teaspoon finely chopped fresh tarragon (or ½ teaspoon dried basil, oregano, sage or tarragon)—optional
Salt and pepper
½ cup white wine or vermouth
1 cup chicken stock or broth

Bring a large pot of water to a boil. Slice off pointed and root ends of onions. Peel off skin and first layer of onion. Using a teaspoon, hollow out from pointed end to form cups, leaving sides and bottoms ½ inch thick. Do not get sides and bottoms too thin. Reserve insides of onions. Drop onions into boiling water. Lower heat and simmer for 10 to 15 minutes, until they are just tender when pierced with a knife. Remove carefully and drain upside down in colander. Reserve onion water. Chop onion cores fine and cook in butter over low heat in a covered pan until tender, 8 to 10 minutes. Measure out 1 cup—do whatever you want with the leftovers. After onions have been blanched, cook rice in boiling onion water for 10 minutes. Drain rice thoroughly and add to onions. Stir in cheese, cream, bread crumbs, parsley, pecans and seasonings. If mixture does not hold together well, add more breadcrumbs. Preheat oven to 375°. Bring wine and stock to a boil on top of stove. While liquid is heating, fill onions with stuffing and place in a buttered casserole. Pour liquid around onions, place in oven and bake for 1 to 1¼ hours, basting onions several times.

NOTE: If you have any leftover stuffing, use it for tomatoes. Hollow out tomatoes, stuff, and bake at 350° until heated through. Serves 6.

CHIVE-CHEESE POTATOES

1 (8 oz.) package cream
  cheese
1 cup milk
¼ teaspoon salt

1 tablespoon chives
  (freeze-dried are fine)
4 cups cooked potatoes,
  cubed

Preheat oven to 350°. In a saucepan over low heat, whisk together cream cheese and milk until smooth. Add chives and salt. Carefully fold in potatoes. Pour into 1½-quart casserole. Bake for 30 minutes.

NOTE: For added color and zip, sprinkle ½ cup grated Cheddar cheese on top before baking.

Jean Roche

POTATOES O'BRIEN

2 pounds cooked potatoes,
  peeled and cubed
4 slices bacon
½ cup chopped onion
½ cup chopped bell
  pepper

2 tablespoons chopped
  pimientos
1 teaspoon paprika
1 teaspoon salt
1 teaspoon black pepper

Fry bacon in a heavy skillet until crisp. Remove from pan. Sauté onion and bell pepper in bacon grease until soft. Add remaining ingredients, including potatoes and crumbled bacon, and cook until potatoes are browned and hot. Serves 4.

FOOL-PROOF RICE

Follow these directions and proportions exactly and you will not fail. I like Mahatma rice, but any good quality rice will do (not Uncle Ben's—that requires a different approach).

Rice	Water
1 cup	1¾ cups
2 cups	3¼ cups
3 cups	4 cups
4 cups	5 cups
5 cups	6 cups

. . . and on up, using 1 cup more water than rice. Salt to taste. Do not wash rice. Place in a heavy pot. Pour cold water on rice; add salt. Bring to a boil, cover and lower heat until water is barely simmering. Set timer for 20 minutes. At end of 20 minutes, remove rice from heat and let stand covered 20 minutes. Do not peek. Remove lid, fluff rice with fork and serve.

LEMON RICE

1 cup raw Uncle Ben's rice
2 cups water
1 teaspoon salt
1 tablespoon butter
2 to 3 tablespoons lemon juice
Grated rind of 1 lemon

Bring water to boil; stir in rice, salt, butter and lemon juice. Lower heat, cover, and simmer until all water is absorbed, about 20 minutes. Sprinkle with lemon rind before serving. Great with fish. Serves 4.

Fay Wiggers

RANCH RICE

¼ cup butter or margarine
1 clove garlic, crushed
1 cup raw rice
1 (11 oz.) can beef bouillon

1 (11 oz.) can onion soup
1 (3 oz.) can mushrooms,
  juice and all

Preheat oven to 350°. Melt butter in a 1½-quart casserole in oven and add garlic. Add rice and stir to coat with butter. Add rest of ingredients and stir to combine. Bake covered for 1 hour, stirring occasionally. Serves 4 to 6.

RED RICE

4 slices bacon
1 medium onion, chopped
2 ribs celery, chopped
1 small bell pepper,
  chopped
2 cups raw rice
1 (1 lb.) can tomatoes,
  drained and chopped
  (reserve juice)

1 (8 oz.) can tomato sauce
1 teaspoon sugar
1 teaspoon salt
Black pepper to taste
Tabasco to taste (should
  be spicy)

Fry bacon in a heavy pot until crisp; remove. Sauté onions, celery, and bell pepper in bacon grease until onions are translucent. Crumble bacon; return to pot. Add rice; stir to coat with grease. Add tomatoes. Measure reserved tomato juice and tomato sauce; add water to make 2½ cups (total) liquid. Pour over rice and bring to a boil, stirring occasionally. Immediately lower until barely simmering, cover pot and set timer for 20 minutes. After 20 minutes, remove from heat and let sit at least 20 minutes. Do not peek. After 20 minutes, fluff with a fork and serve.

PARSLIED RICE

3 cups raw rice
6 cups water
1 teaspoon salt

6 tablespoons butter
1 cup chopped fresh
parsley

Combine rice, water, salt and butter and cook according to package directions. When done, stir in parsley and serve. Serves 10.

WILD RICE

½ cup butter
1 cup wild rice, washed
and drained
½ cup toasted sliced or
slivered almonds
3 tablespoons finely
chopped chives, onion
or bell pepper

¼ pound mushrooms,
sliced
1 tablespoon finely
chopped fresh parsley
3 cups chicken stock
1 teaspoon salt (do not add
if using canned stock)

Melt butter in skillet. Add wild rice, almonds, chives, mushrooms and parsley. Sauté, stirring frequently, until mushrooms are cooked, about 5 minutes. Put mixture in a casserole dish with stock, cover tightly and bake at 350° for 2 hours, or until all liquid is absorbed.
NOTE: If dinner time is drawing nigh and rice is cooked but still juicy, remove lid and bake until dry. Or cook on low heat on top of stove in a heavy pot, checking occasionally. This should take about 1 hour. Serves 4 to 6.

Martha Summerour

RICE PILAF

½ cup butter
1 cup chopped celery
1 cup chopped green
  onions
1 (2½ oz.) package sliced
  or slivered almonds

1 cup uncooked rice
1 (11 oz.) can beef bouillon
2 teaspoons instant beef
  flavor

Preheat oven to 350°. Sauté celery, onions and almonds in butter until onions are translucent. Stir in rice. Add bouillon and beef flavor. Pour into a casserole dish. Cover and bake for 1 hour and 15 minutes, stirring halfway through baking time. Serves 4.

Brenda Lain

CREAMED SPINACH AND ARTICHOKES

1 small jar marinated
  artichoke hearts, drained
1 small onion, finely
  chopped
2 tablespoons butter
2 packages frozen
  creamed spinach,
  cooked

½ cup freshly grated
  Parmesan cheese
¼ teaspoon nutmeg

Place artichoke hearts in bottom of a casserole. Sauté onion in butter until transparent. Mix spinach with onion, ¼ cup cheese and nutmeg; pour over artichoke hearts. Sprinkle remaining ¼ cup cheese on top. Bake at 350° until hot, about 15 minutes. May be prepared in advance. Serves 6 to 8.

Edith Rhodes

SQUASH CASSEROLE

3 cups yellow or zucchini
  squash, sliced
¼ cup sour cream
1 tablespoon butter or
  margarine
2 tablespoons grated
  Cheddar cheese
½ teaspoon salt
⅛ teaspoon paprika

1 egg yolk, beaten
1 tablespoon chopped
  chives or green onion
  tops
¼ cup fresh bread crumbs
¼ cup grated Cheddar
  cheese
3 tablespoons butter,
  melted

Preheat oven to 350°. Place squash in a small amount of water; cover pan. Bring to a boil, lower heat, and simmer until tender, about 6 to 8 minutes. Shake the pan to keep squash from sticking (or use a steamer rack). Drain well. Combine sour cream, butter, grated cheese, salt and paprika. Stir this mixture over low heat until the cheese is melted. Remove from heat and stir in beaten egg yolk and chives or green onions. Add the squash and stir gently to mix. Place the mixture in a baking dish. Cover with breadcrumbs mixed with ¼ cup cheese and 3 tablespoons butter. Bake for 20 minutes, or until top is brown. Let sit 5 minutes before serving. Serves 4.

SOUR CREAM SQUASH

2 pounds yellow squash,
  sliced
1 (8 oz.) carton sour cream
2 tablespoons butter
1 small onion, chopped
  fine

½ teaspoon dill weed
1 teaspoon salt
Pepper to taste

Cook squash and drain well. Mix with remaining ingredients. Pour into greased casserole and bake at 350° for 30 minutes. Serves 6.

GINGER BAKED SQUASH

3 medium acorn squash,
　halved and seeded
¼ cup water
3 tablespoons butter or
　margarine

3 tablespoons brown
　sugar, packed
2 tablespoons sherry
½ teaspoon ground ginger
½ teaspoon salt

Preheat oven to 400°. Place squash halves, cut side down, in baking dish. Add water. Bake 20 minutes. Meanwhile, combine other ingredients in small saucepan and stir over low heat until well-blended. Simmer 5 minutes uncovered. Turn squash cut side up; fill hollows with ginger syrup. Bake 25 minutes longer until fork tender, basting with syrup during last 5 minutes. Serves 6.

Suzanne W. Peterson

SWEET POTATO CASSEROLE I

1 (2½ lb.) can sweet
　potatoes, drained
1 cup sugar
¼ cup butter
2 eggs

½ teaspoon salt
1 teaspoon vanilla extract
½ teaspoon cinnamon
½ teaspoon nutmeg

Preheat oven to 350°. Beat ingredients together in electric mixer or food processor until smooth. Pour into greased 2-quart casserole.

Topping

1 cup coconut
1 cup firmly packed light
　brown sugar
⅓ cup self-rising flour

1 cup chopped nuts
¼ cup butter or margarine,
　melted

Mix together and spread on top of sweet potatoes. Bake for 30 to 35 minutes.

SWEET POTATO CASSEROLE II

2 (1 lb. 13 oz.) cans sweet
  potatoes, drained
½ cup butter or margarine,
  softened
2 eggs
1 teaspoon vanilla

1 tablespoon orange juice
  concentrate
1 tablespoon bourbon
Sugar to taste
½ cup chopped pecans

Preheat oven to 350°. Beat sweet potatoes until smooth in mixer or food processor, add remaining ingredients and beat until well-blended. Bake 30 minutes.
NOTE: If your kids demand it, go ahead and put miniature marshmallows on top! Serves 6 to 8.

Lynn Barnes

 ## SWEET POTATO SOUFFLÉ À LA GUSSIE

1 (1 lb. 13 oz.) can sweet
  potatoes
⅔ cup sugar
¼ cup margarine or butter
1 egg
1 (8 oz.) can crushed
  pineapple, drained—
  reserve juice

1 cup orange juice and
  pineapple juice mixed
1 teaspoon vanilla extract
1 apple, cored and
  chopped fine
¼ cup chopped pecans
Miniature marshmallows

Preheat oven to 350°. Beat sweet potatoes in electric mixer or food processor until very smooth. Beat in sugar, margarine or butter, egg, orange and pineapple juice, and vanilla extract, blending well after each addition. Stir in pineapple, apple and pecans. Pour into buttered 1-quart casserole, top with marshmallows. Bake until marshmallows are brown, 25 to 30 minutes. Serves 4 to 6.

Gussie Stoney

ORANGE-CANDIED YAMS

2 cups water
2 cups sugar
¼ teaspoon yellow food
  coloring
1 small orange, seeded
  and finely chopped in
  food processor or
  blender
½ cup margarine
½ cup firmly packed light
  brown sugar

½ teaspoon cinnamon
½ teaspoon nutmeg
½ teaspoon lemon juice
½ teaspoon salt
½ teaspoon vanilla extract
4 tablespoons cornstarch
4 tablespoons water
Sweet potatoes, baked or
  boiled, peeled and sliced
  (1 medium per person)

Combine water, sugar, food coloring and chopped orange. Bring to a boil, stirring to dissolve sugar. Boil for 5 minutes. Add all remaining ingredients except water, cornstarch and sweet potatoes. Cook until margarine is melted. Dissolve cornstarch in water and add to sauce. Boil until thick and syrupy, about 20 minutes. Pour over sweet potatoes in a casserole dish to taste and bake at 350° for about 30 minutes, or until bubbly.
NOTE: You decide how much sauce you want to use, and refrigerate leftovers. Sauce keeps indefinitely in refrigerator.

CANDIED SWEET POTATOES

4 medium sweet potatoes
1 cup sugar
½ cup butter
Water

Pinch salt
1 tablespoon light Karo
  syrup

Peel potatoes. Cut in half lengthwise. Cut each half into fourths lengthwise. Place potato wedges in a open skillet. Add water to come ¼ up sides of pan and cook potatoes slowly until just tender, when they can be pierced with a fork. Drain water from pan. Sprinkle sugar over potatoes, add butter, salt and Karo syrup. Cook slowly until juice is sticky. Taste for seasoning. Serves 4.

Martha Summerour

MOTHER EDEL'S SHREDDED YAM CASSEROLE

2 pounds raw sweet
   potatoes
1 cup sugar
½ cup light Karo syrup
½ cup water
¼ cup butter
1 cup pineapple juice, or

1 (8 oz.) can crushed
   pineapple—drain juice
   and add enough water to
   make 1 cup liquid
Freshly grated nutmeg,
   optional

Fill a large pot with 1 gallon cold water and 1 teaspoon salt. Peel and shred raw sweet potatoes (use a food processor if you have one) and drop into salted water. Wash and drain well. Combine sugar, Karo syrup and water. Bring to a boil and boil 5 minutes, or until the consistency of heavy cream. Remove from heat, add butter and stir until melted. Put sweet potatoes in a 9x13 inch casserole dish. Pour pineapple juice (or pineapple and juice) over sweet potatoes, then sugar syrup. Grate nutmeg over top if desired. Bake uncovered at 350° for 60 minutes, or until sweet potatoes are transparent. Serves 10 to 12.

Danyse Edel

STEWED TOMATOES

1 (1 lb. 12 oz.) can
   tomatoes
3 tablespoons cider
   vinegar
3 tablespoons sugar
¼ bell pepper, finely
   chopped

1 small onion, chopped
1 rib celery, sliced thin
Salt
Freshly ground pepper

Combine all ingredients, except salt, in a heavy saucepan. Bring to a boil and turn down to low immediately. Simmer for several hours or until mixture gets thick, stirring occasionally, and squashing tomatoes against side of pan with spoon. Add salt to taste. If a sweeter dish is desired, add more sugar. Serve with blackeyed peas, field peas or butter beans.

NOTE: If you have an abundance of fresh tomatoes, use them. If you are in a canning mood, increase the recipe and put some up in sterilized jars. Good served hot or cold.

Martha Summerour

TURNIP GRATIN

1 clove garlic, peeled
3 tablespoons butter
1½ pounds turnips, peeled
   and cut in ⅛-inch slices
Salt
Freshly ground pepper
1 teaspoon tarragon

½ cup grated Swiss
   cheese
½ cup freshly grated
   Parmesan cheese
½ cup heavy cream
¼ cup breadcrumbs

Preheat oven to 400°. Bring a pot of water to a boil. Drop turnip slices into boiling water, boil for 2 to 3 minutes and drain. Rub a small casserole dish with garlic, butter well (save remaining butter for top) and arrange ⅓ of the turnip slices in a layer. Sprinkle with salt and freshly ground pepper, ⅓ of the herbs and ⅓ of the cheese. Repeat, making three layers in all, and finishing with cheese on top. Pour the cream over the turnips; sprinkle with breadcrumbs and bits of butter. Bake 45 minutes.

NOTE: Even if you hate turnips, try this. It's a great alternative to scalloped potatoes. Serves 4 to 6.

BREADS

BEATEN BISCUITS

4 cups all-purpose flour
(preferably White Lily)
1 cup Crisco

1 teaspoon salt
1 cup cold water

Place flour, shortening and salt in bowl of food processor with metal blade. Process until the shortening disappears into flour. Pour water through feed tube while machine is running; process until food processor shuts off. Dough will be slightly sticky. Lightly flour counter and turn out dough. Roll out dough with a floured pin. Beat the dough with the pin until ¼ inch thick. Lightly flour the top, fold over, turn over, and flour other side. Flour pin as needed. Continue beating, folding and flouring until mixture begins to blister and pop, and feels tender. Do not overflour. This process will take approximately 5 minutes. The best rolling pin to use is one without handles. Preheat oven to 350°. Roll dough ⅜ inch thick, and cut with a 1 inch cutter, flouring cutter as needed. (A shot glass works well.) Gather up dough scraps, roll out, fold, and beat until smooth. Continue until all dough is used. Place on lightly greased baking sheets. Prick tops with a fork, going all the way through the biscuit to the pan. Center fork prongs to make 4 holes or use a 3-pronged fork and make a square by pricking 3 times. Bake one sheet at a time for 30 to 35 minutes, or until a pale golden color. Split one to test—biscuits should be dry in center. Serve with thinly sliced country ham. Store in airtight container. Do not freeze. **NOTE:** These are great to make when you are feeling hostile. Pretend the dough is someone you don't like and beat the ___ out of it! Makes approximately 5 dozen.

 Always proof yeast. Let it soften in the warm water until it starts foaming. Better to find out at the beginning if yeast has lost its oomph.

BUTTERMILK BISCUITS

3 cups White Lily self-
   rising flour
3 rounded tablespoons
   Crisco

⅔ cup buttermilk

Preheat oven to 500°. Sift flour into a bowl; mix in Crisco with fingers until crumbly. Make a well in center of flour. Pour in buttermilk and mix with fingers until a soft dough is formed. There should be extra flour left in bowl. Coat ball of dough with flour, turn out on floured counter and knead 10 times. Roll out between ¼ inch and ½ inch thick, cut with a 2 inch cutter and place on greased baking sheet with sides touching. For crusty sides, place ½ inch apart. Combine scraps gently, roll out and cut until all dough is used. Sift flour left in bowl to remove Crisco crumbs and return to flour sack. Bake 8 to 10 minutes, or until golden brown.

NOTE: The secret of good biscuits is in the flour and the handling. Flour made from soft winter wheat is best, and you must handle the dough as gently and as little as possible. Don't despair if your first batch isn't all you expect—practice makes perfect. Makes approximately 16.

Martha Summerour

SHERON'S BISCUITS

4 cups self-rising White
   Lily flour
½ cup lard (no substitute)

1¾ to 2 cups buttermilk
Bacon grease

Preheat oven to 450°. Grease a baking sheet with bacon grease. Sift flour into a mixing bowl. Work in lard with fingers until crumbly. Make a well in center of flour and work in buttermilk a little at a time until a wet dough is formed. Try to work dough as little as possible. De-gunk fingers. Sift a thin layer of flour over dough. Scoop up a blob of dough and work it into a biscuit shape, bouncing dough lightly from palm to palm. Plop it down on baking sheet. Biscuits should be from 2 to 3 inches in diameter, and fairly thick. Repeat until dough is used up, sifting more flour on top if necessary. Biscuits should have sides touching. Bake for 15 to 20 minutes, or until golden brown.

NOTE: These are big, rough, blobby-looking biscuits; not beautiful at all, but they taste absolutely wonderful. The results are well worth the effort to master the technique. As an added bonus, they freeze well. Just toss in a Zip-loc bag and heat as needed. Makes 10 to 12 biscuits.

Sheron George

CORNSTICKS I

1 cup self-rising cornmeal (preferably stoneground)	2 tablespoons oil or melted bacon grease
1 cup buttermilk	Oil or bacon grease for pans
1 egg	

Preheat oven to 500°. Put ½ teaspoon oil or bacon grease in each section of 2 cornstick pans. Heat pans in oven until very hot. Combine all ingredients in a mixing bowl and mix with a spoon until smooth. Remove hot pans from oven and fill each section ½ full of batter. Bake cornsticks for 20 minutes or until golden brown.

NOTE: Preheating the (preferably) cast iron pans produces a cornstick that has the crunchy outside so beloved of Southern ladies and gentlemen. You may also make this recipe into muffins. Prepare muffin pans the same as cornstick pans.

Martha Summerour

CORNSTICKS II

1 cup self-rising flour
1 cup self-rising corn meal
¼ cup sugar
1 teaspoon baking powder

1 cup milk
1 egg
¼ cup butter, melted

Preheat oven to 500°. Grease 2 cornstick pans. Mix all ingredients together with a fork until smooth. Pour into cornstick pans. Bake for 15 minutes or until golden brown. Makes 1 dozen and 3 if you fill pans to the top, or 1½ dozen if you fill pans ⅔ full. If you only have 1 cornstick pan, that's fine. Just keep cornsticks warm as they finish baking and re-use pans. If you don't have enough batter to fill up a whole pan, put water in the empty spaces.

Martha Buttimer

PIRATES' HOUSE CORNBREAD

1½ cups self-rising
   cornmeal
1½ cups self-rising flour
1 teaspoon baking powder
⅓ cup sugar

1 cup half-and-half
1 cup milk
2 eggs
½ cup margarine, melted

Preheat oven to 425°. Grease an 8x8 inch pan and place in oven. Combine dry ingredients in a mixing bowl. Whisk in milk and half-and-half, eggs and melted margarine. Batter should be a little thicker than heavy cream. If it is too thick, add more milk. Remove hot pan from oven, pour in batter and return to oven. Bake at 425° for 20 minutes, then lower heat to 350° and bake until a knife inserted in the center comes out clean, about 15 to 20 minutes. Cut in squares and serve hot.
NOTE: This recipe makes a lot of cornbread. You can easily cut it in half. Bake in an 8x8 inch pan at 425° for 25 to 30 minutes, or until golden brown. Your squares will be thinner, but just as tasty. Or bake a full recipe in a 9x13 inch pan for thinner squares.

MEXICAN CORNBREAD

1 cup margarine
¼ cup sugar
4 eggs
1 (4 oz.) can green chili peppers, seeded and chopped
1 (17 oz.) can creamed corn
½ cup grated Monterey Jack cheese

½ cup grated Cheddar cheese
1 cup all-purpose flour
1 cup plain cornmeal
4 teaspoons baking powder
½ teaspoon salt

Have margarine and eggs at room temperature. Preheat oven to 325°. Grease and flour a 9x13 inch baking dish. Cream margarine and sugar; blend in eggs. Stir in chilies, corn and cheese. Combine remaining ingredients. Add to corn mixture, stirring until well blended. Pour into baking dish. Bake for 50 to 60 minutes or until toothpick inserted in center comes out clean. Cut into squares and serve warm.

HUSH PUPPIES

1 cup plain cornmeal
1½ tablespoons all-purpose flour
¼ teaspoon baking soda
½ teaspoon baking powder

1 teaspoon salt
3 tablespoons finely chopped onion
1 egg, beaten
½ cup buttermilk

Mix dry ingredients together. Add onions, egg and milk. Stir to blend. Drop by spoonfuls into deep fat in which fish is frying. Cook until golden brown. Hush puppies will float to the top when done.

Martha Summerour

SOUR CREAM MUFFINS

1 cup self-rising flour   **½ cup butter, melted**
1 cup sour cream

Preheat oven to 450°. Grease 2 tiny muffin tins (a total of 24 muffins.) Combine all ingredients in bowl or food processor until well-mixed. Bake for 15 minutes; until golden brown. Serve hot. Leftovers may be reheated, but there probably won't be any.
NOTE: These are unbelievably delicious. No need to spread with extra butter, although a little spot of jam is good. Makes 24 tiny muffins.

MAYONNAISE MUFFINS

¼ cup mayonnaise   **2 cups self-rising flour**
¼ cup sugar   **1 cup milk**

Preheat oven to 400°. Grease muffin tins. Mix mayonnaise and sugar together until smooth; stir in flour. Add milk; stir just until flour is moistened—batter should be lumpy. Fill muffin cups ⅔ full. Bake 20 to 25 minutes, until golden brown. Serve hot with butter and jelly. Makes 12 muffins.

Suzanne D. Peterson

BEER BREAD

3 cups self-rising flour   **1 (12 oz.) can cold beer**
3 tablespoons sugar   **½ cup butter, melted**

Preheat oven to 350°. Grease a 9x5 inch loaf pan. Mix flour, sugar and beer until well-blended. Pour into pan; bake for 30 minutes. Remove pan from oven, pour melted butter over top and return to oven for 10 minutes more, or until brown. Best served warm.

QUICK SALLY LUNN

½ cup Crisco
½ cup sugar
3 eggs
2 cups all-purpose flour

4 teaspoons baking
powder
¾ teaspoon salt
1 cup milk

Grease a 9 inch round cake pan or large muffin pans. Preheat oven to 425°. Cream shortening and sugar together until light and fluffy. Beat in eggs 1 at a time; continue beating until smooth. Sift dry ingredients together. Add flour and milk alternately to creamed mixture, beating only until smooth and free of lumps. Pour into pan, bake for 30 minutes (15 minutes for muffins) or until golden brown and a cake tester inserted in the middle comes out clean.

BRITTLE BREAD

2¾ cups all-purpose flour
¼ cup sugar
½ teaspoon salt
½ teaspoon baking powder

½ cup butter
1 cup (8 oz. container)
plain yogurt
Salt

Blend dry ingredients in a mixing bowl. Cut in butter with fingers until crumbly. Stir in yogurt and mix until dough holds together. This may be done in a food processor. If dough is sticky, add more flour. Dust lightly with flour, cover and *refrigerate overnight.* Preheat oven to 425°. Break off walnut-sized pieces of dough, roll in hands, then roll out *very thin* on floured surface, to 5 inch or 6 inch rounds. If dough sticks, use more flour. Place on ungreased cookie sheets, sprinkle generously with salt, and bake 5 to 8 minutes in middle of oven, 1 sheet at a time, until puffed and lightly browned. *Watch carefully!* When all are baked, turn off oven, let oven cool slightly, pile bread onto one sheet and return to warm oven. Leave in oven overnight. Store in a plastic bag in the refrigerator up to 1 month, or freeze.
NOTE: It's easier to make brittle bread with another person, one to roll it out, and one to salt it and watch the oven. Good with Stuffed Brie, see Index, or as an accompaniment for drinks or light summer meals.

Adapted by Danyse Edel

BONANZA BREAD

1 cup unbleached all-
   purpose flour
1 cup whole wheat flour
½ teaspoon salt
½ teaspoon baking soda
2 teaspoons baking
   powder
⅔ cup nonfat dry milk
   powder
⅓ cup wheat germ
½ cup firmly packed light
   brown sugar

¼ cup pecans or walnuts
½ cup unsalted dry
   roasted peanuts
½ cup raisins
3 eggs
½ cup vegetable oil
½ cup molasses
¾ cup orange juice
2 medium bananas, cut up
⅓ cup dried apricots

Preheat oven to 325°. Grease two 8½x4½ inch loaf pans. In food processor, combine flours, salt, soda, baking powder, dry milk, wheat germ, sugar, nuts and raisins. Process by turning machine on and off several times, until nuts and raisins are coarsely chopped. Do not over-process. Transfer flour mixture to large mixing bowl. Put bowl back on food processor—no need to rinse. Process eggs until foamy. Add oil, molasses, orange juice and bananas, processing after each addition, and until bananas are puréed. Add apricots; process just to chop coarsely. Pour liquid ingredients onto flour mixture; blend just until moistened. (If you have a large food processor, dump the flour mixture back in on top of the liquid ingredients and process with a few on-off turns until just moistened.) Pour into pans. Bake for 1 hour or until bread shrinks from sides of pans and center is firm when pressed lightly with finger tip. Cool for 10 minutes in pans on wire rack, then turn out on rack and cool to room temperature. When cool, wrap tightly and store overnight to mellow flavors.

NOTE: If you don't have a food processor, chop nuts and raisins coarsely and mix dry ingredients well with a spoon or fork. Beat liquid ingredients well with a whisk or electric mixer, mash bananas on a plate and beat in. Snip apricots coarsely with oiled kitchen shears.

Variations: Add ½ small orange, peel and all, to the liquid ingredients and chop fine (or chop in blender). Substitute 1 cup
raw chopped apples, applesauce, fresh puréed apricots,
peaches, pears or grated carrot or zucchini for bananas.

One serving (two ⅓ inch slices) supplies 12% of the daily protein requirement for an adult, 15% for 7 to 10 year olds, and
18% for 4 to 6 year olds. For extra protein, spread with cream
cheese. Makes 2 loaves.

DATE-NUT BREAD

6 tablespoons butter or
  margarine, softened
¾ cup sugar
2 eggs
2 cups sifted all-purpose
  flour
2 teaspoons baking
  powder

½ teaspoon cinnamon
¼ teaspoon mace
⅛ teaspoon nutmeg
½ teaspoon salt
½ cup milk
1⅓ cups (8 oz. package)
  chopped, pitted dates
½ cup chopped nuts

Preheat oven to 325° Grease a 9 inch loaf pan. Cream butter
or margarine until soft, add sugar and beat until fluffy. Beat in
eggs. Sift dry ingredients together and add alternately with milk,
starting and ending with dry ingredients. Fold in dates and nuts.
Bake for 60 to 70 minutes or until a cake tester inserted in center comes out clean. Cool in pan on wire rack for 5 minutes;
remove from pan and cool completely on wire rack before slicing. Serve with cream cheese.
NOTE: The best way to cut dates (or any dried fruit) is with
oiled scissors. Toss with ¼ cup of the flour called for in the
recipe and they won't sink to the bottom. You may omit dates
and increase nuts to 1 cup, and you will have a good spicy nut
bread.

BANANA NUT BREAD

2 very ripe medium
  bananas
1 teaspoon lemon juice
⅓ cup butter
⅔ cup sugar
2 eggs

1¾ cups all-purpose flour
2¼ teaspoons baking
  powder
½ teaspoon salt
½ cup pecans, coarsely
  chopped

Have butter and eggs at room temperature. Grease a 9x5x3 inch bread pan. Mash bananas; stir in lemon juice. Preheat oven to 350°. Cream butter until soft. Add sugar; beat until fluffy. Add eggs 1 at a time, beating well after each addition. Beat in bananas. Sift dry ingredients together. Beat into creamed mixture just until flour disappears. Stir in nuts. Pour into pan; bake for 1 hour or until a knife inserted in the center comes out clean. Cool on a wire rack for 5 minutes; remove bread from pan. Cool to room temperature before slicing. Makes 1 loaf.
NOTE: If using a food processor, just throw cut-up bananas in after creaming butter and sugar and process until smooth. Don't forget lemon juice. You can also throw unchopped nuts in at the end and process on and off a few times to chop.

YOGURT BRAN BREAD

¾ cup unbleached all-
  purpose flour
¾ cup whole wheat flour
⅓ cup bran
⅓ cup wheat germ
¾ teaspoon baking powder
1 teaspoon baking soda
½ teaspoon cinnamon
¼ teaspoon salt
1 egg

½ cup firmly packed light
  brown sugar
⅓ cup vegetable oil
⅔ cup plain yogurt
Grated rind of one lemon
  or orange
1 cup chopped nuts
  (optional)
½ cup raisins (optional)

Preheat oven to 375°. Grease and flour a 9x5 inch loaf pan. Place flours, bran, wheat germ, baking powder, soda, cinnamon and salt in food processor (or large bowl). Give processor a few quick on-off turns to mix ingredients, or mix with fork. Beat together egg, sugar, oil, yogurt and rind. Add to dry ingredients. Process with on-off turns until just blended, or stir with fork until just blended. Stir in nuts and/or raisins. Pour into loaf pan. Bake in center of oven for 50 to 60 minutes, until brown and cooked through. Cool in pan on wire rack for 10 minutes, then turn out and cool to room temperature.

SOUR CREAM COFFEE CAKE

½ cup butter	1 teaspoon baking soda
1 cup sugar	½ teaspoon salt
2 eggs	1 cup sour cream
2 cups sifted all-purpose flour	1 teaspoon vanilla
1 teaspoon baking powder	

Nut Mixture

⅓ cup firmly packed light brown sugar	1 tablespoon cinnamon
¼ cup sugar	1 cup chopped nuts

Have butter and eggs at room temperature. Preheat oven to 325°. Grease a bundt pan or 9 inch tube pan. Cream butter until soft; add sugar and beat until fluffy. Add eggs 1 at a time, beating well after each addition. Sift dry ingredients together. Add to creamed mixture in 3 batches, alternating with sour cream and starting and ending with flour. Add vanilla and blend well. Pour ½ batter into pan. Cover with nut mixture; pour remaining batter over nut mixture. Bake for 40 minutes or until golden brown. Serve warm.

Susan Provost

LEMON BREAD

6 tablespoons butter,
  softened
1 cup sugar
Grated rind of 1 lemon
2 eggs

1½ cups all-purpose flour
1½ teaspoons baking
  powder
½ teaspoon salt
½ cup milk

Butter and flour an 8½x4½ inch loaf pan. Preheat oven to 350°. Cream butter and sugar together until light and fluffy. Add lemon rind. Add the eggs 1 at a time, beating well after each addition. Add the flour and beat in just until incorporated. Pour in milk and blend in. Pour into pan and bake for 1 hour or until golden brown, bread shrinks slightly from sides of pan, and a cake tester inserted in the center comes out clean. Cool on wire rack for 10 minutes, turn out, and cool to room temperature.

Lemon Glaze

½ cup sifted
  confectioners' sugar

1 tablespoon lemon juice

Mix sugar and lemon juice to make a glaze. Brush over bread when cool.
NOTE: This is really more of a cake than a bread. It freezes well; however, omit the glaze when freezing or glaze after thawing.

ZUCCHINI BREAD

2 medium unpeeled
  zucchini, grated
  (about 2 cups)
3 eggs
1 cup vegetable oil
1 tablespoon vanilla
  extract

2¼ cups sugar
3 cups all-purpose flour
1 teaspoon salt
1 teaspoon baking soda
1 teaspoon baking powder
3 teaspoons cinnamon
1 cup nuts

Squeeze grated zucchini by handfuls to remove excess water. Grease two 8½x4½x2½ inch bread pans, line bottoms with wax paper, and grease paper. Preheat oven to 350°. Beat eggs in electric mixer or food processor. Add oil and vanilla and beat well. Sift dry ingredients together. Mix with eggs and oil just until flour disappears. Stir in zucchini and nuts. Batter will be stiff. Pour into pans; bake for 1 hour or until a knife inserted in the center comes out clean. Cool on wire racks for 5 minutes; remove bread from pans. Cool to room temperature before slicing. Good served plain or with cream cheese icing.

POPOVERS

2 eggs
1 cup milk

1 cup all-purpose flour
½ teaspoon salt

Break eggs into bowl; beat well with a fork or whisk. Add milk, flour and salt. Beat well, but don't worry about a few lumps. Fill greased large muffin tins or custard cups ¾ full. Put in rack in middle of oven. Set oven at 450° and turn on. Bake 30 minutes without opening door. Serve with lots of butter. Jam, syrup or honey are good too!

NOTE: These popovers are so good it is almost unbelievable that they are so simple to make. The secret is starting with a cold oven. And don't peek for the full 30 minutes (of course you can look if you have an oven window), when your success is ready to serve amid cheers. Makes 6.

Suzanne W. Peterson

CUBAN BREAD

2 packages dry yeast
1¼ tablespoons salt
1 tablespoon sugar
2 cups warm water
    (110° to 115°)

6 to 7 cups unbleached all-
    purpose flour or bread
    flour
1 egg, beaten

Add yeast, salt and sugar to warm water. Stir gently with a wooden spoon to dissolve. Let stand 5 to 10 minutes until mixture is foamy. Pour yeast mixture into a large bowl. Add flour 1 cup at a time, mixing well with a wooden spoon. When dough gets too stiff to stir, mix with your hands. Knead on a lightly floured surface, adding flour as needed, just until dough is smooth and not sticky, about 5 minutes. Shape into a ball and place in an oiled bowl, turning dough to coat all sides. Cover bowl with plastic wrap and let rise in a warm place until doubled. When dough has risen, punch down, divide in half, turn out on a floured surface and shape into two loaves; flatten bread into a 12x8 inch rectangle, roll up tightly, and pinch edges and ends under. You can make fat round loaves or long skinny ones. Arrange on a greased baking sheet. Brush tops with beaten egg. Slash tops 5 or 6 times with a sharp knife or razor blade and sprinkle with sesame or poppy seeds, or leave plain. Place loaves in a *cold* oven. Place a pan of boiling water on the bottom of the oven. Set oven at 400°. Bake for 30 to 40 minutes, until golden brown and crusty. Remove to wire racks.

Food Processor Method

1 package dry yeast
½ tablespoon salt
½ tablespoon sugar
1 cup warm water
    (110° to 115°)

3 to 3½ cups unbleached
    all-purpose flour or
    bread flour

Add yeast, salt and sugar to warm water. Stir gently with a wooden spoon to dissolve. Let stand 5 to 10 minutes, until mixture is foamy. Put 1 cup flour in food processor fitted with metal blade. With processor running, gradually pour yeast mixture through feed tube. Process until well blended. Dump in 2 cups flour; process until dough forms a ball on top of blade. If dough feels sticky, sprinkle with flour and continue processing until smooth and not sticky. You may need to add more flour, but don't add too much. Remove dough from processor and knead on lightly floured surface 20 to 30 times. Proceed as for handmade bread.

NOTE: If you have a large capacity food processor you can make a full recipe. For a minimum effort, this is one of the best breads you can make. Serve with lots of real butter.

ANGEL BISCUITS

1 package yeast
3 tablespoons warm water
   (110-115°)
5 cups White Lily all-
   purpose flour
1 teaspoon baking soda

3 teaspoons baking
   powder
1 teaspoon salt
¼ cup sugar
1 cup Crisco
2 cups buttermilk

Dissolve yeast in warm water with a pinch of the sugar and let stand for 10 minutes, or until foamy. Sift dry ingredients together. Rub Crisco into dry ingredients with fingers until the size of peas. Add yeast to buttermilk. Stir buttermilk mixture into flour mixture just until all flour is moistened. Dough will be sticky. Cover with plastic wrap and refrigerate overnight before using. To make biscuits: Preheat oven to 425°. Place about 1 cup flour on a piece of wax paper. Dust hands with flour, pinch off a piece of dough the size of a small egg, roll lightly in hands to shape. Handle as little as possible. Place with sides touching on a lightly greased baking sheet. Bake for 10 to 15 minutes or until brown. Dough will keep for a week in the refrigerator, so bake as needed. Makes 3 to 4 dozen small biscuits.

ORANGE BUTTER COFFEE CAKE

1 package yeast
¼ cup very warm water
  (110° to 115°)
¼ cup sugar, divided
1 teaspoon salt
2 eggs
½ cup sour cream
6 tablespoons butter,
  softened

2¾ to 3 cups all-purpose
  flour
¾ cup sugar
1 cup coconut, divided
2 tablespoons grated
  orange rind
2 tablespoons butter,
  melted

Sprinkle yeast over warm water in bowl of electric mixer or large bowl; stir in 1 tablespoon sugar and stir to dissolve yeast. Let mixture stand until foamy, about 10 minutes. Beat in 3 tablespoons sugar, salt, eggs, sour cream and 6 tablespoons butter. Gradually add enough flour to form a stiff dough. Dough will be slightly sticky. Place dough in a greased bowl and turn to coat all sides. Cover bowl with plastic wrap and let rise in a warm place until doubled, about 2 hours. Combine ¾ cup sugar, ¾ cup coconut and orange rind. Punch down dough; knead on floured surface 15 times. Divide in half. Roll out each half on a floured surface into a 12 inch circle. Brush each circle with 1 tablespoon melted butter and sprinkle with half of sugar-coconut mixture. Cut into 12 wedges. Roll wedges up, starting with wide end. Place rolls point-side down in 3 rows in a buttered 9x13 inch baking dish. Cover and let rise at room temperature for 1 hour. Preheat oven to 350°. Bake for 25 to 30 minutes until golden brown. Leave rolls in pan, pour glaze over rolls and sprinkle with remaining ¼ cup coconut. Serve warm.

Glaze

¼ cup butter, melted
¾ cup sugar
½ cup sour cream

2 tablespoons orange juice
  (from grated orange)

Whisk until smooth in small saucepan. Bring to boil, stirring occasionally. Boil for 3 minutes.
NOTE: These are great the next day. Just cover tightly with aluminum foil and heat at 350° for 10 to 15 minutes.

Jean Roche

SALLY LUNN

1 cup milk
¼ cup water
½ cup Crisco
2 packages yeast
⅓ cup sugar

2 teaspoons salt
4 cups all-purpose flour
3 eggs
2 tablespoons butter,
    softened

Heat the milk, water and Crisco together until very warm— 115°. Shortening does not need to melt. Stir in yeast and 1 tablespoon of the sugar. Let stand 5 to 10 minutes, until foamy. Pour liquids into the bowl of an electric mixer. Add 1⅓ cups flour, remaining sugar and salt. Beat at medium speed for 2 minutes, scraping sides occasionally. Gradually add ⅔ cup of the remaining flour and eggs and beat at high speed for 2 minutes. Add the remaining flour and mix well. Batter will be thick but still sticky. Scrape down sides of bowl, cover with plastic wrap and let rise in a warm place until doubled, about 1½ hours. Beat dough down with a spatula or wooden spoon. Grease hands and place dough in a greased 9 inch tube pan or bundt pan. Spread softened butter on top of dough with hands, smoothing the top of the dough as you go. Cover with plastic wrap and let rise about 30 minutes in a warm place. Bake in a preheated 350° oven about 40 to 50 minutes, or until golden brown and hollow-sounding when tapped on top. Run knife around center and outer edges and turn out on a rack. Serve warm with lots of butter. Good reheated for breakfast the next day with homemade jam.

CAKES

Baking Tips

Use only the best ingredients—real butter, real chocolate, real vanilla extract. Why go to all the trouble for an inferior product? Eggs called for in these recipes are always large—don't substitute small, medium or jumbo.

Use unbleached all-purpose flour for baking bread, cookies, sauces, and cakes which call for it. White Lily all-purpose flour is ideal for most cakes, and can usually be substituted for cake flour. White Lily self-rising flour is the perfect biscuit flour. White Lily flour is made from soft winter wheat, and is the only flour of its kind in the United States. If you can't find it where you live, write:

The White Lily Foods Company
P. O. Box 871
Knoxville, Tennessee 37901
Or call (615)546-5511

Explain your predicament, and they will arrange to send you what you need.

Always have your butter and eggs at room temperature. Preheat the oven. If you bake your cakes in three 8 inch pans rather than two 9 inch pans, you will find that your layers won't hump in the middle, and will be easier to ice. It's best to bake cakes in the center of the oven, however, if you have 4 layers, divide the oven in thirds with the 2 racks and put layers in alternating corners, so that no layer is directly under another one. You may have to switch them around halfway through the baking time. Always cool cakes on wire racks.

When baking cookies, you will have the best results if you use shiny aluminum sheets and bake them 1 sheet at a time in the middle of the oven. Turn the baking sheet around 180° halfway through the baking time, so that cookies will brown evenly.

If you suspect that your oven thermostat is off, buy an oven thermometer and adjust the oven setting accordingly. All the recipes in this book were baked in an accurate oven.

APPLE-DATE-NUT CAKE

2 cups sugar
1½ cups vegetable oil
2 teaspoons vanilla extract
2 eggs
Juice of ½ lemon
3 cups sifted all-purpose
    flour
1 teaspoon cinnamon

1 teaspoon salt
1¼ teaspoons baking soda
2 large apples, peeled,
    cored and chopped
1 cup chopped dates
1½ to 2 cups chopped
    pecans

Preheat oven to 325°. Grease and flour a 10 inch tube pan. Beat first 5 ingredients together until smooth. Stir ½ cup flour into apples, dates and nuts. Sift remaining flour, cinnamon, salt and baking soda together. Gradually add to first mixture. Add apples, dates and nuts. Mix well. Batter will be very thick, and may have to be mixed by hand. Spoon into pan, smooth top and bake for 1½ hours, or until a cake tester inserted in the middle comes out clean. Cool on wire rack before turning out.

CARROT CAKE

2 cups all-purpose flour
    (White Lily is best)
2 cups sugar
¼ teaspoon baking soda
1 teaspoon baking powder

2½ teaspoons cinnamon
1½ cups vegetable oil
4 eggs
3 cups grated carrots

Grease and flour three 8 inch round cake pans. Preheat oven to 375°. Sift first 5 ingredients together. Beat eggs with oil; add dry ingredients; beat until smooth. Fold in carrots. Pour batter into pans. Bake for 25 minutes, or until tops spring back when touched lightly and cake shrinks from sides of pan. Cool on wire racks before icing.

Icing

1 (8 oz.) package cream cheese, softened
½ cup butter or margarine, softened

1 box confectioners' sugar
2 teaspoons vanilla extract
1 cup chopped pecans
1 cup coconut

Mix first 4 ingredients until smooth. Add pecans and coconut. Ice between layers and on top.

Margaret Faulkner

TRIPLE CHOCOLATE CAKE

1 box chocolate cake mix—*not* pudding mix style
1 (3 oz.) box instant chocolate pudding

1 (12 oz.) bag semi-sweet chocolate chips
1¾ cups milk
2 eggs

Preheat oven to 350°. Grease and flour a bundt pan or 10 inch tube pan. Combine all ingredients in electric mixer. Beat on low speed to blend. Beat at medium speed for 2 minutes. Pour into pan. Bake 60 minutes or until a cake tester inserted in the middle comes out clean. Cool on wire rack for 10 minutes, remove cake from pan and cool to room temperature before slicing— if you can stand to wait. No need for icing.

NOTE: This is a simple recipe for an incredibly good cake. If you are a purist, just pretend you are not letting a cake mix in your house. You'll be glad you did!

Sally-Byrd Newton Combs

CHOCOLATE-CHOCOLATE-CHOCOLATE CAKE

4 ounces unsweetened
  baking chocolate, melted
¾ cup butter
2½ cups sugar
5 eggs, separated

2½ cups sifted all-purpose
  White Lily or cake flour
1 teaspoon baking soda
1 cup buttermilk
1 teaspoon vanilla extract

Have butter and eggs at room temperature. Grease, line bottoms with wax paper, grease paper and flour three 8 inch round cake pans. Preheat oven to 350°. Cream butter and sugar until light and fluffy. Beat in egg yolks 1 at a time; beat in melted chocolate. Sift flour and baking soda together. Beat in alternately with buttermilk, starting and ending with flour. Beat in vanilla. Beat egg whites until stiff but not dry. Beat ¼ of the egg whites into chocolate mixture to lighten it, then fold chocolate mixture into egg whites gently but thoroughly. Chocolate batter is very heavy and doesn't want to cooperate, but be firm. Divide batter among pans, smooth tops and bake for 30 to 35 minutes, until tops spring back when lightly touched and cake shrinks from sides of pan. Cool on wire racks and turn out. You may have to slip a finger under the wax paper to get it started. Fill and ice.

Filling

½ cup sugar
3 tablespoons flour
Pinch salt
2 ounces unsweetened
  baking chocolate

1 cup milk
1 egg
1 tablespoon butter
½ teaspoon vanilla extract

Mix dry ingredients. Whisk in egg until smooth. Melt chocolate in milk in a heavy saucepan, stirring constantly. Gradually pour milk into egg mixture, whisking rapidly and constantly. Return mixture to saucepan and cook, stirring constantly with a wooden spoon, until mixture thickens and comes to a boil. Remove from heat; beat in butter and vanilla. Pour into a bowl, place a piece of plastic wrap directly on the surface of the filling and refrigerate until cool. Use between layers of cake.

Icing

2 ounces unsweetened	**1 cup milk**
baking chocolate	**2 cups sugar**
⅓ cup butter	**1 teaspoon vanilla extract**
1 teaspoon flour	

Melt chocolate and butter in a large, heavy saucepan over low heat, stirring constantly. Dissolve flour in part of the milk; add milk, flour and sugar to chocolate. Bring to a boil, stirring frequently, and boil until mixture reaches soft ball stage on a candy thermometer (234°). Remove from heat, stir in vanilla, and beat with an electric mixer until icing becomes just thick enough to spread. Do not let it harden too much. If icing does become too hard, beat in a little milk. Ice entire outside of cake. Dip spatula or knife in hot water to smooth icing.

NOTE: Don't let the length of this recipe intimidate you. For true chocolate lovers, it is well worth the effort.

Edna Traub

 When adding flour and liquid to cake batter, add flour in 4 batches and liquid in 3, starting and ending with flour.

COCA COLA CAKE

2 cups sugar
2 cups all-purpose White
  Lily or cake flour
½ cup vegetable oil
½ cup butter or margarine
½ cup Coca Cola
3 tablespoons cocoa

½ cup buttermilk
2 eggs
1 teaspoon baking soda
1 teaspoon vanilla extract
1½ cups miniature
  marshmallows

Preheat oven to 350°. Grease and flour a 9x13 inch baking pan. Sift together sugar and flour in a large mixing bowl. Mix oil, butter or margarine, Coke and cocoa in a saucepan. Bring to a boil and pour over dry mixture. Beat well with electric mixer, whisk or wooden spoon until smooth. Beat in buttermilk, eggs, soda, vanilla extract and marshmallows. Batter will be thin. Pour into pan; marshmallows will float on top. Bake 45 minutes, or until a cake tester inserted in middle comes out clean. Remove from oven; ice while still warm.

Icing

½ cup butter or margarine
⅓ cup Coca Cola
6 tablespoons cocoa
1 (1 lb.) box confectioners'
  sugar, sifted

1 teaspoon vanilla extract
1 cup chopped pecans

Mix butter, Coke and cocoa in a saucepan and bring to a boil. Remove from heat. Add confectioners' sugar and vanilla; beat until smooth. (If you have a food processor, dump sugar in bowl, turn on machine and pour liquids in. Process until smooth.) Stir in nuts. Spread over cake while icing is hot and cake is warm.

Tammy Farrow

FRESH COCONUT CAKE

1 large or 2 small coconuts
1 recipe 1,2,3,4 Cake,
  see Index; substituting
  coconut milk for milk

1 recipe 7-Minute Icing, see
  Index

Open coconuts and reserve milk; peel and grate. A food processor will save you lots of time and grated knuckles. If you don't have 1 cup coconut milk, add water to make 1 cup. Bake cake and cool. Ice cake, placing icing and coconut between layers and pressing coconut firmly over icing on entire outside surface. You should use about 3 cups coconut—freeze leftover for another use.
NOTE: You can use store-bought grated coconut and use milk instead of coconut milk in the cake, but it won't be the same.

SOUR CREAM AND COCONUT CAKE

1 (18½ oz.) box Duncan
  Hines Golden Butter
  cake mix
2 cups sour cream
1 cup sugar

3 (6 oz.) or 2 (9 oz.)
  packages frozen
  coconut, thawed
1 (8 oz.) container Cool
  Whip, thawed

Bake cake as directed. Cool. Split cake layers in half horizontally. Combine sour cream, sugar and coconut. Reserve 1 cup for frosting; spread remainder between layers of cake. Combine reserved sour cream mixture and Cool Whip. Spread on top and sides of cake. Store in air-tight container in refrigerator for 3 days before serving—do not cheat! It takes 3 days for this unlikely combination of store-bought ingredients to realize its tasty potential.

Brenda Lain
Ginny Barnett

DADDY'S FAVORITE CAKE

¼ cup butter
¼ cup shortening
1½ cups sugar
½ teaspoon vanilla extract
3 eggs
2 cups sifted all-purpose
   White Lily or cake flour

2 teaspoons nutmeg
1 teaspoon baking powder
1 teaspoon baking soda
¼ teaspoon salt
1 cup buttermilk

Have butter and eggs at room temperature. Grease and flour three 8 inch or two 9 inch round cake pans. Preheat oven to 350°. Cream butter, shortening and sugar together until light and fluffy. Add vanilla extract. Add eggs 1 at a time, beating well after each addition. Sift dry ingredients together 3 times. Add to creamed mixture alternately with buttermilk, starting and ending with flour. Divide evenly among pans. Bake for 25 to 30 minutes, until golden, tops spring back when touched, and cake shrinks from sides of pan. Cool on wire racks. Turn out when cool. Fill and ice.

Seven Minute Icing

2 unbeaten egg whites
1½ cups sugar
5 tablespoons cold water
¼ teaspoon cream of tartar

1½ teaspoons light corn
   syrup
1 teaspoon vanilla extract

Place egg whites, sugar, water, cream of tartar and corn syrup in the top of a double boiler. Beat until thoroughly blended. Place over rapidly boiling water. Beat with electric mixer or rotary beater for 7 minutes. Remove icing from heat and beat in vanilla extract. (If icing thickens too quickly, while cooking, add a small amount of boiling water.) Continue beating until icing is the proper consistency for spreading.

Filling

½ **cup chopped pecans**
½ **cup chopped raisins**
½ **cup coconut**

½ **cup drained and**
  chopped maraschino
  cherries

Mix together with approximately ½ cup icing—enough to hold ingredients together. Spread filling between cake layers. Spread icing over top and sides of cake.

NOTE: Try using freshly grated nutmeg. It makes a big difference.

Suzanne W. Peterson

DATE NUT CAKE

1 **cup butter**
1 **cup sugar**
4 **eggs**
1½ **cups sifted all-purpose**
  flour

3 **cups chopped pecans**
1 **(1 lb.) package pitted**
  dates, snipped with
  scissors

Have butter and eggs at room temperature. Place a pan of hot water on the bottom rack of the oven. Preheat oven to 300°. Grease and flour a 9 inch tube pan. Stir ¼ cup of the flour in with dates. Cream butter and sugar until light and fluffy. Beat in eggs 1 at a time. Beat in remaining 1¼ cups flour gradually. Stir in nuts and dates. Pour into pan; smooth top. Place on rack above hot water. Bake for 1 hour and check. If top is browning too rapidly, cover with aluminum foil. Continue baking another 30 to 45 minutes, or until cake springs back when touched lightly and a cake tester inserted in center comes out clean. Cool completely on a wire rack before turning out.

Carolyn Farrow

LIGHT FRUITCAKE

½ pound candied cherries
½ pound candied pineapple
1 cup snipped dried apricots
1 cup snipped dried figs
1 cup white raisins
1 cup snipped dates
2 cups chopped pecans
1½ cups butter

4 cups sugar
10 eggs
2 teaspoons vanilla extract
2 teaspoons almond extract
8 cups sifted all-purpose flour
2 teaspoons baking powder
1 teaspoon salt

Place candied fruit in a mixing bowl. Pour boiling water over fruit to cover and stir 20 to 30 seconds; drain. This washes off preservatives and excess gunk. Chop or snip cherries and pineapple. Combine fruit, nuts and 1 cup flour in a *large* mixing bowl. Sift remaining flour with baking powder and salt. Cream butter and sugar until light and fluffy. Beat in eggs 1 at a time. Add flavorings and beat until well-blended. Beat in dry ingredients gradually, and beat until smooth. Combine batter and fruit. Pour into pans that have been greased, lined on the bottoms with wax paper, greased again and floured. Bake at 325° for 1 to 1½ hours, until golden brown and a cake tester inserted in the center comes out clean. Cool on wire racks in pans for 30 minutes. Remove from pans, peel off paper and cool completely. Poke holes in cakes with a toothpick and pour brandy or rum over cakes (⅓ cup for a big cake). Store in air-tight tins or wrap tightly in plastic wrap and aluminum foil.

NOTE: Bake in mini-loaf pans, regular loaf pans or tube pans. Fill pans to within ½ inch of the top.

Sally-Byrd Newton Combs

MAMMY'S DARK FRUITCAKE

½ pound candied citron
½ pound candied cherries
½ pound candied pineapple
¼ pound candied orange peel
¼ pound candied lemon peel
2 (15 oz.) boxes raisins
1 (10 oz.) box currants
1 cup port wine
4 cups chopped pecans
4 apples, peeled, cored and finely chopped
1 tablespoon molasses
2 cups butter, softened
2 cups sugar
8 eggs
5 cups sifted all-purpose flour (preferably White Lily)
2 teaspoons baking powder
1 teaspoon baking soda
2 teaspoons each cinnamon, nutmeg and ground cloves
1 cup buttermilk

Place candied fruit in a large bowl. Pour boiling water over fruit to cover and stir 20 to 30 seconds. Drain. This washes off the preservatives and surplus gunk. Mix candied fruit, raisins and currants with port in a large mixing bowl or pot; let stand covered at least 4 hours or overnight. Add nuts, apples and molasses. Cream butter and sugar until light and fluffy. Beat in eggs 1 at a time. Sift dry ingredients together; add alternately to creamed mixture with buttermilk, starting and ending with dry ingredients. Combine batter and fruit. Pour into pans which have been greased, lined on the bottom with wax paper, greased again, and floured. Bake at 300° for 2 to 3 hours, until browned and a cake tester inserted in the center comes out clean. Cool on wire racks. Pour extra port over cakes while still warm. Wrap tightly in plastic wrap and foil or store in air-tight tins.

NOTE: Makes about 10 pounds of fruitcake. You may bake fruitcake in mini-loaf pans, regular loaf pans, tube pans, or even soup or coffee cans, depending on your needs. Just fill pans to within ½ inch of top. Fruitcake is better if made 2 to 3 months in advance and stored in a cool place. The best dark fruitcake ever!

May DeMaurice

GERMAN CHOCOLATE CAKE

1 package (4 oz.) Baker's
   German Sweet
   Chocolate
½ cup boiling water
1 cup butter
2 cups sugar
4 eggs, separated

1 teaspoon vanilla extract
2½ cups sifted all-purpose
   White Lily or cake flour
1 teaspoon baking soda
½ teaspoon salt
1 cup buttermilk

Have butter and eggs at room temperature. Preheat oven to 350°. Grease and flour three 9 inch round cake pans (8 inch pans are too small!). Melt chocolate in boiling water. Cool. Cream butter and sugar until light and fluffy. Add egg yolks 1 at a time, beating well after each addition. Beat in vanilla and chocolate. Sift flour with salt and soda; add alternately with buttermilk to chocolate mixture, starting and ending with flour. Beat until smooth. Beat egg whites until stiff but not dry. Fold into chocolate mixture. Pour into pans and bake for 30 to 35 minutes, or until tops spring back when lightly touched and cake shrinks from sides of pan. Cool on wire racks.

Filling

1 cup evaporated milk
1 cup sugar
3 egg yolks
½ cup butter

1 teaspoon vanilla
1½ cups coconut
1 cup chopped pecans

Combine evaporated milk, sugar, egg yolks, butter and vanilla in a saucepan. Cook over medium heat, stirring constantly, until thickened. Add coconut and pecans. Cool until thick enough to spread, beating occasionally. Spread between layers and on top.

ITALIAN CREAM CAKE

½ cup butter
½ cup Crisco
2 cups sugar
5 eggs, separated
2 cups all-purpose White
  Lily or cake flour

1 teaspoon baking soda
1 cup buttermilk
1 teaspoon vanilla extract
2 cups coconut
1 cup chopped pecans

Have butter and eggs at room temperature. Preheat oven to 350°. Grease and flour a 9x13 inch pan or three 8 inch round pans. Cream butter and Crisco. Add sugar; beat until light and fluffy. Beat in egg yolks one at a time. Sift flour and soda together; add to creamed mixture alternately with buttermilk, starting and ending with flour. Beat in vanilla, coconut and nuts. Beat egg whites until stiff but not dry; fold into batter—may be done on low speed of mixer. Pour into pan or pans. Bake 30 to 35 minutes for 8 inch pans or 1 hour to 1 hour and 15 minutes for 9x13 inch pan, or until golden brown, cake shrinks from sides of pan, and a cake tester inserted in the middle comes out clean. Cool on rack; ice—you may leave the 9x13 inch cake in the pan.

Icing

1 (8 oz.) package cream
  cheese, softened
½ cup butter, softened

1 (1 lb.) box confectioners'
  sugar, sifted
1 teaspoon vanilla extract

Beat together until smooth. Spread on cooled cake.
NOTE: This cake is much better the next day. Lock it in the refrigerator overnight before serving.

Susan Provost
Bonnie Youmans

FINNISH SOUR CREAM CAKE

2 eggs, beaten
2 cups sour cream
2 cups sugar
2 to 3 drops almond
　extract
3 cups all-purpose flour

1 teaspoon baking soda
½ teaspoon salt
½ teaspoon cinnamon
½ teaspoon ground
　cardamom

Preheat oven to 350°. Grease a 9 inch tube pan or bundt pan and dust with granulated sugar (not the 2 cups in recipe). Combine eggs, sour cream, sugar and almond extract. Beat until well-blended. Sift together dry ingredients and beat into sour cream mixture until smooth. Pour into pan and bake for 1 hour. Cool on a wire rack for 10 minutes, turn out and cool to room temperature before slicing.
NOTE: Easy to make in a food processor.

Suzanne W. Peterson

HERSHEY CHOCOLATE CAKE

6 tablespoons butter
1 cup sugar
4 eggs
1 cup all-purpose flour
1 teaspoon baking powder

¼ teaspoon salt
1 (16 oz.) can Hershey's
　chocolate syrup
1 teaspoon vanilla extract

Have butter and eggs at room temperature. Grease and flour a 9x13 inch pan. Preheat oven to 350°. Cream butter and sugar until light and fluffy; add eggs 1 at a time, beating well after each addition. Sift dry ingredients together; add alternately to creamed mixture with chocolate syrup, starting and ending with flour. Beat in vanilla. Pour into pan; bake 30 minutes or until cake springs back when touched lightly. Ice while warm.

Icing

1 cup sugar
⅓ cup evaporated milk
6 tablespoons butter

½ cup chocolate chips
1 cup chopped pecans

Cook, stirring constantly, over medium heat until chocolate is melted and sugar is dissolved—icing should not be grainy. Pour hot over warm cake.

Suzanne D. Peterson

MISSISSIPPI MUD CAKE

1 cup butter or margarine
2 cups sugar
4 eggs
1½ cups sifted all-purpose
    flour
⅓ cup cocoa

¼ teaspoon salt
3 teaspoons vanilla extract
1 cup chopped nuts
3 cups (6¼ oz. bag)
    miniature marshmallows

Have butter and eggs at room temperature. Preheat oven to 350°. Grease and flour a 9x13 inch pan. Cream butter and sugar together until light and fluffy. Add eggs 1 at a time, beating well after each addition. Sift flour, cocoa and salt together. Add to creamed mixture gradually. Mix well. Beat in vanilla extract and nuts. Pour into pan and bake for 30 to 35 minutes. Remove from oven and pour marshmallows over top. Return to oven for 10 minutes, until marshmallows are soft but not brown. Cool on wire rack to room temperature before frosting.

Frosting

1 box confectioners' sugar
⅓ cup cocoa
½ cup butter or margarine
1 teaspoon vanilla

¼ to ⅓ cup evaporated
    milk
½ cup nuts

Mix well and spread on cake. Easy to do in a food processor.
NOTE: This is a very sweet cake—serve small pieces.

JAPANESE FRUIT CAKE

1 cup butter
2 cups sugar
6 eggs
3 cups sifted all-purpose
  flour (White Lily is best)

2 teaspoons baking
  powder
¼ teaspoon salt
1 cup milk
1 teaspoon vanilla extract

Dark Part

1 teaspoon allspice
1 teaspoon cloves
1 teaspoon cinnamon

1 teaspoon nutmeg
1 cup raisins, tossed with
  ¼ cup flour

Have butter and eggs at room temperature Preheat oven to 350°. Grease and flour four 8 inch round cake pans. Cream butter and sugar until light and fluffy. Beat in eggs 1 at a time, beating well after each addition. Sift together flour, baking powder and soda. Add alternately to creamed mixture with milk, starting and ending with flour. Add vanilla extract and beat until smooth. Divide batter in half. Fill 2 cake pans with one half of batter. Stir spices and raisins into other half and fill remaining 2 cake pans. Distribute pans evenly in oven and bake 30 to 35 minutes, turning and redistributing pans halfway through baking time if necessary, until golden brown, tops spring back when lightly touched, and cake shrinks from sides of pan. Cool on wire racks.

Filling

1 cup sugar
1 cup boiling water
4 tablespoons cornstarch
1 (20 oz.) can crushed
  pineapple, drained

2 cups coconut
Juice and rind of 2 lemons

Combine in saucepan and simmer, stirring constantly, until thick. Cool. Spread between layers and on top, alternating light and dark layers.

LANE CAKE

1 cup butter
2 cups sugar
8 egg whites
3¼ cups sifted all-purpose White Lily or cake flour

2 teaspoons baking powder
1 cup milk
2 teaspoons vanilla extract

Have butter and eggs at room temperature. Preheat oven to 375°. Line bottoms of three 9 inch round cake pans or four 8 inch pans with wax paper. Cream butter and sugar until very light and fluffy. Sift flour and baking powder 3 times and add alternately with milk to creamed mixture, starting and ending with flour. Beat in vanilla. Beat egg whites until stiff but not dry and fold gently but thoroughly into creamed mixture. Divide among pans; bake for 20 minutes or until golden brown and cake shrinks from sides of pan. Cool on wire racks for 10 minutes, turn out, remove wax paper, turn right side up and finish cooling on racks.

Filling

½ cup butter, softened
1 cup sugar
8 egg yolks
⅓ to ½ cup bourbon or brandy

1 teaspoon vanilla extract
1 cup raisins
1 cup pecan pieces, optional

Cream butter and sugar together. Beat in eggs. Place in a heavy non-aluminum pot over medium heat and cook, stirring constantly with a wooden spoon, until very thick. Stir in bourbon, vanilla, raisins and nuts. Cool. Spread between layers of cake. Frost entire cake with 7-Minute Icing, see Index. Refrigerate.

LEMONADE CAKE

1 box Duncan Hines plain
  yellow cake mix
1 (3 oz.) package lemon
  gelatin
¾ cup boiling water
¼ cup vegetable oil

4 eggs
1 (6 oz.) can lemonade
  concentrate, thawed
  (do not dilute)
¾ cup sugar

Preheat oven to 350°. Grease and flour a 9 inch tube pan. Pour boiling water over gelatin and stir to dissolve. Set aside. Beat cake mix, oil and eggs until smooth. Add gelatin and beat until smooth. Pour into pan and bake for 1 hour, or until golden brown, top springs back when touched lightly and cake shrinks from sides of pan. While cake is baking, add sugar to lemonade. As soon as cake comes out of the oven, spoon lemonade over the cake, pulling cake away from sides of pan so lemonade can run down sides. Refrigerate until cool. Remove cake from pan and return to refrigerator.

Donna Kay McLaurin

GLAZED ORANGE CAKE

1 cup butter
2 cups sugar
½ teaspoon vanilla extract
2 tablespoons grated
  orange rind
5 eggs

3 cups sifted all-purpose
  White Lily or cake flour
1 tablespoon baking
  powder
⅛ teaspoon salt
¾ cup milk

Have butter and eggs at room temperature. Grease and flour a 9 inch tube pan. Preheat oven to 350°. Cream butter and sugar until light and fluffy. Add vanilla extract and orange rind. Add eggs 1 at a time, beating well after each addition. Sift dry ingredients together twice. Add to the creamed mixture alternately with milk, starting and ending with flour. Beat until smooth. Pour into pan. Bake for 1 hour or until brown and top of cake springs back when touched. Cool on wire rack for 5 minutes.

Glaze

¼ cup butter
½ cup sugar

⅓ cup orange juice (use grated orange)

Heat ingredients for glaze in a saucepan until sugar dissolves. Pour evenly over cake in pan while cake is still hot. Allow cake to cool completely before removing from pan. Place on cake plate with top up or glaze will stick to the plate.

Gladys Pickens

1,2,3,4 CAKE

1 cup butter
2 cups sugar
3 cups sifted all-purpose flour (White Lily is best)
4 eggs

2 teaspoons baking powder
1 cup milk
1 teaspoon vanilla extract

Have butter and eggs at room temperature. Grease, line bottoms with wax paper, then grease again and flour, three 8 inch, two 9 inch, or a 9x13 inch cake pan. Preheat oven to 350°. Cream butter and sugar well. Add eggs one at a time, beating well after each addition. Sift flour together with baking powder. Add flour alternately with milk, starting and ending with flour. Add vanilla. Beat until smooth. Divide batter between pans. Bang pans 5 or 6 times on counter to remove air bubbles. Turn and shake pans to level batter. Bake for 30 minutes or until cake is golden brown, springs back when touched, begins to shrink from sides of pans, and a cake tester inserted in the middle comes out clean. Cool on wire racks for 30 minutes, then turn out and cool to room temperature before icing. Be sure to remove wax paper!
NOTE: A good basic cake to frost many different ways.

RED VELVET CAKE I

½ cup butter
1½ cups sugar
2 eggs
2 (1 oz.) bottles red food
  coloring
2 tablespoons cocoa
2½ cups sifted all-purpose
  flour (White Lily is best)

½ teaspoon salt
1 cup buttermilk
1 teaspoon vanilla extract
1 teaspoon baking soda
1 tablespoon vinegar

Have butter and eggs at room temperature. Grease and flour two 8 inch or 9 inch round cake pans. Preheat oven to 350°. Cream butter and sugar together until light and fluffy. Beat in eggs 1 at a time. Mix food coloring and cocoa together until well-combined; add to creamed mixture. Sift flour and salt together; add flour and buttermilk alternately to creamed mixture, starting and ending with flour. Beat until smooth; stir in vanilla. Remove from mixer, add vinegar and baking soda and beat by hand until smooth. Divide evenly between pans and bake for 30 to 35 minutes, or until cake shrinks from sides of pan and springs back when touched lightly. Cool on wire racks to room temperature.

Icing

1 cup milk
3 tablespoons flour
1 cup butter, softened

1 cup sugar
1 tablespoon vanilla
  extract

Whisk milk and flour together until smooth. Bring to a boil, whisking constantly, and boil until thick, 3 to 4 minutes. Remove from heat, place a piece of plastic wrap directly on surface, and cool to room temperature. Cream butter, sugar and vanilla together until light and fluffy. Beat in cooled milk and flour mixture and beat until very fluffy. Split cake layers horizontally with a serrated bread knife or dental floss; ice. (You don't have to split layers, of course, but it does look pretty.)

Susan Provost
Brenda Lain

RED VELVET CAKE II

1½ cups sugar
1 cup vegetable oil
2 eggs
1¼ cups buttermilk
1 teaspoon vinegar
1 teaspoon vanilla extract

1 (1 oz.) bottle red food
  coloring
2½ cups sifted self-rising
  flour (White Lily is best)
1 teaspoon baking soda

Grease and flour three 8 inch or two 9 inch round cake pans. Preheat oven to 350°. Mix sugar and oil and beat until smooth. Beat in eggs 1 at a time. Beat in milk, vinegar, vanilla and food coloring. Sift flour and baking soda together; beat into liquid ingredients until smooth. Divide batter among pans and bake 25 to 30 minutes, until tops spring back when touched lightly and cake shrinks from sides of pan. Cool on wire racks before icing.

Icing

1 (8 oz.) package cream
  cheese, softened
½ cup butter, softened
1 (1 lb.) box confectioners'
  sugar

1 teaspoon vanilla extract
1 cup pecans, finely
  chopped

Mix cream cheese and butter in food processor or mixer until smooth. Add remaining ingredients. Spread between layers and over outside of cake.
NOTE: Use 1 bottle of green food coloring for St. Patrick's Day.

Sheron George

Before you put that cake or bread in the oven, ask yourself— "Have I left anything out? What is going to make this rise? Are the salt, sugar, eggs, flour, etc. all in?" A simple way to avoid disaster, and it does happen to the best of us!

TOASTED BUTTER PECAN CAKE

1 recipe 1,2,3,4 Cake,
   see Index

2 cups chopped pecans
¼ cup butter

Melt butter in a jelly roll pan in a 350° oven. Stir in pecans; toast for 20 to 25 minutes, stirring frequently. Stir 1⅓ cups toasted pecans into cake batter. Bake and cool on wire racks. Ice.

Icing

¼ cup butter, softened
1 (1 lb.) box confectioners'
   sugar, sifted
1 teaspoon vanilla extract

4 to 6 tablespoons heavy
   cream
⅔ cup toasted pecans

Beat butter, sugar, vanilla extract and cream together until smooth and a good spreading consistency. Stir in pecans and ice cake.

PLUM CAKE

3 eggs
1 cup Wesson oil
2 small jars plum baby
   food
2 cups self-rising flour
   (preferably White Lily)

2 cups sugar
½ teaspoon cinnamon
½ teaspoon ground cloves
½ teaspoon nutmeg
⅛ teaspoon salt
1 cup chopped pecans

Preheat oven to 350°. Grease and flour a 9 inch tube pan or bundt pan. Beat eggs, add oil and baby food and beat until smooth. Sift flour, sugar and spices together. Add to wet ingredients; beat only until smooth. Stir in pecans. Pour into pan and bake for 1 hour and 10 to 15 minutes, until browned, cake shrinks from sides of pan, and a cake tester inserted in the center comes out clean. Cool on wire rack for 10 minutes, turn out and finish cooling.

NOTE: Wrapped tightly, this cake will keep moist and fresh for days. Good as a coffee cake too.

Gladys Pickens

PUMPKIN CAKE

2 cups sugar
1½ cups vegetable oil
4 eggs
2½ cups all-purpose flour
2 teaspoons baking soda

1 teaspoon salt
2 teaspoons cinnamon
1 (1 lb.) can pumpkin
1 cup chopped nuts

Preheat oven to 350°. Grease and flour a 9 inch tube pan or bundt pan. Beat together sugar, oil and eggs until smooth. Sift together flour, soda, salt and cinnamon. Add to liquid ingredients; beat until smooth. Beat in vanilla and pumpkin until smooth. Add nuts. Pour into pan and bake for 1 hour, or until a cake tester inserted in the middle comes out clean. Cool on wire rack.

Icing

1 (8 oz.) package cream
  cheese, softened
½ cup butter, softened

1 (1 lb.) box confectioners'
  sugar, sifted
1 teaspoon vanilla

Beat together until smooth.
NOTE: This cake is fine without the icing, and a lot less caloric!

Susan Provost

LEMON SUPREME LAYER CAKE

1 cup butter
1½ cups sugar
4 eggs
3 cups sifted all-purpose
   White Lily or cake flour
2 teaspoons baking
   powder

1 scant cup water
1 teaspoon lemon extract
1 box Duncan Hines
   Lemon Supreme cake
   mix

Have butter and eggs at room temperature. Grease three 9 inch or four 8 inch round cake pans, line bottoms with wax paper, grease again and flour. Preheat oven to 350°. Cream butter and sugar until fluffy. Beat in eggs 1 at a time. Sift flour and baking powder together. Add alternately with water to creamed mixture, starting and ending with flour. Add lemon extract. Beat on high for 1 minute. Add cake mix and beat on medium speed until well blended. Divide batter evenly among pans; bake 30 to 40 minutes until golden, tops spring back when touched, cake shrinks from sides of pan and a toothpick inserted in the center comes out clean. Cool on wire racks to room temperature. Turn out. Trim sides with a serrated knife to even out. Brush off crumbs.

Icing

¼ cup butter, softened
1 box confectioners' sugar,
   sifted

Grated rind of 2 lemons
Juice of 2 lemons
Milk

Cream butter and sugar together. Add lemon rind and juice. Add enough milk to reach desired spreading consistency. Spread icing between layers and over cake. There will be enough, it just won't be very thick.

Eloise Kelly

COCONUT POUND CAKE

1 cup butter
½ cup Crisco
3 cups sugar
6 eggs
3 cups sifted all-purpose
    flour (White Lily is best)
¼ teaspoon salt

1 cup milk
½ teaspoon almond
    extract
½ teaspoon coconut
    extract
1 (3½ oz.) can grated
    coconut

Have butter and eggs at room temperature. Grease, line bottom with wax paper, grease paper and flour a 10 inch tube pan. Preheat oven to 325°. Cream butter, shortening and sugar until light and fluffy. Add eggs 1 at a time, beating well after each addition. Sift flour and salt together; add alternately to creamed mixture with milk, starting and ending with flour. Beat until smooth. Add flavorings. Remove bowl from mixer; fold in coconut. Pour into prepared pan and smooth top. Bake for 1 hour and 30 to 35 minutes, until golden brown, top springs back when touched lightly, cake shrinks from sides of pan and a cake tester inserted in center comes out clean. Place on wire rack, poke holes all over with a toothpick and pour topping over while cake is still warm. Cool cake completely before removing from pan.

Topping

1 cup sugar
1 cup water

1 teaspoon coconut extract

Combine ingredients in saucepan and stir over heat to dissolve sugar. Boil hard until mixture becomes syrupy. Pour over hot cake.

APRICOT BRANDY POUND CAKE

1 cup butter
3 cups sugar
6 eggs
3 cups all-purpose flour
   (preferably White Lily)
1/4 teaspoon baking soda
1/2 teaspoon salt
1 cup sour cream

1/2 teaspoon rum flavoring
1 teaspoon orange extract
1/4 teaspoon almond
   extract
1/2 teaspoon lemon extract
1 teaspoon vanilla extract
1/2 cup apricot brandy

Have butter and eggs at room temperature. Grease and flour a 10 inch tube pan. Preheat oven to 325°. Cream butter and sugar until light and fluffy. Add eggs 1 at a time, beating well after each addition. Sift dry ingredients together. Mix sour cream, flavorings and brandy together. Add flour to creamed mixture in 4 batches, alternating with sour cream mixture and starting and ending with flour. Beat until smooth. Pour into pan; smooth top. Bake for 1 hour and 20 to 30 minutes, until golden brown, top springs back from touch, sides shrink from pan, and a cake tester inserted in the center comes out clean. Cool to room temperature on a wire rack before turning out.

Suzanne W. Peterson

AUNT NELLIE'S POUND CAKE

3/4 pound butter
1 1/2 cups sugar
7 eggs
3 cups sifted all-purpose
   flour (White Lily is best)

1/2 teaspoon almond
   extract
1 teaspoon fresh lemon
   juice
1 teaspoon warm water

Have butter and eggs at room temperature. Preheat oven to 325°. Grease a 9 inch tube pan, line bottom with wax paper, grease paper and flour pan. Cream butter and sugar until light and fluffy. Beat in eggs 1 at a time, beating well after each addition. Sift flour 3 times. Gradually add to creamed mixture. Beat on high for 30 seconds, or until well blended. Beat in flavorings and water. Pour into pan, smooth top and bake for 1½ to 1¾ hours until golden, cake shrinks from sides of pan, and a cake tester inserted in the center comes out clean. Cool on a rack for 30 minutes, turn out, and finish cooling.
NOTE: Let cake mellow overnight before slicing and it will be even better.

Suzanne W. Peterson

CONFECTIONERS' SUGAR POUND CAKE

1½ cups butter
1 (1 lb.) box confectioners' sugar, sifted
6 eggs
3⅓ cups sifted all-purpose flour (White Lily is best)

½ teaspoon salt
½ teaspoon baking powder
½ cup milk or water
1 teaspoon vanilla extract
¼ teaspoon almond extract

Have butter and eggs at room temperature. Grease and flour a 10-inch tube pan. Preheat oven to 325°. Cream butter until soft. Beat in sugar; cream until light and fluffy. Add eggs 1 at a time, beating well after each addition. Sift together flour, salt and baking powder. Add to creamed mixture alternately with milk or water, starting and ending with flour. Beat until smooth. Beat in flavorings. Pour into pan; smooth top. Bake for 1 hour and 20 to 30 minutes, or until golden brown, top springs back when touched and cake shrinks from sides of pan. Cool on wire rack. Slice thin to serve.

CHRISTMAS POUND CAKE

1 (8 oz.) package cream cheese
1 cup butter
1¾ cup sugar
1 teaspoon vanilla extract
1 tablespoon brandy
4 eggs
2¼ cups sifted all-purpose flour, divided (White Lily is best)
½ teaspoon baking powder
1 tablespoon cornstarch
1 cup (8 oz.) chopped candied fruit—red and green cherries and yellow pineapple
½ cup chopped pecans (in cake)
½ cup finely chopped pecans (for bottom of pan)

Have cream cheese, butter and eggs at room temperature. Preheat oven to 325°. Grease a 9 inch tube pan or bundt pan. Sprinkle ½ cup finely chopped pecans on bottom of pan. Toss candied fruit and ½ cup chopped pecans in ¼ cup flour. This keeps them from sticking together or sinking to bottom of pan. Beat cream cheese and butter together until soft. Add sugar; beat until light and fluffy. Beat in vanilla extract and brandy. Add eggs 1 at a time, beating well after each addition. Sift together 2 cups flour, baking powder and cornstarch. Add flour gradually until well blended, beating until smooth. Fold in candied fruit and nuts. Pour into pan. Smooth top. Bake at 325° for 30 minutes, then reduce oven to 300°. Bake for another 45 to 60 minutes, until golden brown and a cake tester inserted in center comes out clean. Cake does not rise very high. Cool on wire rack. Cut in thin slices. This cake freezes well.

SOUR CREAM POUND CAKE

1 cup butter
3 cups sugar
6 eggs
3 cups sifted all-purpose flour (White Lily is best)
1 cup sour cream
½ teaspoon baking soda
2 teaspoons vanilla extract
½ teaspoon almond extract

Have butter and eggs at room temperature. Grease and flour a 10-inch pan. Preheat oven to 325°. Cream butter until soft. Beat in sugar and beat until light and fluffy. Add eggs 1 at a time, beating well after each addition. Sift together flour and baking soda. Add flour and sour cream alternately to creamed mixture, starting and ending with flour. Add flavorings and beat until smooth. Pour into pan, smooth top and bake for 1½ hours or until golden brown, top springs back when touched, cake shrinks from sides of pan and a cake tester inserted in the middle comes out clean. Cool on wire rack before turning out. Slice thin to serve.

CHOCOLATE POUND CAKE I

1 cup butter
3 cups sugar
3 eggs
1 tablespoon vanilla
extract
3 cups sifted all-purpose
flour (preferably White
Lily)

1 cup cocoa
3 teaspoons baking
powder
1 teaspoon salt
1¾ cups half-and-half

Have butter and eggs at room temperature. Preheat oven to 325°. Oil well a 10 inch tube pan. Beat butter and sugar together until light and fluffy. Add eggs 1 at a time, beating well after each addition. Add vanilla extract. Sift dry ingredients together. Add alternately to creamed mixture with half-and-half, starting and ending with dry ingredients. Scrape down sides of bowl and beat at high speed for 1 minute, until batter is smooth. Pour batter into pan and bake for 1½ to 2 hours, or until a cake tester inserted in the middle comes out clean. Cool completely on a wire rack before turning out.
NOTE: You must use a 10 inch tube pan—this is a big cake.

CHOCOLATE POUND CAKE II

1 cup margarine
½ cup Crisco
3 cups sugar
5 eggs
3 cups sifted all-purpose
flour (White Lily is best)

⅓ cup cocoa
1 teaspoon baking powder
½ teaspoon salt
1¼ cups milk
1 tablespoon vanilla
extract

Have margarine and eggs at room temperature. Grease and flour a 10 inch tube pan. Preheat oven to 325°. Cream margarine, Crisco and sugar together until light and fluffy. Beat in eggs 1 at a time, beating well after each addition. Sift dry ingredients together. Add alternately to creamed mixture with milk, starting and ending with dry ingredients. Beat in vanilla; beat until smooth. Pour into prepared pan; smooth top. Bake for 1½ to 2 hours, until top springs back when lightly touched, cake shrinks from sides of pan, and a cake tester inserted in the center comes out clean. Cool cake completely on a wire rack before turning out.

Icing

2 cups sugar
¾ cup evaporated milk
¼ cup light Karo syrup
2 ounces unsweetened
chocolate

½ cup margarine
1 teaspoon vanilla extract

Combine sugar, milk, Karo syrup and chocolate in a *large* heavy pot. Cook over low heat, stirring, until chocolate melts. Bring to a boil; boil until mixture reaches soft ball stage (238°) on a candy thermometer. Beat in vanilla extract and margarine and cool. Beat until a good spreading consistency (be sure not to overbeat) and ice cake.

Lola Park

PIES

BANANA CREAM PIE

9 inch pie crust, baked and
  cooled
2 cups milk
6 tablespoons flour
1 cup sugar
¼ teaspoon salt
4 egg yolks

4 tablespoons unsalted
  butter, softened
1 teaspoon vanilla extract
4 small bananas
1 cup heavy cream
⅓ cup confectioners' sugar

Bring milk to a full rolling boil in a heavy saucepan. Meanwhile, beat flour, sugar, salt and egg yolks together until smooth. When milk comes to a boil (watch carefully so it doesn't boil over) pour gradually into egg yolk mixture, whisking constantly. When all the milk has been added and mixture is smooth, return to saucepan and cook over medium heat, stirring constantly with a wooden spoon, until mixture comes to a boil and is very thick. Remove from heat and stir in butter and vanilla. Strain if custard is lumpy. Place a piece of plastic wrap directly on the surface of the custard and cool 15 minutes. Slice 2 of the bananas in ¼ inch slices and arrange on the bottom of the pie shell. Cover evenly with half the custard. Arrange remaining bananas over custard layer and cover evenly with remaining custard. Cover with wax paper and refrigerate 2 hours. Beat heavy cream with an electric mixer on high speed until soft peaks form. Gradually add confectioners' sugar on low speed, then beat on high speed until cream is thick. Spread over pie and serve.

BOURBON PIE

9 inch pie crust, unbaked
3 eggs
1 cup firmly packed light
  brown sugar

½ cup light Karo syrup
¼ cup butter, melted
½ teaspoon salt
¼ cup bourbon

Preheat oven to 375°. Whisk ingredients together until smooth. Pour into pie crust. Bake 40 to 50 minutes, until set and a knife inserted in the center comes out clean. Cool on a wire rack.

COFFEE ICE CREAM SUNDAE PIE

Crust

½ **package Nabisco Famous Chocolate Wafers, crushed**

¼ **cup butter or margarine, melted**

Preheat oven to 350°. Combine cookie crumbs and butter. This can be done in a food processor. Press onto bottom and sides of a 9 inch pie pan. Bake for 7 to 8 minutes, until set. Cool.

Filling

½ **gallon best-quality coffee ice cream, slightly softened**

1 **cup fudge sauce, store-bought or homemade, see Index**

Spoon half of ice cream into pie crust. Spread fudge sauce over ice cream. Spoon remaining ice cream on top, mounding it in center and pressing down to firm. Freeze until hard.

Topping

1 **cup heavy cream, whipped and sweetened to taste**

Fudge sauce, heated
½ **cup chopped pecans**
8 **maraschino cherries**

To serve, cut pie in 8 slices. Spoon or pipe whipped cream on each slice; spoon hot fudge over whipped cream. Sprinkle with nuts. Top with a cherry.

PEANUT BUTTER CREAM PIE

9 inch pie crust, baked and cooled
¼ cup creamy peanut butter
½ cup confectioners' sugar
1 cup sugar
4 tablespoons cornstarch
¼ teaspoon salt
1 (13 oz.) can evaporated milk
4 egg yolks, beaten
1½ cups hot water
¼ cup butter, softened
1 teaspoon vanilla extract
4 egg whites
¼ teaspoon cream of tartar
4 tablespoons sugar

Rub peanut butter and confectioners' sugar between fingers until crumbly and well combined. Spread in bottom of pie shell, reserving 1 tablespoon if desired for garnish. Mix sugar, cornstarch and salt in heavy saucepan until well mixed. Whisk in evaporated milk and egg yolks. Place over medium heat; whisk in hot water slowly. Cook, whisking constantly, until mixture comes to a boil and thickens enough to stand a spoon in. Remove from heat, stir in butter and vanilla and beat until smooth. Pour custard over peanut butter in pie shell. Beat egg whites and cream of tartar until soft peaks form. Beat in sugar 1 tablespoon at a time and continue beating until stiff but not dry. Spread meringue over custard filling, making sure to bring all the way out to crust. Bake at 350° for 10 to 15 minutes, until meringue is browned.

Lisa Bonfield

BLACK BOTTOM PIE

Crust

½ package Nabisco Famous Chocolate Wafers, crushed
¼ cup butter or margarine, melted

Preheat oven to 350°. Combine cookie crumbs and butter. This can be done in a food processor. Press onto bottom and sides of a 9 inch pie pan. Bake for 7 to 8 minutes, until set. Cool.

Filling

1 envelope unflavored gelatin	½ cup all-purpose flour
¼ cup cold water	2 ounces baking chocolate
4 cups milk	1 teaspoon vanilla extract
5 eggs, separated	½ cup Myers's dark rum
¾ cup sugar	¼ teaspoon cream of tartar
	¼ cup sugar

Dissolve gelatin in cold water and set aside to soften. Bring the milk to a rolling boil in a heavy saucepan. Be careful that it doesn't boil over. Meanwhile, beat the egg yolks and ¾ cup sugar with a wire whisk until thick. Beat in the flour until smooth. When the milk boils, pour it slowly and carefully into the egg mixture, whisking constantly. Whisk until smooth, pour the mixture back into the milk pan and return to heat. Bring to a boil over medium heat, whisking constantly. Reduce heat and cook for 2 to 3 minutes, stirring constantly to prevent scorching. Place the chocolate in a bowl. Pour 2½ cups of hot custard over the chocolate. Immediately place a piece of plastic wrap directly onto the surface of the custard to prevent a skin from forming. If you fail to do this, you will have lumps in your pie. Let sit until chocolate is melted, add vanilla extract, and stir to blend. Replace plastic wrap. Cool to room temperature and fill pie crust, spreading chocolate custard up to edge of crust. Refrigerate. Add gelatin to remaining hot custard to melt. Cover with plastic wrap as for chocolate custard. Cool. Add rum. Refrigerate, stirring occasionally, until custard begins to thicken to about the consistency of unbeaten egg whites. Beat egg whites and cream of tartar until they form soft peaks. Beat in sugar; continue beating until peaks are stiff but not dry. Fold thickened rum custard into egg whites and mound on top of chocolate custard. If the rum mixture does not set up—highly possible in a hot kitchen—refrigerate, stirring frequently with a rubber spatula, until it thickens enough to mound. Refrigerate uncovered 4 to 6 hours or overnight. Garnish with whipped cream and tiny chocolate chips—and a cherry! Serves 8.

FROZEN LEMON PIE

Crust

30 vanilla wafers, crushed
½ cup blanched almonds,
ground
¼ teaspoon almond
extract

¼ cup butter or margarine,
melted

Mix cookie crumbs, ground almonds and almond extract with butter or margarine. This can be done in a food processor. Press into a 9 inch pie pan. Bake at 375° for 8 minutes. Cool on rack.

Filling

4 eggs, separated
1 (15 oz.) can sweetened
condensed milk
1 (6 oz.) can frozen
lemonade concentrate,
thawed

½ cup heavy cream,
whipped

Beat egg yolks with a whisk. Add sweetened condensed milk and lemonade and whisk until smooth. Beat egg whites until stiff but not dry. Fold whipped cream into lemon mixture. Fold lemon mixture into egg whites. Pour into pie crust and freeze 8 hours or overnight. 10 to 15 minutes before serving, remove pie from freezer. Garnish if desired with sweetened whipped cream, twisted lemon slices and maraschino cherries.
NOTE: The Pirates' House uses a special almond meal which is not available in stores. This is a fairly close approximation of the crust. Serves 8.

PRALINE ICE CREAM SUNDAE PIE

Crust

½ package Nabisco
  Famous Chocolate
  Wafers, crushed

¼ cup butter or margarine,
  melted

Preheat oven to 350°. Combine cookie crumbs and butter. This can be done in a food processor. Press onto bottom and sides of a 9 inch pie pan. Bake for 7 to 8 minutes, until set. Cool.

Filling

½ gallon best-quality
  praline ice cream,
  slightly softened

1 cup (½ package) Heath
  Bits 'o Brickle

Spoon half of ice cream into pie crust. Sprinkle Bits 'o Brickle over ice cream. Spoon remaining ice cream on top, mounding it in center and pressing down to firm. Freeze until hard.

Topping

1 cup heavy cream,
  whipped and sweetened
  to taste
Fudge sauce, homemade
  or store-bought, heated
  (see Index)

½ cup chopped pecans, or
  leftover Bits 'o Brickle
8 maraschino cherries

To serve, cut pie into 8 slices. Spoon or pipe whipped cream on each slice; spoon hot fudge sauce over whipped cream. Sprinkle 1 tablespoon pecans or Bits 'o Brickle on top. And of course, no Pirates' House dessert would be complete without a cherry!

SWEET POTATO PIE

Two 8 inch pie crusts,
   unbaked
3 cups mashed, boiled and
   peeled sweet potatoes
   (use food processor or
   mixer)

¼ cup butter
1 cup sugar
2 eggs
3 to 4 teaspoons allspice

Preheat oven to 325°. Mix all ingredients in food processor or mixer until smooth. Pour into pie crusts. Bake until crust is brown, about 45 minutes. Cool and refrigerate.

Marie Driggers

GRASSHOPPER PIE

Crust

½ package Nabisco
   Famous Chocolate
   Wafers, crushed

¼ cup butter or margarine,
   melted

Preheat oven to 350°. Combine cookie crumbs and butter. This can be done in a food processor. Press onto bottom and sides of a 9 inch pie pan. Bake for 7 to 8 minutes, until set. Cool.

Filling

1 envelope unflavored
   gelatin
¼ cup cold water
4 cups milk
5 eggs, separated
¾ cup sugar
½ cup all-purpose flour
2 ounces unsweetened
   chocolate
1 teaspoon vanilla extract

2 tablespoons creme de
   cacao
4 tablespoons green crème
   de menthe
2 to 3 drops oil of
   peppermint (buy at
   drugstore)
¼ teaspoon cream of tartar
¼ cup sugar

Dissolve gelatin in cold water and set aside to soften. Bring the milk to a rolling boil in a heavy saucepan. Be careful that it doesn't boil over. Meanwhile, beat the egg yolks and ¾ cup sugar with a wire whisk until thick. Beat in the flour until smooth. When the milk boils, pour it slowly and carefully into the egg mixture, whisking constantly. Whisk until smooth, pour the mixture back into the milk pan, and return to heat. Bring to a boil over medium heat, whisking constantly. Reduce heat and cook for 2 to 3 minutes, stirring constantly to prevent scorching. Place the chocolate in a bowl. Pour 2½ cups of hot custard over the chocolate. Immediately place a piece of plastic wrap directly onto the surface of the custard to prevent a skin from forming. If you fail to do this, you will have lumps in your pie. Let sit until chocolate is melted, add vanilla extract, and stir to blend. Replace plastic wrap. Cool to room temperature and fill pie crust, spreading chocolate custard up to edge of crust. Refrigerate. Add gelatin to remaining hot custard to melt. Cover with plastic wrap as for chocolate custard. Cool. Add crème de cacao, crème de menthe, and oil of peppermint. Refrigerate, stirring occasionally, until custard begins to thicken to about the consistency of unbeaten egg whites. Beat egg whites and cream of tartar until they form soft peaks. Beat in sugar 1 tablespoon at a time; continue beating until peaks are stiff but not dry. Fold thickened green custard into egg whites and mound on top of chocolate custard. If the green mixture does not set up—highly possible in a hot kitchen—refrigerate, stirring frequently with a rubber spatula, until it thickens enough to mound. Refrigerate uncovered 4 to 6 hours or overnight. Garnish with whipped cream and tiny chocolate chips—and a cherry! Serves 8.

 Freeze extra egg whites in ice cube trays, 1 egg white per cube. Pop into Zip-loc bags to have on hand for soufflés, meringues, angel food cake, etc. Bring to room temperature before using.

PECAN PIE I

9 inch pie crust, unbaked
1 cup sugar
⅔ cup light Karo syrup
3 eggs
¼ teaspoon salt

1 teaspoon vanilla extract
¼ cup butter, melted
1 tablespoon flour
1 cup pecan halves or
    pieces

Preheat oven to 350°. Mix all ingredients except pecans together until smooth. Stir in pecans. Pour into pie crust and bake for 1 hour, or until set. Cool on wire rack to room temperature before slicing.

NOTE: This pie was most popular with our testers.

PECAN PIE II

9 inch pie crust, unbaked
1 cup sugar
½ cup dark Karo syrup
¼ cup butter, melted

3 eggs, well beaten
1 cup pecan halves or
    pieces

Preheat oven to 400°. Mix syrup, sugar and butter. Add eggs and pecans. Pour into pie crust. Bake at 400° for 10 minutes. Reduce heat to 350° and continue baking for 30 to 35 minutes, until set around edges. Pie will not be completely set in middle when done. Cool on a wire rack to room temperature before serving. Refrigerate left-overs.
NOTE: Makes a dark, rich, old-fashioned pie.

Martha Summerour

Sweeten whipped cream with confectioners' sugar. The cornstarch in the sugar helps stabilize the cream, and it holds up longer.

PIRATES' HOUSE PECAN PIE

9 inch pie crust, unbaked
3 eggs
½ cup dark Karo syrup
½ cup whipping cream
1 teaspoon vanilla extract
3 tablespoons bourbon

1 cup sugar
⅛ teaspoon salt
2 tablespoons butter, melted
2 cups chopped pecans

Preheat oven to 375°. Beat eggs well. Beat in all other ingredients until well-blended. Pour into pie shell. Bake on a cookie sheet for 40 minutes, or until center is set. Pie will puff up and then settle. Cool to room temperature and refrigerate. Serve with whipped cream or vanilla or coffee ice cream, or plain.

TOLLHOUSE COOKIE PIE

9 inch pie crust, unbaked
½ cup butter, softened
½ cup sugar
½ cup firmly packed light brown sugar
1 egg
½ teaspoon vanilla extract

1 cup all-purpose flour
½ teaspoon baking soda
½ teaspoon salt
1 (6 oz.) package chocolate chips
½ cup chopped pecans

Preheat oven to 350°. Cream butter and sugar together until light and fluffy. Beat in egg and vanilla until well-blended. Sift dry ingredients together; beat into creamed mixture until smooth. Add chocolate chips and nuts. Spoon into pie crust; bake for 40 to 45 minutes, or until puffed, golden brown, and set on edges. Pie should be set but not hard in middle; it should feel like a quiche. Serve warm with vanilla ice cream or whipped cream.

LEMON CHESS PIE

9 inch pie crust, unbaked
2 cups sugar
1 tablespoon all-purpose
   flour
1 tablespoon cornmeal

4 eggs
¼ cup butter, melted
¼ cup milk
¼ cup grated lemon rind
¼ cup lemon juice

Preheat oven to 350°. Mix ingredients well and pour into pie crust. Bake until brown and set, about 40 to 45 minutes. Cool to room temperature before cutting.
NOTE: ¼ cup lemon rind sounds overpowering, but it's good. You can cheat and give up after grating 4 lemons if it's not quite ¼ cup—close enough!

Lurline Coggeshall

SOUR CREAM PUMPKIN PIE

9 inch pie crust, unbaked
1 (1 lb.) can pumpkin
3 eggs, slightly beaten
1½ cups sour cream
½ cup sugar
½ cup firmly packed light
   brown sugar
2 tablespoons molasses

1 teaspoon cinnamon
½ teaspoon ginger
¼ teaspoon nutmeg
¼ teaspoon ground cloves
1 cup heavy cream,
   whipped and sweetened
   to taste, for garnish

Preheat oven to 425°. Combine filling ingredients and mix well. Pour into pie shell and bake for 15 minutes at 425°. Lower heat to 350° and bake about 50 minutes longer, until firm and a knife inserted in center comes out clean. Cool on wire rack to room temperature and refrigerate. Serve with whipped cream.

Suzanne W. Peterson

FRIED PIES

Filling

½ pound dried peaches   **⅓ to ½ cup sugar**

Cover dried peaches with cold water in a heavy sauce pan. Soak 5 minutes. Pour off water. Barely cover with cold water, bring to a boil, reduce to a simmer, cover and cook until tender, about 1 hour. Add sugar to taste. Mash with a potato masher (do *not* use a food processor.) Chill.

Dough

2 cups White Lily self-   **4 rounded tablespoons**
**   rising flour**   **Crisco**
¾ to 1 cup buttermilk   **Crisco for frying**

Sift flour into a mixing bowl. Add shortening and mix with fingers until crumbly. Add milk as needed until a soft dough is formed. It should not be too wet. Knead on a floured surface until firm and not sticky, about 1 minute. Wrap dough in plastic wrap and let rest in refrigerator at least 30 minutes. Melt enough Crisco to come ½ inch up side of electric skillet. Heat to 375°. Pinch off a piece of dough the size of an egg and roll into a smooth ball with your hands. Roll out on a floured surface, flouring as necessary to keep from sticking, into a 5 to 6 inch circle. Place 2 tablespoons filling on one half of the circle, leaving a 1 inch border. Fold plain half over. Run the edge of a saucer around the edge of the pie to trim. Seal edges with a floured fork. Pierce top of pie with fork. Place carefully in hot fat, cook on 1 side until golden, turn and cook other side until golden. You can cook 3 to 4 pies at a time. They are rather difficult to turn—try sliding them up the side of the pan and flipping them over. Drain on paper towels. You may spread the tops with butter if desired.
NOTE: Try dried apples, pears, or apricots for a change. Makes 8 pies.

Lola Park

MAMMY'S PIE CRUST

3½ cups all-purpose flour
1½ teaspoons salt
1 cup Crisco
1 egg

1 teaspoon vinegar
8 tablespoons
(approximately) cold
water

Sift flour and salt into a bowl. Add Crisco; work into flour with fingers or pastry blender until crumbly. Beat egg and vinegar together, add water and mix well. Make a well in center of flour mixture, pour in liquid and mix until dough is formed. Add more water if necessary. It's okay to have some flour left in bowl. Knead dough on floured counter about 10 times, just to mix well. Do not overwork dough. Divide in thirds, press each third out into a 5 inch circle, wrap and refrigerate at least 1 hour before rolling out on a floured surface. Extra pie crust may be wrapped tightly and frozen. Bring to room temperature before rolling out. **NOTE:** This is an easy pie crust to handle. It rarely sticks or cracks, but it must be refrigerated before rolling out.

May DeMaurice

 Always refrigerate pie crust at least 1 hour before rolling out. It won't fight you, or shrink while baking.

DESSERTS

PIRATES' HOUSE CHEESECAKE

Crust

30 vanilla wafers, crushed
½ cup blanched almonds, ground

¼ teaspoon almond extract
¼ cup butter or margarine, melted

Filling

3 (8 oz.) packages cream cheese, softened
1 cup sugar, divided

4 eggs, separated
1 teaspoon vanilla extract

Topping

2 cups sour cream
1 teaspoon vanilla extract

⅔ cup sugar

Mix cookie crumbs, ground almonds and almond extract with butter. Press into bottom of a 10 inch springform pan. Preheat oven to 350°. Beat cream cheese until smooth. Beat in ½ cup sugar. Add egg yolks 1 at a time. Add vanilla extract. This can be done in a food processor. Beat egg whites in an electric mixer until they form soft peaks. Beat in ½ cup sugar 1 tablespoon at a time; continue beating until peaks are stiff but not dry. Fold cream cheese mixture into egg whites on low speed. Pour into pan. Bake for 50 to 60 minutes, until cake is set but still soft in the middle, and top is golden brown. Cake will puff up, then sink and crack. Do not be alarmed. Cool on a rack for 30 to 40 minutes. Mix topping ingredients together until smooth. Pour topping over cake; return to oven for 10 minutes to glaze. Cool to room temperature and refrigerate, preferably overnight. Top with fresh or frozen strawberries or peaches, sweetened to taste, or with cherry or blueberry pie filling. Serves 10.

CHOCOLATE CHEESECAKE

Crust

½ package (20) Nabisco
Famous Chocolate
Wafers, crushed

¼ cup butter or margarine,
melted

Combine cookie crumbs and butter. This can be done in a food processor. Press onto bottom of a 10 inch springform pan.

Filling

3 (8 oz.) packages cream
cheese, softened
1 cup sugar, divided
4 eggs, separated
1 teaspoon vanilla extract
1 (12 oz.) package semi-
sweet chocolate chips,
melted

1 cup heavy cream,
whipped and sweetened
to taste
Cocoa

Preheat oven to 350°. Beat cream cheese until smooth. Beat in ½ cup sugar. Beat in egg yolks 1 at a time. Add vanilla extract. Beat in melted chocolate. This all can be done in a food processor. Beat egg whites in an electric mixer until they form soft peaks. Beat in ½ cup sugar 1 tablespoon at a time; continue beating until peaks are stiff but not dry. Fold chocolate-cream cheese mixture into egg whites on low speed. Pour into pan. Bake for 50 to 60 minutes, until set. Cake will puff up and then sink and crack. Do not be alarmed. Cool on wire rack to room temperature, preferably overnight. Serve with whipped cream (necessary to cut richness) with cocoa sifted on top. Mr. Traub says for a super great treat, freeze the cheesecake for several hours, then serve with whipped cream. Serves 8 to 10—cut slices thin or you may overdose on chocolate.

BANANAS WITH COCONUT

4 to 6 medium bananas   **1 cup coconut**
½ cup orange juice   **1 tablespoon butter**
¼ cup light brown sugar

Preheat oven to 425°. Peel bananas and cut in half lengthwise. Arrange cut-side down in a well-buttered 9x13 inch baking dish, 1 layer deep. Combine orange juice and brown sugar; pour over bananas. Dot with butter. Sprinkle coconut over top. Bake until bananas are soft and coconut is browned, about 15 minutes. Serve hot with cold custard, see below.
NOTE: Really delicious—and so simple! Makes a good brunch dish.

Nancy McWhinnie

CUSTARD SAUCE

4 egg yolks   **1½ cups milk**
½ cup sugar   **¼ cup cold milk or cream**
½ teaspoon vanilla extract

Place egg yolks, sugar and vanilla extract in a bowl. Whisk 3 to 4 minutes until pale yellow and very thick. When mixture is lifted with the whisk, it should fall back on itself like a ribbon. Bring milk to a rolling boil. Pour gradually into egg mixture, whisking constantly and rapidly so eggs won't scramble. Combine well and pour into milk pan. Cook for a few minutes over medium heat, stirring with a wooden spoon, until the mixture thickens slightly and coats the spoon. Test by running your finger across the spoon—there should be a distinct mark. Do not overcook or eggs will scramble. When sauce is done, add the cold milk. Strain into a cold bowl. Cool, stirring once in a while. Refrigerate until ready to serve.

BANANAS FOSTER

1 banana, sliced
1 tablespoon butter
⅓ cup dark brown sugar
Dash cinnamon
2 tablespoons banana
   liqueur

2 tablespoons brandy
Best-quality vanilla ice
   cream

Heat a heavy skillet. Add butter, sugar, cinnamon and banana liqueur. Cook sauce, stirring constantly, until bubbling—don't let it get too thick. Add bananas and stir to coat with sauce. Push bananas to back of pan and pull sauce forward. Pour brandy into pan, heat and ignite. Serve hot over vanilla ice cream. Serves 1 glutton or 2 normal people. Doubles easily.

NOTE: If you have a chafing dish with a good hot flame you may do the cooking tableside, but it's easier to invite your guests into the kitchen. Make sure someone is strategically placed by the switch to douse the lights when it's time to flame the brandy.

Scott Zeitler

FRUIT COBBLER

½ cup butter
1 cup sugar
1 cup self-rising flour

¾ cup milk
1 quart fruit

Preheat oven to 350°. Melt butter in a 9x13 inch baking dish. Mix dry ingredients, add milk and pour over melted butter. Spread fruit on top and bake for 1 hour, or until very brown. Serve with your favorite hard sauce or vanilla ice cream.

NOTE: Jenne uses fruit her mother puts up, but fresh peaches, blackberries or blueberries, sweetened to taste, are great. Try frozen peaches or blackberries or canned cherries too.

Jenne Ficke

APPLE CRISP

4 cups baking apples,
　peeled, cored and sliced
1 tablespoon lemon juice
⅓ cup all-purpose flour
1 cup quick oats,
　uncooked

½ cup firmly packed light
　brown sugar
½ teaspoon salt
1 teaspoon cinnamon
⅓ cup butter, melted

Preheat oven to 375°. Combine apple slices and lemon juice; spread in bottom of flat casserole dish. Combine remaining ingredients until well blended. Spread on top of apples. Bake for 30 to 45 minutes, or until apples are soft and topping is brown. Serve warm with vanilla ice cream. Great cold, too, straight out of the refrigerator. Serves 4.

Suzanne W. Peterson

PERSIMMON PUDDING

2 cups persimmon pulp
1 cup firmly packed light
　brown sugar
3 eggs, beaten
½ cup butter or margarine,
　melted
2½ cups milk
1¼ cups all-purpose flour

1 teaspoon baking powder
1 teaspoon baking soda
½ teaspoon salt
2 teaspoons cinnamon
¼ teaspoon nutmeg
1 cup heavy cream,
　whipped and sweetened
　to taste, for garnish

Preheat oven to 325°. Sift dry ingredients together. Combine all ingredients until smooth. Pour into a 9x9 inch baking dish. Bake for 1 hour, or until firm. Serve warm or cold with whipped cream.

Suzanne W. Peterson

FRUIT PIZZA

Dough

1 cup butter, softened
1 cup sugar
1 cup firmly packed light
   brown sugar
2 eggs
1 teaspoon vanilla

2 cups all-purpose flour
1 cup whole-wheat flour
1 teaspoon baking soda
½ teaspoon baking powder
1 teaspoon salt

Preheat oven to 375°. Cream butter and sugar together. Beat in eggs and vanilla until smooth. Sift dry ingredients together; beat into creamed mixture. Form into ball; flatten onto a 12 inch round baking sheet. Bake until golden brown, about 15 minutes. Cool on sheet.

Topping

1 (8 oz.) package cream
   cheese, softened
1 cup honey

Fresh fruit in season
   (blueberries, green
   grapes, cherries,
   strawberries, peaches,
   bananas, plums, kiwi
   fruit, etc.)

Mix cream cheese and honey until smooth. Spread on cookie right before serving, and top with whatever fruits you want, laid out in a decorative pattern.

Henry Gaede

 The best way to melt chocolate is on a plate over a pot of simmering water. Baking chocolate can be melted in its wrapper.

CAFÉ GLACÉ

1½ cups milk
¾ cup sugar
1 teaspoon vanilla extract
1½ cups cold coffee

¾ cup heavy cream
Sweetened whipped cream
   for garnish

Combine milk and sugar in a saucepan and bring to a boil, stirring until sugar is dissolved. Remove from heat, add vanilla extract and let stand until cold. Combine milk mixture, coffee and cream, mixing well; pour into a metal pan. Freeze until hard. Put in blender or food processor and process until mushy. Spoon into wine glasses or champagne flutes. Top with spirals of whipped cream. Serve immediately. Serves 4 to 6.

PLUM PUDDING

3 cups dark raisins
1½ cups golden raisins
1 cup dry sherry
¾ cup butter, softened
1 cup firmly packed dark
   brown sugar
2 cups breadcrumbs
2 cups self-rising flour
½ teaspoon salt
1 teaspoon cinnamon
½ teaspoon nutmeg
½ teaspoon ground cloves
½ teaspoon allspice

½ teaspoon mace
Rind of 1 orange
Rind of 1 lemon
¾ cup finely chopped suet
1½ cups currants
1 cup shredded carrots
1 large tart apple, peeled,
   cored and finely
   chopped
2 cups pecans
4 eggs
Juice of 1 orange
½ cup ale or stout

Heat sherry until steaming. Pour over raisins and let soak a few hours or overnight. In a very large mixing bowl, cream butter and brown sugar with a wooden spoon until smooth. Sift flour with salt and spices. Add breadcrumbs, flour, orange and lemon rind, suet, currants, carrots, apple and pecans to bowl. Mix with hands until well blended. Make a well in the center of the mixture. Beat eggs until frothy; beat in orange juice and ale. Pour into well; mix with hands until well blended. Butter a 2½ to 3 quart pudding bowl, or 2 or 3 smaller ones. Pour pudding into bowl; mixture should fill mold completely. Cut a large circle of parchment paper or brown paper 8 to 10 inches wider than diameter of bowl. Cut a circle of aluminum foil the same size as the paper. Butter parchment paper, place over pudding and cover with aluminum foil. Tie very securely around bowl with string—cover must be on tight. Or, use a pudding mold with a tight-fitting lid. Place a small round rack (a vegetable steamer works fine) in a large deep stock pot or kettle. Place pudding bowl on rack and fill halfway up side of bowl with boiling water. Cover pot and steam pudding 7 hours for large bowl or 5 hours for smaller ones. Water must remain boiling and you will need to add more boiling water occasionally to maintain correct water level. When pudding is done, remove from pot and cool. Replace paper and foil with plastic wrap and foil and store in a cool dark place. You may pour on brandy from time to time if you like. Before serving, steam pudding for 1 hour to heat through. Turn out on a platter, pour ½ cup warm brandy over the pudding, ignite and bear triumphantly to the table. Serve with your favorite hard sauce.

NOTE: Your butcher will probably give you some suet if you ask nicely. Chop it in a food processor or grind it in a meat grinder. You may wrap a small favor of some kind (a dime store ring is perfect) in foil and stir into batter. The person who finds it will have luck in the coming year. Plum pudding should be made at least 2 months before Christmas. Some people make it a year ahead. Dousing it occasionally with brandy improves the product, plus it reminds you of Christmas even in July! Serves at least 20.

PIRATES' HOUSE TRIFLE

1 (6 oz.) box instant vanilla
 pudding
3 cups milk
1 cup sherry
1 Duncan Hines angel food
 cake, made according to
 package directions (or
 bought or leftover angel,
 sponge or pound cake)

1 cup heavy cream
2 tablespoons
 confectioners' sugar
¼ teaspoon vanilla extract

Mix pudding according to package directions. Refrigerate until thickened. Add sherry and blend well. Refrigerate. Whip cream with sugar and vanilla until it stands in soft peaks. Do not let it get too stiff. Using a serrated knife, slice cake horizontally in ½ inch thick slices. Pour half the pudding into a glass soufflé dish or serving dish. Cover with a layer of cake slices, piecing them together to fit. Cover cake with half the whipped cream. Repeat with pudding, cake and whipped cream. Cover and refrigerate until serving time.
NOTE: This is pretty in a glass bowl, especially layered with fresh or frozen raspberries or raspberry jam (or any other seasonal fruit.) It improves with age—within reason! If you are feeling especially profligate, flavor the whipped cream with cognac!

PINEAPPLE ICE BOX CAKE

1 (12 oz.) box vanilla
 wafers, crushed
1 (8 oz.) can crushed
 pineapple
2 envelopes unflavored
 gelatin
¼ cup cold water
1 cup sugar

1 cup butter or margarine,
 softened
3 eggs, separated
1 cup chopped pecans
½ pint heavy cream,
 whipped and sweetened
 to taste

Drain pineapple and add enough water to juice to make 1 cup. Soften gelatin in ¼ cup cold water. Heat 1 cup juice and water. Dissolve gelatin in hot liquid; cool. Set aside 1 cup vanilla wafers. Cover the bottom of a 9x13 inch dish with more crumbs, reserving some for topping. Cream sugar and butter until fluffy; add egg yolks and beat until smooth. Add cooled gelatin mixture. Fold in pineapple, 1 cup crumbs and nuts. Beat egg whites until stiff but not dry; fold into pineapple mixture. Pour over crumbs in dish and top with remaining crumbs. Refrigerate until set. Cut in squares and serve with whipped cream. Serves 8 to 10.

May DeMaurice

POTS DE CRÈME AU CHOCOLAT

**1 (6 oz.) package semi-
   sweet chocolate chips**
2 eggs
**2 tablespoons very strong
   coffee**
1 tablespoon dark rum

**1 tablespoon Grand
   Marnier**
¾ cup milk
**Sweetened whipped cream
   for garnish (optional)**

Place chocolate chips, eggs, coffee, rum and Grand Marnier in blender or food processor and process until chocolate is finely ground. Bring milk to a *full* boil. Turn on blender or food processor and pour boiling milk onto chocolate mixture. Process until chocolate is dissolved. Pour into pots de crème cups, custard cups or Chinese tea cups, or a small soufflé dish, and chill for 2 hours. Serve with whipped cream if desired.
NOTE: If you use skim milk and omit the whipped cream, you will have a delicious diet dessert at 80 calories per serving. This is one dessert that works better in a blender than a food processor, but the secret is in having the milk hot enough. Serves 8 dieters or 4 to 6 piggies.

FRENCH BREAD PUDDING

1 loaf stale French bread, torn in chunks (about 6 cups)
1 quart milk
3 eggs, beaten

2 cups sugar
1 tablespoon vanilla extract
1 cup raisins
2 tablespoons butter

Soak bread in milk for 30 minutes. Mush up with hands until well-mixed. Add eggs, sugar and vanilla and stir until well blended. Stir in raisins. Preheat oven to 350°. Melt butter in baking dish; pour in bread mixture. Bake for about 1 hour, or until firm and golden brown and a knife inserted in the center comes out clean. Serve warm with whiskey sauce. Refrigerate leftovers.

NOTE: Great for breakfast!

Whiskey Sauce

½ cup butter, softened
1 cup sugar

1 egg, well beaten
1 to 2 ounces bourbon

In a heavy pan over low heat, beat sugar and butter until fluffy and hot with a wooden spoon. Remove from heat; whisk in egg rapidly drop by drop so it doesn't curdle. Cool and whisk in bourbon.

NOTE: Sauce may separate but will whisk right back up. Refrigerate leftover sauce.

BEST VANILLA ICE CREAM

4 eggs
2½ cups sugar
1½ quarts milk
1 quart heavy cream
1½ tablespoons vanilla extract

½ teaspoon salt
4 cups crushed peaches, strawberries, bananas, etc., sweetened to taste, optional

Beat eggs until light and fluffy. Add sugar gradually, ¼ cup at a time, beating well after each addition. If mixture becomes too stiff, add a little milk to make beating easier. Add remaining ingredients and pour into a gallon freezer. If freezer is not ⅔ full, add more milk. Freeze in ice cream churn according to manufacturer's instructions.

NOTE: If you add fresh fruit, omit the vanilla, crush fruit, sweeten it well, and let stand 30 minutes. If fruit is not well-sweetened, it will freeze harder than the ice cream. (If using peaches or bananas, add juice of 1 lemon.) Either stir fruit into ice cream half-way through churning, or fold in at the end before packing.

Martha Summerour

ELEGANT ICE CREAM

5 egg yolks
2 cups sugar
1 tablespoon flour
2 cups milk
4 teaspoons lemon juice
2 cups sour cream

1 quart strawberries,
    crushed and sweetened
or
1 quart peaches, peeled,
    crushed and sweetened

Whisk egg yolks, sugar and flour together until thick and smooth. Heat milk in a large saucepan to a full rolling boil. Pour slowly into sugar-egg yolk mixture, whisking constantly, until well-blended. Return mixture to milk pan and cook, stirring with a wooden spoon, until mixture thickens slightly and a finger drawn across the spoon leaves a clear trail. Strain into a bowl, cool, and combine with lemon juice, sour cream and fruit. Freeze in ice cream churn according to manufacturer's instructions.

Edna Traub

GINGER ICE CREAM

4 cups milk
10 egg yolks
1½ cups sugar
5 tablespoons chopped
  candied ginger

1 to 1½ cups heavy cream,
  whipped until it holds a
  soft shape

Bring the milk to a full rolling boil. Beat the egg yolks with the sugar in a bowl until thick and light. Whisk in the hot milk slowly—don't whisk too hard or you will get too much foam—pour into milk pan, and return to heat. Heat gently, stirring constantly with a wooden spoon, until the custard thickens slightly; if you draw your finger across the back of the spoon, it will leave a clear trail. The foam should subside by the time the custard is done. Do not overcook or boil the custard or it will curdle. Remove the custard at once from the heat, strain it into a bowl, and stir in the chopped candied ginger. Let cool and pour into a churn. After about 5 minutes of churning, or when the ice cream is partly set, add the lightly whipped cream to the mixture and continue churning until set. Remove dasher, taste, and either stir in ginger from bottom of freezer or throw away if ice cream is flavored enough. Serve immediately or replace lid covered with aluminum foil, repack freezer with ice and salt, wrap freezer in towels or a blanket, and let ice cream cure 1 to 2 hours. Serve plain or in cream puffs, with raspberry or strawberry purée—use blender or food processor to purée fresh berries, sweetened lightly if necessary.

No need to buy a double boiler. Just put a heat-proof bowl in a skillet full of water and go from there. If you are brave and stir carefully, there aren't many recipes you need to use a double boiler for.

COFFEE ICE CREAM

4 eggs
1½ cups sugar
½ cup sweetened
  condensed milk
¼ teaspoon salt

2 quarts heavy cream,
  divided
2 cups milk
1 teaspoon vanilla extract
¼ cup instant coffee

Whisk eggs, sugar, condensed milk and salt together until thick and smooth. Heat 2 cups cream with milk to a full rolling boil. Slowly pour into egg mixture, whisking constantly. Return to milk pan; cook, stirring with a wooden spoon, until mixture thickens slightly and a finger drawn across the spoon leaves a clear trail. Strain into a bowl; whisk in coffee until dissolved. Add vanilla and remaining cream. Cool; freeze in ice cream churn according to manufacturer's instructions.

Julia Roberts

FUDGE SAUCE

4 ounces unsweetened
  baking chocolate
1½ cups sugar
1 cup cream or evaporated
  milk

4 tablespoons butter
1 teaspoon vanilla extract

Combine chocolate, sugar and cream in a heavy saucepan. Cook, stirring constantly, over medium heat until chocolate is melted. Raise heat, bring to a boil and boil 6 minutes, stirring constantly. Remove from heat; beat in butter and vanilla. Serve hot or cold. Keeps indefinitely in the refrigerator. Reheat in a bowl or pan over hot water, or in a microwave oven.
NOTE: Easy to make, and a lot better than store-bought.

Edna Traub

COOKIES
AND
CANDY

MOTHER EDEL'S CHOCOLATE BROWNIES

3 ounces unsweetened
  baking chocolate
¾ cup butter
1½ cups sugar
3 eggs, well-beaten

¾ cup all-purpose flour
⅛ teaspoon salt
1 teaspoon vanilla extract
¾ cup chopped pecans

Preheat oven to 350°. Melt chocolate and butter over low heat in a heavy saucepan, stirring often. Watch carefully—chocolate burns easily. When melted, remove from heat and stir in sugar. Beat in eggs. Add flour and salt; beat until smooth. Beat in vanilla and nuts. Pour into an 8x8 inch pan—batter will be thin. Bake 30 minutes. Remove from oven and cool on wire rack before cutting.

NOTE: These are gooey brownies—a veritable piece of heaven for chocolate lovers. Store in the refrigerator. Makes 16 brownies.

Danyse Edel

BUTTERSCOTCH BROWNIES

½ cup butter, softened
1 (1 lb.) box light brown
  sugar
2 eggs
2 cups all-purpose flour

1 teaspoon baking powder
½ teaspoon salt
2 teaspoons vanilla
1½ cups chopped pecans

Preheat oven to 350°. Grease an 8x8 inch baking pan. Cream butter and sugar together until light and fluffy. Beat in eggs 1 at a time. Sift dry ingredients together, add to creamed mixture and beat until smooth. Beat in vanilla and nuts. Pour batter into baking pan; smooth top. Bake for 40 minutes, or until golden brown, brownies shrink from side of pan, and a cake tester inserted in center comes out clean. Cool on wire rack. Cut into 16 squares.

CHOCOLATE CRINKLES

½ cup Crisco
1⅔ cups sugar
2 teaspoons vanilla extract
2 eggs
2 ounces unsweetened
  chocolate, melted
2 cups sifted all-purpose
  flour

2 teaspoons baking
  powder
½ teaspoon salt
¼ cup milk
½ cup chopped walnuts or
  pecans
Sifted confectioners' sugar

Cream shortening and sugar until fluffy. Beat in eggs and vanilla until well blended. Beat in chocolate. Sift dry ingredients together. Add alternately with milk to chocolate mixture. Beat until smooth. Add nuts. Chill for 3 hours. Preheat oven to 350°. Form cookies into 1 inch balls; roll in confectioners' sugar. Place 2 inches apart on greased cookie sheets. Bake for 12 to 15 minutes. Let cookies set on sheets for 2 to 3 minutes; remove and cool on wire racks. Cookies should be soft—do not overbake. Makes approximately 4 dozen cookies.

Jean Roche

CHRISTMAS BOURBON BALLS

1 (12 oz.) box vanilla
  wafers, crushed—3 cups
1 cup confectioners' sugar
2 tablespoons cocoa
1½ cups finely chopped
  pecans

3 tablespoons light Karo
  syrup
½ cup bourbon

Combine ingredients and mix well. Roll into 1-inch balls. Roll in sifted confectioners' sugar. Store in an airtight container.
NOTE: Definitely not for the kiddies. These improve with age—within reason. Makes approximately 4 dozen.

Suzanne D. Peterson

DATE PINWHEELS

½ cup butter, softened
½ cup sugar
½ cup firmly packed light
   brown sugar
1 egg

½ teaspoon vanilla
2 cups all-purpose flour
½ teaspoon salt
½ teaspoon soda

Cream butter and sugar together until fluffy. Add egg and vanilla; beat well. Sift dry ingredients together; beat into creamed mixture until well blended. Chill. Divide chilled dough in half. On a floured surface, roll each half into a 12x8 inch rectangle. Dough is not easy to work with—flour the rolling pin as well as the work surface, and be patient. You may have to resort to piecing it together and squashing it with your fingers. Spread each half gently with half the filling. Roll up like a jelly roll, starting with the long side. Wrap in plastic wrap and chill several hours, or freeze. Preheat oven to 400°. Slice rolls ¼ inch thick and place 2 inches apart on well-greased cookie sheets. Bake for 8 minutes. Let cookies set on sheets 3 to 4 minutes before removing. The filling wants to stick to the cookie sheets—wipe your spatula often and be firm. Cool on wire racks and store in airtight container.

Date Filling

1 pound chopped pitted
   dates
½ cup sugar

½ cup water
½ cup finely chopped
   walnuts or pecans

Combine dates, sugar and water and cook over medium heat until mixture boils and thickens slightly. Just before using, stir in nuts. Makes 4 dozen cookies.

Jean Roche

In the South, "nuts" in a recipe means pecans; in the North, it means walnuts.

SARAH'S CHOCOLATE CHIP COOKIES

½ cup unsalted butter
½ cup Crisco
¾ cup sugar
¾ cup firmly packed light
 brown sugar
1 teaspoon vanilla extract
2 eggs
1¼ cups all-purpose flour

1 cup whole-wheat flour
1 teaspoon baking soda
1 teaspoon salt
½ cup wheat germ
1 (12 oz.) bag *real* semi-
 sweet chocolate chips
1 cup chopped nuts

Have butter and eggs at room temperature. Place oven rack in middle of oven. Preheat oven to 375°. In an electric mixer, cream butter and Crisco until soft. Add sugar, brown sugar and vanilla extract; beat until fluffy. Add eggs 1 at a time, beating well after each addition. Sift together all-purpose flour, baking soda and salt. Stir in whole-wheat flour and wheat germ. Add flour to creamed mixture; beat well. Stir in chocolate chips and nuts. Drop by teaspoonfuls onto ungreased cookie sheets, leaving 1½ inches between cookies. Bake one sheet at a time for 8 to 10 minutes, turning cookie sheet around after 5 minutes to ensure even browning. Remove cookies from sheet and cool on wire racks. Store in an airtight container. Makes 80 to 100 2 inch cookies.

CAROLYN'S COOKIES

½ pound candied
 pineapple, chopped
1 pound candied cherries,
 chopped
1 pound pitted dates,
 snipped
½ cup sherry
1 cup butter, softened

1 cup firmly packed light
 brown sugar
3 eggs
3 cups unbleached all-
 purpose flour
½ teaspoon baking soda
1 tablespoon cinnamon
4 cups chopped pecans

Before chopping, place candied fruit (not dates) in a large bowl. Pour boiling water over fruit to cover, and stir for 20 to 30 seconds to remove preservatives. Drain well and chop. Combine fruit and dates, pour sherry over and stir to mix well. Let stand 30 minutes. Preheat oven to 325°. Cream butter and sugar until light and fluffy. Beat in eggs 1 at a time. Sift dry ingredients together and beat into creamed mixture until smooth. Stir in fruit and nuts. Drop by teaspoonfuls on greased cookie sheets, or bake in 2 inch foil baking cups until golden brown, 25 to 30 minutes. Cool on wire racks. Sprinkle more sherry on top after baking if desired. These keep indefinitely stored in an airtight container—in fact, they improve with age. Makes approximately 72 2 inch cookies.

Brenda Lain

COCONUT CUTIES

1 cup Crisco
1 cup firmly packed light
  brown sugar
1 cup sugar
2 eggs
1 teaspoon vanilla extract
1½ cups all-purpose flour

1 teaspoon baking soda
1 teaspoon salt
3 cups quick oats,
  uncooked
1 cup coconut
Sugar

Preheat oven to 375°. Cream Crisco and sugars together until fluffy. Beat in eggs 1 at a time; beat in vanilla extract. Sift dry ingredients together. Beat into creamed mixture. Beat in coconut and oatmeal. Form into small balls. Roll in sugar and place 2 inches apart on ungreased cookie sheets. Bake for 10 to 12 minutes, depending on whether you like soft or crisp cookies. Let cookies set for 1 minute before removing from sheets; then work quickly before cookies become glued to sheets. Cool on wire racks; store in airtight container. Makes 4 dozen.

Jean Roche

GRANDMA'S COOKIES

1 cup butter
2 cups firmly packed light
   brown sugar
2 eggs

3½ cups all-purpose flour
1 teaspoon baking soda
1 cup chopped pecans

Have butter and eggs at room temperature. Cream butter and sugar until light and fluffy. Add eggs 1 at a time, beating well after each addition. Sift together flour and baking soda. Beat into creamed mixture. Stir in nuts. Roll into logs, wrap in waxed paper and chill. Dough must be firm to slice correctly. Cut *very* thin and bake on greased cookie sheets at 400° until lightly browned, about 6 to 8 minutes. Bake one sheet at a time in middle of oven, turn sheet around halfway through baking time and *watch carefully.* Cool on wire racks and store in an airtight container.
NOTE: To freeze, wrap logs in aluminum foil before freezing. Thaw before slicing. Makes approximately 200.

Marsha Peterson

LEMON SPICE BARS

1 cup all-purpose flour
1 teaspoon baking powder
¼ teaspoon cinnamon
¼ teaspoon nutmeg
1 cup quick oats,
   uncooked
1⅓ cups firmly packed
   light brown sugar

¾ cup vegetable oil
2 eggs, slightly beaten
2 teaspoons lemon juice
½ teaspoon vanilla extract
½ cup chopped pecans

Preheat oven to 350°. Grease and flour a 9x13 inch baking pan. Combine first 6 ingredients; stir well. Add oil, eggs, flavorings and nuts; mix thoroughly. Spoon batter into pan; bake for 25 minutes. Remove from oven; spread glaze over top. Let cool and cut into 1x2 inch bars.

Lemon Glaze

1½ to 2 cups confectioners' sugar, sifted	1 tablespoon lemon juice ¼ teaspoon cinnamon 3 tablespoons milk

Combine 1½ cups confectioners' sugar with remaining ingredients and mix until smooth. Beat in more sugar if glaze is not thick enough.

Kit Traub

JONHAGEL

2¼ cups flour	1 cup butter, cut in small
¾ cup sugar	pieces
1 teaspoon baking powder	1 egg yolk
¼ teaspoon salt	1 tablespoon milk
½ teaspoon cinnamon	1 tablespoon cinnamon
2 teaspoons vanilla extract	3 tablespoons sugar
1 egg white	1 cup sliced almonds
1 tablespoon milk	

Sift dry ingredients into a large bowl or straight onto countertop. Make a hole in the center. Place vanilla, egg white and milk in hole. Work in butter with fingers until dough is well-mixed. Divide dough in half, shape into rectangles, wrap and chill. Preheat oven to 375°. Spread half of dough with fingers onto a jelly roll pan. Dough will be thin, but will cover pan, so don't give up. Beat egg yolk and milk together to form a glaze. Brush half the glaze onto dough, sprinkle with half the combined cinnamon and sugar and ½ cup almonds. Bake until brown around the edges, about 15 minutes. Immediately cut into pieces about 2 inches x 3 inches. Cool on wire racks. Repeat process with remaining dough. Makes approximately 48 cookies.

Mia Dietvorst

LEMON SQUARES

1 cup all-purpose flour
½ cup butter, softened
¼ cup confectioners' sugar
2 eggs
1 cup granulated sugar

½ teaspoon baking powder
¼ teaspoon salt
Grated rind of 1 lemon
2 tablespoons lemon juice

Preheat oven to 350⁰. Blend flour, butter and sugar thoroughly. Press evenly on bottom of 8x8 inch pan. Bake 20 minutes. Meanwhile, beat remaining ingredients together until light. Pour over hot crust. Bake about 30 to 35 minutes longer, or until top is golden and *no* imprint remains when touched lightly in center. Cool on wire rack. Cut in 36 squares. Store in refrigerator.

NOTE: For those who like lemon and chocolate, chop 2 (1 oz.) squares unsweetened baking chocolate in food processor. Sprinkle over hot crust before pouring filling over.

GERMAN SPICE COOKIES

2 eggs
1 cup sugar
1 cup all-purpose flour
¼ teaspoon cinnamon
⅛ teaspoon ground cloves
⅛ teaspoon ground
  cardamom

¾ cup blanched almonds,
  ground
¼ cup candied lemon peel,
  chopped fine
½ teaspoon grated lemon
  rind.

Preheat oven to 325°. Beat eggs, gradually adding sugar; beat until thick. Sift flour and spices together; add gradually to egg mixture. Add almonds, lemon peel and rind. Drop by teaspoon-fuls on well-greased cookie sheets. Bake 15 to 20 minutes, or until edges are brown. Cool on racks; sprinkle with confection-ers' sugar. Makes approximately 4 dozen cookies.

Cindy Miller

MINCEMEAT SQUARES

¼ cup butter or margarine, melted
1 cup firmly packed light brown sugar
1 egg
1 teaspoon vanilla extract
1 cup all-purpose flour
¼ teaspoon salt
¼ teaspoon baking powder
½ cup mincemeat
Confectioners' sugar

Preheat oven to 350°. Grease and flour an 8x8 inch baking dish. Mix butter and brown sugar together until smooth. Beat in egg and vanilla extract. Sift dry ingredients together, add to butter-brown sugar mixture and beat until smooth. Stir in mincemeat. Pour into pan and bake for 40 minutes. Cool on wire rack; cut into 16 squares. Remove squares from pan and roll in sifted confectioners' sugar.

Jean Roche

SNICKERDOODLES

1 cup Crisco
1½ cups sugar
2 eggs
1 teaspoon vanilla
2¾ cups all-purpose flour
2 teaspoons cream of tartar
1 teaspoon baking soda
2 tablespoons sugar
2 tablespoons cinnamon

Cream Crisco and sugar together until fluffy. Beat in eggs 1 at a time; beat in vanilla. Sift flour, cream of tartar and baking soda together; add to creamed mixture and beat until smooth. Chill dough. Preheat oven to 400°. Combine cinnamon and sugar. Roll dough into walnut-size balls; roll in cinnamon and sugar mixture. Place 2 inches apart on ungreased cookie sheets. Bake for 10 minutes; cool on wire racks. Makes 4½ to 5 dozen.

Jean Roche

SEVEN-LAYER COOKIES

¼ cup butter or margarine
1½ cups (1 individual
   package) crushed
   graham crackers
1 (3½ oz.) can coconut
1 (6 oz.) package chocolate
   chips

1 (6 oz.) package
   butterscotch chips
1 can sweetened
   condensed milk
1 cup chopped pecans or
   walnuts

Preheat oven to 325° for glass dish, or 350° for metal. Melt butter in a 9x13 inch baking dish in oven. When butter is melted, remove from oven, stir in crumbs and pat out to cover bottom of dish. Sprinkle coconut over crumbs, then chocolate chips, then butterscotch chips. Pour sweetened condensed milk evenly over all. Sprinkle nuts over all; press down gently. Bake 30 minutes. Cool completely before cutting. Cut into 24 or 32 pieces.

NOTE: More like candy than cookies. *Very* fattening and very good.

PECAN TASSIES

Pastry

1 (3 oz.) package cream
   cheese, softened
½ cup butter or margarine,
   softened

1½ cups all-purpose flour

Blend together cream cheese and butter. Stir in flour. Chill for about 1 hour. Shape into 36 balls; place in tiny ungreased muffin pans. Press dough against bottom and sides of pans. If using miniature fluted tart pans, double pastry recipe and fill 72 tart pans. You will have some dough left over. Lay tart pans out on a baking sheet.

Filling

1 egg
1 cup firmly packed light
 brown sugar
1 tablespoon butter or
 margarine, softened

1 teaspoon vanilla extract
Dash salt
1 cup coarsely broken
 pecans

Beat together egg, sugar, butter, vanilla and salt, just until smooth. Stir in pecans. Fill pastry-lined muffin pans or tart pans half full, making sure no filling touches the edges of the pans. Bake in a preheated 350° oven for 20 to 25 minutes or until filling is set. Remove from pans. These freeze beautifully, so they can be made well ahead.

NOTE: Much prettier made in miniature tart pans. If you make them for a party, hide them well. A friend's husband searches them out and eats them frozen!

WALNUT SPICE COOKIES

½ cup butter
1 cup sugar
4 eggs
½ teaspoon vanilla
2 cups all-purpose flour
2 teaspoons baking
 powder

1 teaspoon cinnamon
1 teaspoon nutmeg
½ teaspoon cloves
Dash salt
1 cup black walnuts,
 coarsely chopped
1 cup currants or raisins

Have butter and eggs at room temperature. Preheat oven to 350°. Cream butter until soft. Add sugar and beat until fluffy. Add eggs 1 at a time, beating well after each addition. Sift dry ingredients together. Gradually beat dry ingredients into creamed mixture until smooth. Add nuts and currants or raisins. Drop from teaspoon onto greased cookie sheets. Bake for 15 minutes, or until golden. Cool on wire racks; store in airtight container.

Suzanne W. Peterson

WHITE MICE

1 cup butter
½ cup confectioners' sugar
2¼ cups all-purpose flour
1 teaspoon salt

1 teaspoon vanilla extract
1 cup ground pecans
Confectioners' sugar

Cream butter and sugar together until light and fluffy. Add flour, salt and vanilla extract and beat until smooth. Add nuts. Chill. Form into 2 inch long mouse bodies—like short, fat cigars. Bake on ungreased cookie sheets at 325° for 20 to 25 minutes, until light brown on the bottom. Roll in sifted confectioners' sugar while still warm.

NOTE: Try substituting almond extract and ground almonds for vanilla and pecans, or use almond extract and pecans. A food processor grinds nuts in a flash. Makes approximately 4 dozen.

Suzanne W. Peterson

PULLED MINTS

Butter
2½ cups sugar
1 cup cold water
4 tablespoons butter

Oil of peppermint (buy at
   drugstore)
Green or red food coloring

Butter a marble slab heavily and place in freezer. Combine sugar, water and 4 tablespoons butter and cook, stirring gently, over medium heat until sugar is dissolved. Raise heat and boil until syrup reaches 260° on a candy thermometer. Pour immediately onto buttered marble. Drop 6 drops oil of peppermint and about 6 drops food coloring on top. Mints should be pastel colored, not day-glo. Pull in from sides with metal spatula until cool enough to work with hands. Be careful not to burn yourself. Pick up, twist and pull. Pull until you can't pull any more, and fine lines appear. Don't give up too soon, or your mints won't be light and fluffy. Pull out into a rope and cut into pieces with scissors. Leave mints out on a towel overnight to mellow. Store in an airtight container—do not freeze.

NOTE: Try your local quarry for a marble slab, but make sure you don't purchase one too heavy to pick up, or too large to fit in your freezer. Some cooking stores also have them. Or you could do as one of our friends, who uses her husband's onyx chess board. Make sure your marriage is solid before trying this!

DIVINITY

2½ cups sugar
½ cup light Karo syrup
½ cup water
¼ teaspoon salt
2 egg whites

1 teaspoon vanilla extract
1 cup pecans, finely
    chopped (use food
    processor or nut grinder)

Combine sugar, Karo syrup, water and salt in a large sauce-pan. Bring to a boil over high heat, stirring until sugar is dis-solved. Do not stir after mixture comes to a boil. While sugar syrup is cooking, beat egg whites with an electric mixer until they form soft peaks. When sugar syrup reaches 248° on a candy thermometer, pour half slowly into egg whites while mixer is running. Heat remaining sugar syrup to 272°, pour over egg whites while mixer is running and beat until firm. Beat in vanilla and pecans. Quickly drop candy by spoonfuls onto wax paper—it will still be hot, so be careful. As candy cools and hardens, you can press it together with your hands. Store in an airtight container.

NOTE: Quick, easy and delicious—but you must use a thermometer.

May DeMaurice

HELLENBURG TOFFEE

2 cups sugar
2 cups Lyle's Golden
   Syrup or light Karo
   syrup

¼ teaspoon salt
6 tablespoons butter
1 (13 oz.) can evaporated
   milk

Butter a jelly roll pan or 9x13 inch pan. Combine sugar, syrup and salt in a *large* heavy saucepan. Stir over medium heat until sugar is dissolved. Add butter 1 tablespoon at a time. Bring to a slow boil and add milk in droplets, stirring constantly. Boil mixture, stirring frequently, until it reaches 250° on a candy thermometer. Pour toffee into pan and cool completely. *Do not touch* until cool—you could burn yourself badly. Cut toffee into small rectangles and wrap each piece in cellophane.
NOTE: Lyle's Golden Syrup can sometimes be found in gourmet food shops. It's an English syrup for which there is no real American equivalent, but light Karo will do for this toffee.

Paula Sullivan

PEANUT BRITTLE

2 cups raw peanuts
1 cup sugar
½ cup light Karo syrup

Few grains of salt
2 teaspoons baking soda

Prepare a buttered surface before starting—a no-stick baking sheet, a piece of foil, a platter, or even your counter. Combine peanuts, sugar, corn syrup and salt in a large saucepan. Cook over medium heat to at least 300° on a candy thermometer, or until mixture is a deep rich brown and peanuts smell done. Add baking soda, stir madly, and pour out onto buttered surface—do not spread out. Break up when cool.
NOTE: Recipe doubles easily, but do not double baking soda measurement.

Emmeline Cooper

INDEX

And Now...A Few Vital Statistics About

The Pirates' House.

Savannah's Award-winning Restaurant

with

23 Unique Dining Rooms

Spectacular Rain Forest Bar

Elegant Gift Shop

Savannah's famous Pirates' House is located on one of the most historic spots in Georgia, for it is here that Trustees' Garden, the first public agricultural experimental garden in America, was located.

When General James Edward Oglethorpe and his little band of colonists arrived from England in 1733, they came ashore in the vicinity of the present City Hall on Bull and Bay Streets, approximately seven blocks due west of The Pirates' House, and there pitched their tents to found the city of Savannah. Within one month, Oglethorpe established this large experimental garden on what was then the outskirts of Savannah and named it in honor of the men in his native England who were the trustees of the infant state of Georgia.

The garden was modeled very closely after the Chelsea Botanical Garden in London, a diagram of which can be seen hanging in our Jolly Roger Room. Consisting of ten acres, it was bounded on the north by the Savannah River, on the south by what is now Broughton Street and on the East by old Fort Wayne. Botanists were sent from England to the four corners of the world to procure plants for the new project and soon vine cuttings, fruit trees, flax, hemp, spices, cotton, indigo, olives and medicinal herbs were all taking root on the banks of the Savannah River. The greatest hopes, however, were centered on the wine industry and on the mulberry trees which are essential to the culture of silk; but both of these crops failed due to the unsuitable soil and weather conditions. From this garden, however, were distributed the peach trees which have since given Georgia and South Carolina a major commercial crop, and also the upland cotton which later comprised the greater part of the world's cotton commerce.

The small building adjoining The Pirates' House was erected in 1734 and is said to be the oldest house in Georgia. This building originally housed the gardener of Trustees' Garden. His office and tool room were in the front section; his stable occupied the back room and a hayloft was upstairs. The bricks used in the construction of this old "Herb House", as it is called even today, were manufactured only a short block away under the bluff by the Savannah River where brickmaking was begun by the colonists as early as 1733.

Around 1753, when Georgia had become firmly established and the need for the experimental garden no longer existed, the site was developed as a residential section, and since Savannah had become a thriving seaport town, one of the first buildings constructed on the former garden site was naturally an inn for visiting seamen. Situated a scant block from the Savannah River, the inn became a rendezvous for bloodthirsty pirates and sailors from the Seven Seas. Here seamen drank their fiery grog and discoursed, sailor fashion, on their adventures from Singapore to Shanghai and from San Francisco to Port Said. This very same building has been converted into one of Savannah's most unique restaurants, The Pirates' House, and even though every modern restaurant facility has been installed, the atmosphere of those exciting days of "wooden ships and iron men" has been carefully preserved.

In the chamber known as the Captain's Room with its hand hewn ceiling beams joined with wooden pegs, negotiations were made by shorthanded ship's masters to shanghai unwary seamen to complete their crews. Stories still persist of a tunnel, extending from the old Rum Cellar beneath the Captain's Room to the river, through which these men were carried, drugged and unconscious, to ships waiting in the harbor. Indeed, many a sailor drinking in carefree abandon at The Pirates' House awoke to find himself at sea on a strange ship bound for a port half a world away. A Savannah policeman, so legend has it, stopped by The Pirates' House for a friendly drink and awoke on a four-masted scooner sailing to China, from where it took him two years to make his way back to Savannah!

Hanging on the walls in the Captain's Room and the Treasure Room are framed pages from an early, very rare edition of the book *Treasure Island*. Savannah is mentioned numerous times in this classic by Robert Louis Stevenson; in fact, some of the action is supposed to have taken place in The Pirates' House! 'Tis said that old Cap'n Flint, who originally buried the fabulous treasure on Treasure Island, died here in an upstairs room. In the story, his faithful first mate, Billy Bones, was at his side when he breathed his last, muttering, "Darby, bring aft the rum!" Even now many swear that the ghost of Cap'n Flint still haunts The Pirates' House area on moonless nights.

The validity of The Pirates' House has been recognized by the American Museum Society, which lists this historic tavern as an authentic house museum. The property was acquired by the Savannah Gas Company in 1948 and the building soon fell under the magic wand of Mrs. Hansell (Mary) Hillyer, wife of the president of the company, who with great imagination, perseverance and skill transformed the fascinating old museum into a restaurant. Today it is a mecca for Savannahians and tourists alike who come to enjoy its many delicious Southern specialties served in the original romantic setting of yesteryear.

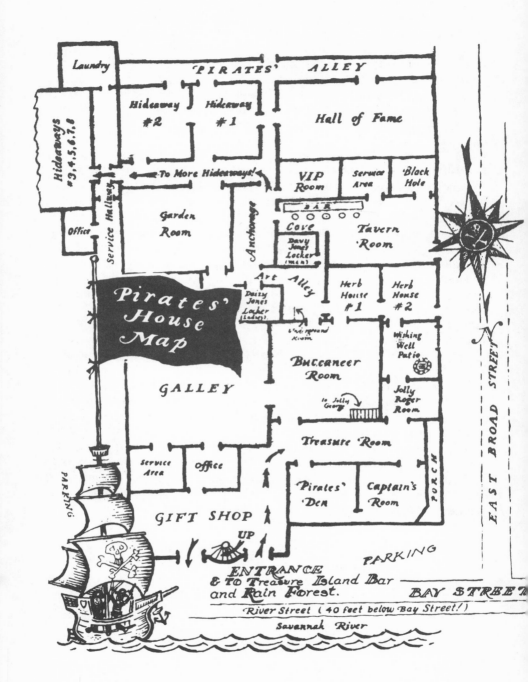

These recipes didn't make the deadline for the first edition, but they were too good to leave out altogether, so here's a bonus for you!

PEACHES-ON-THE-BEACHES

1 liter white wine
4 fresh peaches, peeled
  and sliced

¼ cup sugar
1 lemon, sliced thin and
  seeded

At least 8 hours before serving, mix everything together in a container and refrigerate. Pour into a large thermos, add some ice and hit the beach. When the punch is all gone, don't forget to eat the potent fruit. Serves 4 generously.

Danyse Edel

BETTY PLATT'S FAMOUS CHILI

1 to 1½ pounds lean
  ground beef
1 large or 2 small onions,
  coarsely chopped
1 large or 2 small green
  peppers, coarsely
  chopped
2 to 4 cloves garlic, finely
  chopped
2 tablespoons vegetable oil
1 (8 oz.) can tomato sauce
1 (6 oz.) can tomato paste

1 to 2 tablespoons chili
  powder
Tabasco to taste, optional
3 (15 oz.) cans dark red
  kidney beans
Celery seeds to taste
Parsley flakes to taste
Oregano to taste
Cumin to taste
Dried or fresh basil to taste
Salt and pepper to taste
1 or 2 crushed bay leaves

Heat oil in large frying pan. Sauté meat, onion, green pepper and garlic until meat loses red color. DO NOT BROWN. Add beans and seasonings to taste; cook slowly, stirring occasionally, for about 1 hour. Chili is much better if made the day before, refrigerated and reheated. Skim off fat before reheating. Serve over rice or corn chips; garnish with shredded lettuce, finely chopped onions and Cheddar cheese.

Betty Platt

PASTA SALAD

1 pound pasta—shells, ziti, wheels, or multi-colored fettuccine are all good choices

¼ cup good olive oil or vegetable oil

1 pound meat or seafood, see Note

½ pound Cheddar or Swiss cheese, optional

3 tomatoes, seeded and diced

1 cup fresh parsley, finely chopped

3 cloves garlic, finely chopped

1 teaspoon dried oregano or 1 tablespoon fresh, or to taste

1 teaspoon dried basil or 1 tablespoon fresh, or to taste

Vinaigrette

1 tablespoon Dijon mustard

1 teaspoon salt

½ teaspoon pepper

¼ to ⅓ cup red wine vinegar or balsamic vinegar

⅔ cup good olive oil or vegetable oil, or mix according to taste

Whisk together mustard, salt, pepper and vinegar. Slowly whisk in oil; whisk until emulsified.

Cook pasta in rapidly boiling salted water until it is just done, "al dente". Do not overcook—it is better to err on the slightly crunchy side. Drain in a colander. DO NOT RINSE. Pour into a large bowl and toss with ¼ cup oil until every piece is coated. Add meat or seafood, cheese, tomatoes, parsley, garlic, oregano and basil. Add vinaigrette to taste and toss well. Cover and refrigerate at least 6 hours or overnight. Adjust seasonings to taste.

NOTE: The best thing about pasta salad is that you can add anything to the basic mix (including lightly blanched vegetables) and have a wonderful summery salad. Good meats include: boiled, peeled shrimp, scallops, chunks of fish (even tuna fish in a pinch), diced ham, chicken or turkey, or strips of rare roast beef. Do not mix meat and seafood, because it ends up tasting strange.

PATE IN ASPIC

2 (3 oz.) packages cream
   cheese, softened
2 (4¾ oz.) cans liver paste
   OR
1 (8 oz.) package liverwurst
   (see Note)
2 ounces bourbon

1 (10 oz.) can condensed
   beef broth
lemon juice and/or
   vermouth or Madeira to
   taste
1 envelope unflavored
   gelatin

Mix cream cheese and liver paste or liverwurst in food processor or electric mixer until smooth and fluffy. Add bourbon; beat in well. Line a bowl or mold with slanting sides with plastic wrap; fill with paté mixture. Bang on countertop a few times to eliminate air bubbles; cover and refrigerate several hours or overnight. Carefully remove paté from bowl onto a plate; refrigerate. Lightly oil same bowl or mold. Pour beef broth into a 2-cup glass measuring cup. Add lemon juice and/or wine to make 1½ cups liquid. Pour 1 cup liquid into a saucepan and bring to a boil. Soften gelatin in remaining ½ cup liquid. Add to hot liquid and stir until dissolved. Remove from heat and cool slightly. Pour aspic into mold to a depth of ½ inch. Refrigerate until set. Leave remaining aspic at room temperature. When aspic is firm, gently place paté bottom-side up on aspic. Pour remaining aspic around and over paté—stir up aspic if it has started to set. Cover and refrigerate until aspic is set. Unmold carefully on a platter and serve with crackers or melba toast. Best made a day ahead.

NOTE: Underwood makes liver paste, but it's hard to find. Liverwurst is an acceptable substitute.

Rosemary Colmers

EVA'S SPINACH DIP

2 (10 oz.) packages frozen
  spinach
1 (8 oz.) can water
  chestnuts
1 (1⅝ oz.) package Knorr
  vegetable soup mix

½ cup mayonnaise
1½ cups sour cream

Bring a big pot of water to a boil. Unwrap spinach, place in pot, cover, remove from heat and let sit until spinach is thawed. Drain well; press on spinach with a wooden spoon to remove excess water. Squeeze out by handfuls—spinach must be as dry as possible. Throw everything into a food processor and process until smooth. Or chop spinach and water chestnuts fine and mix well with remaining ingredients. Cover and refrigerate at least 12 hours or overnight.

Eva Colmers

LIPTAUER SPREAD

8 ounces cream cheese,
  softened
8 ounces cottage cheese
1 teaspoon each: mustard,
  caraway seeds, finely
  chopped capers, finely
  chopped green onion or
  onion, and finely
  chopped fresh parsley
  or chives

½ teaspoon paprika
½ teaspoon anchovy paste
salt and pepper to taste

In food processor or electric mixer, combine cream cheese and cottage cheese and mix until smooth. Add remaining ingredients; mix until smooth. Pour into a non-metal bowl, preferably glass, cover and refrigerate overnight. Serve with rye crackers or pumpernickel bread.

Rosemary Colmers

The Pirates' House Cookbook
20 E. Broad St.
Savannah, Ga. 31401

Please send me _____copies of THE PIRATES' HOUSE COOKBOOK at $10.95 per copy, plus $1.55 per book for postage and handling. Georgia residents add 4% sales tax. Make checks payable to The Pirates' House.

Name:_____

Address:_____

City_____State:_____Zip Code:_____

The Pirates' House Cookbook
20 E. Broad St.
Savannah, Ga. 31401

Please send me _____copies of THE PIRATES' HOUSE COOKBOOK at $10.95 per copy, plus $1.55 per book for postage and handling. Georgia residents add 4% sales tax. Make checks payable to The Pirates' House.

Name:_____

Address:_____

City_____State:_____Zip Code:_____

The Pirates' House Cookbook
20 E. Broad St.
Savannah, Ga. 31401

Please send me _____copies of THE PIRATES' HOUSE COOKBOOK at $10.95 per copy, plus $1.55 per book for postage and handling. Georgia residents add 4% sales tax. Make schecks payable to The Pirates' House.

Name:_____

Address:_____

City_____State:_____Zip Code:_____

Reorder Additional Copies